THE TULSA RACE MASSACRE:
THE DEPARTMENT OF JUSTICE REVIEW AND EVALUATION

T0349075

The Tulsa Race Massacre
The Department of Justice Review and Evaluation

Published in 2025 by Melville House
First Melville House Printing: January 2025
The photographs of Tulsa in between the sections are from the
American National Red Cross photograph collection at the Library of Congress.

Melville House Publishing
46 John Street
Brooklyn, NY 11201
and
Melville House UK
Suite 2000
16/18 Woodford Road
London E7 0HA

mhpbooks.com
@melvillehouse

ISBN: 978-1-68589-221-0
ISBN: 978-1-68589-222-7 (eBook)

Printed in the United States of America
1 3 5 7 9 10 8 6 4 2

THE DEPARTMENT OF JUSTICE REVIEW AND EVALUATION

THE TULSA RACE MASSACRE

MELVILLE HOUSE

BROOKLYN · LONDON

JUNE 1st. 1921.

THE BESSEMER GAS ENGINE CO.

CIVIL RIGHTS DIVISION[1]
Review and Evaluation
Tulsa Race Massacre

File No. 144-59N-731

Date: January 17, 2025[*]

To: Chief, Criminal Section
Re: Multiple persons known and unknown – Subjects;
A.C. Jackson – Deceased;
C.L. Daniels – Deceased;
Multiple additional victims who died during the massacre both known[2] and unknown –
Deceased;
Viola Ford Fletcher ("Mother Fletcher")
Lessie Benningfield Randle ("Mother Randle")
Multiple persons who survived the massacre but have since died[3] – Victims;

CIVIL RIGHTS

The following is a Report issued pursuant to a Review and Evaluation undertaken pursuant to the
Emmett Till Unsolved Civil Rights Crime Act.

1. Date of the Incident: May 31 – June 1, 1921

2. Synopsis of Review and Evaluation: The Government has reviewed the events of May 31 and
   June 1, 1921, and issues this Report to officially acknowledge, illuminate, and preserve for
   history the horrible ordeals of the massacre's victims. This Report is the first full accounting of
   the massacre undertaken by the Department of Justice.

   Barbara Kay Bosserman
   Deputy Chief of the Cold Case Unit &
   Senior Legal Counsel

To: Records Section
       Office of Legal Administration

The above numbered file has been closed as of this date.

January 17, 2025
Date

Chief, Criminal Section

---

[*] This is an updated version of a Report previously signed on January 9, 2025 and posted on January 10. This version un-
redacts names of individuals who have submitted a written request to be unredacted and makes minor changes to improve
accuracy.

FORMERLY CVR-3   FORM CL-3

Table of Contents

A.   Executive Summary[4]

On the night of May 31, 1921, a violent attack by as many as 10,000 white Tulsans[5] destroyed the thriving Black community of Greenwood, Oklahoma—a prosperous area often referred to as "Black Wall Street."[6] The attack, which lasted into the afternoon of June 1, was so systematic and coordinated that it transcended mere mob violence. White men murdered hundreds of Black residents, burned businesses and homes to the ground, and left survivors without resources or recourse. In the aftermath, authorities failed to offer meaningful help, and efforts to seek justice through the courts foundered.

Seeking to understand and acknowledge the scope and impact of the massacre, the United States Department of Justice's Civil Rights Division, under the Emmett Till Unsolved Civil Rights Crime Act,[7] recently announced that its Cold Case Unit would review the events of 1921. From the beginning of that effort, it has been clear that no avenue of prosecution now exists for these crimes—the youngest potential defendants would today be more than 115 years old, and the relevant statutes of limitations have long since expired. Nevertheless, as the federal government's first thorough reckoning with this devastating event, our resulting review officially acknowledges, illuminates, and preserves for history the horrible ordeals of the massacre's victims.

The review, conducted by the Cold Case Unit in the Civil Rights Division's Criminal Section, involved speaking with survivors and their families, examining firsthand accounts, and studying primary materials[8]—including an investigative report from June 1921 by the Justice Department's Bureau of Investigation, the precursor to the FBI. The agent's report, attached as Appendix C, was prepared pursuant to an "informal" investigation, took less than a week to research and write, characterized the triggering incident as a "small" and "half-hearted" attempt at a lynching, asserted that the "riot" was not the result of "racial feeling," implied that Black men were ultimately responsible for the massacre, and concluded that its perpetrators had not violated any federal laws.[9] Although flawed in multiple ways, the agent's report contains crucial information not discussed in other sources that describe the massacre. For example, it includes allegations that law enforcement actively recruited white men from outside of Tulsa to participate in a raid on Greenwood. Our Report therefore discusses the agent's 1921 findings at some length, while identifying conclusions and opinions inconsistent with other sources.

The trigger for the violence of the Tulsa Race Massacre was the kind of unfounded condemnation that, at the time, commonly justified unspeakable treatment of Black men. The allegations of a white man led police to arrest 19-year-old Dick Rowland for allegedly assaulting a white woman who operated an elevator he used. A local newspaper then sensationalized the story, and soon a mob of white Tulsans gathered outside the courthouse, demanding a lynching.

Black men from Greenwood came to the courthouse to protect Rowland. The white mob saw this effort to save Rowland as a challenge to the social order and quickly recruited others. The mob grew. A confrontation broke out, and when someone fired a shot, "all hell broke loose."

Violence escalated quickly. Local police deputized hundreds of white residents, many of whom had been advocating for a lynching and had been drinking. Law enforcement officers helped organize these special deputies—as well as other white Tulsans—into the martial forces that ravaged Greenwood. Over the next several hours, they looted, burned, and destroyed 35 city blocks while Greenwood's residents tried desperately to defend their homes. Some Black residents were shot (or otherwise assaulted), and many were arrested or detained. Law enforcement actively participated in the destruction, disarming Black residents, confiscating their weapons, and detaining many in makeshift camps under armed guard. There are allegations that some members of law enforcement participated in arsons and murders.

Contrary to the agent's 1921 report, the situation did not "spontaneously" grow out of control. Rather, what had initially been sporadic and opportunistic violence became systematic, yielding a much more devastating result, due to coordinated efforts among white residents and law enforcement entities. Moreover, although the 1921 report asserts that the massacre (then called a "riot") was not the result of "racial feeling," perpetrators of the massacre overtly expressed and acted upon racial bias.

As the fires consumed Greenwood, many Black families fled for their lives. White residents chased them across and beyond the city, taking men, women, children, the elderly, and the infirm into custody. The destruction of the district was total. The survivors were left with nothing.

After the devastation, city officials promised to help Greenwood rebuild, but the white-led government of Tulsa not only failed to do so but put up obstacles to residential reconstruction. White local leaders rejected outside aid, claiming they could handle the recovery, but then provided little to no financial support. Instead, claiming the area was best suited for industrial use, they imposed harsh new fire codes that priced residents out of the area, although a court later enjoined those provisions.

Compounding the injustice, insurance companies denied Black residents of Greenwood compensation due to the "riot clause" in their policies. Legal attempts to hold the city accountable also failed. Black residents of Tulsa were left with no avenue for redress.

The passage of time did not clear the path to justice. In 2003, victims' families sought compensation in federal court, but the statute of limitations had expired, and their case was dismissed. In 2020, families made another attempt in state court, alleging nuisance and unjust enrichment. That lawsuit also failed.

This Justice Department review concludes that, had today's laws been on the books in 1921, federal prosecutors could have pursued hate crime charges against the massacre's perpetrators under hate crime laws including the Matthew Shepard and James Byrd, Jr. Hate Crimes Prevention Act (18

U.S.C. § 249) and the criminal provisions of the Fair Housing Act (42 U.S.C. § 3631). The government could have prosecuted the destruction of Black churches under the Church Arson Prevention Act (18 U.S.C. § 247). Officers, public officials, and others who participated in the massacre could have faced charges for depriving Greenwood residents of their constitutional rights (18 U.S.C. § 242) or for civil rights conspiracy (18 U.S.C. § 241).

Many of these legal avenues, however, were not available then. Courts narrowly interpreted those federal civil rights laws that then existed, and although there was no shortage of bias-motivated attacks, the existing law did not recognize them as hate crimes.

Now, the perpetrators are long dead, statutes of limitations for all civil rights charges expired decades ago, and there are no viable avenues for further investigation. Furthermore, the Constitution's Confrontation Clause, which requires the government to provide live witnesses who can be cross-examined, presents an insurmountable barrier to prosecution.

Despite yielding what will, for many, be a painful and dissatisfying outcome, this review of the Tulsa Race Massacre corrects the record; it recognizes and documents the trauma and loss suffered by the residents of Greenwood. Although legal and practical limitations prevent the perpetrators of the crimes committed in 1921 from being held criminally accountable in a court of law, the historical reckoning is far from over. Legal limits may have stymied the pursuit of justice, but the work to ensure that future generations understand the magnitude of the atrocity continues.

Many of the matters reviewed by the Cold Case Unit involve systemic racism, state-sanctioned brutality, and the failure of government institutions to protect victims of color. Although this case reflects that same pattern, it was on a scale that multiplied the loss of life and extinguished an entire vibrant community. For the descendants of that lost Greenwood community, the fight for justice, while hindered by time and legal constraints, continues to seek truth and recognition.

As antilynching advocate Ida B. Wells said, "The way to right wrongs is to turn the light of truth upon them." This Report aims to do just that.

B. The Department of Justice Review

We[10] took the following steps in conducting our review:

Interviews with Survivors and Descendants: We personally interviewed survivors named in lawsuits filed following the massacre,[11] as well as several descendants of massacre survivors who learned about the massacre from their parents or grandparents.[12] We also read survivor accounts about the massacre. These included a recent account co-authored by a living massacre survivor[13] and a historical account by Mary Jones Parrish, first published in 1923, which also collected accounts of other survivors.[14] We reviewed an account by Attorney B.C. Franklin written ten years after the massacre,[15] as well as the account in his autobiography.[16] We also viewed, listened to, or read accounts of now-deceased survivors who provided their recollections. These accounts are available in various collections, including the Helmerich Center for American Research ("HCAR")'s Eddie Faye Gates collection and Oklahoma State University's Ruth Sigler Avery collection.[17]

Bureau of Investigation Reports: We reviewed federal reports dated June 3 and June 6, 1921, one written by the federal agent who investigated the massacre and another by that agent's supervisor, which included the investigator's preliminary findings. We discovered these reports through ProQuest, a platform available through many public libraries, universities, and other institutions with subscriptions; the reports are also available through the National Archives.[18] Because neither the Official Commission Report (cited below) nor the leading studies of the massacre cite these reports, and because they may be important to scholars who conduct research into the massacre, we reproduce them in full at Appendix C. In addition, we reviewed two additional Department of Justice files related to the massacre, which include correspondence and secondhand witness accounts; these files are included as Appendices D and E.[19]

Oklahoma Commission Report: We reviewed a report issued in 2001 by the Oklahoma Commission (the "Commission") created to study the massacre (then called a "riot"). This comprehensive report includes multiple articles with in-depth explorations of various aspects of the massacre.[20]

Primary Source Material:[21] We reviewed American Red Cross reports that were written in the wake of the massacre.[22] We reviewed the after-action reports submitted by members of the National Guard,[23] as well as materials related to a 1921 state grand jury investigation that led to charges filed against the Tulsa Police Chief.[24] We also reviewed materials in the Special Collections of McFarlin Library at the University of Tulsa;[25] these materials relate to the massacre and to the Ku Klux Klan as it existed in Tulsa in the 1920s.

Legal Pleadings: We reviewed available legal filings, including pleadings from civil lawsuits seeking insurance compensations and/or compensatory damages, which members of Greenwood's Black community filed in the wake of the massacre.[26] We also reviewed more recent legal pleadings, such as those filed in *Alexander v. Oklahoma*, 382 F.3d 1206 (10th Cir. 2004) and *Randle v. City of Tulsa*, 556 P.3d 612 (Okla. 2024), *reh'g denied* (Sept. 9, 2024).

Secondary Sources:[27] We read books about the massacre, examined a variety of law review articles, reviewed other scholarly publications and dissertations, viewed several documentaries, and listened to podcasts discussing the massacre. Many older materials were available from the Special Collections at the University of Tulsa's McFarlin Library and from the Ruth Sigler Avery Collection at Oklahoma State University. We also consulted several timelines prepared by the Commission and others describing the massacre.[28]

News Articles and Photographs: We obtained and read many contemporaneous news accounts published in the aftermath of the massacre.[29] We also examined several collections of photographs taken during and after the massacre. [30]

Interviews with Experts: We met with over a dozen historians, journalists, and citizen experts who have published accounts of the massacre. Attached at Appendix B is a list of experts who shared their time and expertise with us.

C.   Background

This Report of our review cannot accurately analyze the massacre outside of the historical context in which it occurred. We therefore begin by describing the nation, state, city, and community as it existed at the time of the massacre. We also examine the effect of the First World War (which we call the Great War, as that was the term that would have been used in 1921).

1.   Race Relations in America at the Time of the Massacre

In early twentieth century America, there were multiple incidents in which white mobs attacked Black communities. In 1898, 23 years before the Tulsa Race Massacre, white supremacists violently deposed the duly elected government in Wilmington, North Carolina, because these white supremacists were upset that the government had allowed Black participation in elections and city governance. During this coup, white supremacists killed many Black people.[31] In July 1917, four years before the Tulsa Race Massacre, a white mob attacked a Black community in East St. Louis, Missouri; estimates of the death toll vary widely but the massacre likely killed hundreds of Black residents and caused over $400,000 in property damage.[32] Two years later, between March and October 1919, white mobs committed assaults upon Black communities in at least 26 cities across the country.[33] The summer was so bloody it is remembered as the "Red Summer" of 1919.[34] In 1923, two years *after* the Tulsa Race Massacre, a white mob invaded the Black community in Rosewood, Florida, where they killed at least eight people, burned and looted homes and businesses, and drove many in the Black community out of town.[35] Nearly all white perpetrators evaded accountability.

In addition to violence targeting whole communities, there were countless examples of white mobs murdering individual Black people, a practice known as lynching. According to records kept by the Tuskegee Institute, in 1921, white mobs lynched 59 Black people, which is an average of more than one lynching per week.[36] One law professor writing about the Tulsa Race Massacre notes that, at the time, "[l]ynchings—whether for white sport and family entertainment or to terrorize Black communities deemed too successful and uppity[]—grew not only in number but also in ferocity."[37]

2.   Oklahoma Before the Massacre

During the late nineteenth century, Oklahoma Territory had a reputation for being welcoming to Black Americans.[38] Some Black leaders described Oklahoma as a "promised land" friendly to Black interests.[39] Oklahoma Territory had over 50 all-Black towns, a record number for any state or territory.[40] The amount of land owned by the Black community resulted from the way Black settlers arrived in Oklahoma. Many came to what was then "Indian Territory" by accompanying Native American tribes that had been expelled from the Antebellum South.[41] These Tribes had previously adopted the South's slavery system and brought enslaved Black people with them when the Tribes were forcibly relocated.[42] After post-war emancipation, Freedmen (people formerly enslaved by the Tribes) received land when Congress divided communal Tribal land.[43] Some Freedmen became quite wealthy.[44] Many Black Tulsans whom we interviewed proudly identified themselves by stating their Tribal affiliation in addition to their identification with Greenwood's Black community.

Oklahoma did not remain welcoming to the Black community. After the Civil War, the lure of newly discovered oil fields drew white settlers to Oklahoma Territory.[45] Many of these settlers were the children and grandchildren of the Southerners who had supported Confederate rebels during the war and most of whom adopted their forebearers' attitudes towards Black people.[46] When Congress granted Oklahoma statehood in 1907, these white Oklahomans drafted a constitution and state laws that contained explicit "Jim Crow" provisions, mandating segregation.[47] Thus, despite its description as a promised land while it remained a territory, Oklahoma became segregated when it achieved statehood.

Many Oklahomans adopted other aspects of the Jim Crow system, including the proclivity to commit racial-terror lynchings. From 1877 to 1950, there were approximately 75 reported lynchings in the state.[48] Particularly disturbingly, a white mob abducted a 28-year-old Black woman and her young son from a jail in Okemah, Oklahoma, 10 years before the Tulsa Race Massacre. The mob lynched the two victims and, to intimidate residents, displayed their bodies outside the Black community of Okemah.[49]

3.   **Tulsa Before the Massacre**

Tulsa is a name derived from "Tulasi" or "Tallasi," which meant "old town" in the language of the Creek Indians.[50] Tulsa officially incorporated as a city on January 18, 1898.[51] When oil was discovered nearby, Tulsa had the foresight to build a railroad center and to provide other necessities for oil prospectors.[52] The city grew exponentially. By 1910, Tulsa had a population of more than 10,000, and by 1920, the population of greater Tulsa was more than 100,000.[53] Revenue from oil and supporting industries made the town prosperous, and it soon garnered the name the "Magic City."[54]

Tulsa was also a deeply segregated city. Housing ordinances barred Black people from living in white neighborhoods unless they were "domestics" serving white families.[55] Tulsa had its share of extrajudicial violence, and its victims included those in the white community.[56] Less than a year before the massacre, a crowd of armed men kidnapped a white man named Roy Belton from his jail cell in a Tulsa courthouse and lynched him.[57] The lynching occurred with the apparent complicity of the Tulsa police; in fact, some sources say that police directed traffic during the lynching.[58] It is undisputed that Police Chief John Gustafson ordered police not to intervene.[59] Afterwards, he made a public statement that, although he was opposed to mob justice, his "honest opinion" was that Belton's lynching would "prove of real benefit to Tulsa."[60]

Belton's lynching rattled the Black community. Many thought that if a mob could lynch a white man with official approval, there would be *no* protection for a Black man.[61] A.J. Smitherman, a Greenwood community leader who ran the *Tulsa Star*, a Black newspaper, wrote that Belton's lynching "explodes the theory that a prisoner is safe on the top of the Court House from mob violence."[62]

4.   Greenwood Before the Massacre

Before the massacre, Greenwood was a close-knit, flourishing community. It was a city within a city—a Black enclave inside Tulsa. Mary Jones Parrish, writing shortly after the massacre, described prosperous Black businesses and "homes of beauty and splendor."[63] The community was, in the words of one historian, a "nationally renowned entrepreneurial center."[64] The number of Black-owned businesses from that time are well documented.[65] There were "four well-equipped drug stores," many grocery stores, two "fine hotels," and the Dreamland Theater.[66] Loula Williams owned the Dreamland Theater and a confectionary shop as well as additional theaters elsewhere in Oklahoma.[67] J.B. Stradford owned a hotel.[68] The Nails family owned a shoe shop.[69] The community worshipped in dozens of Black churches.[70] Doctors, lawyers, teachers, and other well-respected and wealthy members of the community lived on Detroit Avenue.[71] Many Black families had accumulated enough wealth to decorate their homes in fashion.[72] Families owned pianos, fine living room furniture, and jewelry.[73]

Survivors' statements reflect the prosperity of Greenwood as it existed before the massacre. Mother Fletcher described Greenwood as a prosperous society, marked by Black wealth, success, and opportunity.[74] Both Mother Fletcher and Mother Randle described living in homes filled with toys, family, and joy.[75] They felt safe and unafraid.[76] Mother Fletcher described the churches, music venues, and sports teams that populated Greenwood.[77] Georgia Walker Hill and Samuel Walker described living in a "really elegant" home.[78] Beatrice Webster described having a piano and a Davenport sofa in her home, as well as double swings in the yard.[79] Kinney Booker described a lovely home with a piano.[80] Olivia Hooker described her family as owning jewelry, furs, and silver, all of which were stolen in the massacre.[81] W.D. Williams, son of John and Loula Williams, remembered his father owning one of the first automobiles in Tulsa.[82]

While undoubtedly a prosperous Black community, Greenwood was not a utopia; it suffered the ill-effects of segregation. Due to white control of Tulsa's tax revenue, Greenwood was not appropriated funds for sanitation and running water, nor were its streets paved to the same extent as those in white Tulsa.[83] Moreover, although remembered as "Wall Street," Greenwood was not a financial center with brokerage firms or banks. It was, however, a center of shopping and other trade. Because Black residents of Greenwood were unable or unwilling to spend money in the white section of Tulsa (those white businesses that would accept Black customers often forced them to endure humiliation), they spent their income almost exclusively in Greenwood.[84] Likewise, Black farmers and residents of small towns outside the city who needed supplies would spend their dollars in Greenwood, not in white businesses in Tulsa.[85]

In spite of its commercial success, Greenwood had a reputation among some in the white community as a place where white men could buy drugs or engage in illicit sexual activity.[86] Part of this reputation may have been based upon nothing more than the fact that some establishments in

Greenwood played jazz music and sold bootlegged, Choctaw ("Choc") alcohol.[87] The year before the massacre, authorities conducted a vice investigation, with then-scandalous allegations of white women dancing with Black men in "Choc joints."[88] These allegations, amplified in editorials in white newspapers,[89] likely increased the prejudice of white Tulsans against the community they referred to derogatorily as "Little Africa" or "Ni**ertown."[90] This may have contributed to their willingness to destroy it.[91]

In sum, Greenwood was a prosperous Black community, even if it was not a financial center. Survivors, descendants, and historians all stressed that what made Greenwood so very special was not so much its wealth but its extraordinary sense of community. Mary Jones Parrish, writing in the years after the massacre, emphasized that her love of Greenwood flowed from the "wonderful cooperation" among the people in the community.[92] A descendant we spoke to during our review likewise stressed that the most important aspects of the community were its strength, pride, and courage.[93]

5. The Effect of The First World War

The massacre took place a few years after the end of the Great War. By 1921, many men from Tulsa had served in that war.[94] America's Black soldiers had distinguished themselves and earned appreciation from the highest levels of the French government following their military service.[95] Following their service, these veterans were less willing than their elders had been to accept second-class treatment.[96] W.E.B. Du Bois, a Black civil rights leader, captured this post-war sentiment within the Black community in an article he wrote for *The Crisis*. In it, Du Bois expressed dismay that Black men who had served so honorably during the war had returned to insults and lynchings, and encouraged Black Americans to resist white violence, concluding: "We *return from fighting*. We *return fighting*."[97] Greenwood's Black newspaper editor A.J. Smitherman agreed, running articles in his *Tulsa Star* urging Black residents to forcefully oppose all attempts at lynching.[98]

In white Tulsa, a "Home Guard" was formed during the war whose purpose was to replace members of the National Guard who had gone overseas during the Great War.[99] The men of the Home Guard drilled together and prepared to defend Tulsa from attack from foreign or domestic sources.[100] Members of the Home Guard, acting for Tulsa's wartime "Council of Defense" and with the "Knights of Liberty," also took on the role of morality police, intimidating (and occasionally tarring and feathering) those suspected of communism and labor organizing.[101] These extrajudicial actions may have acclimated some members of the group to vigilante "justice."[102] In addition, these joint ventures may explain the efficiency with which these white men organized during the massacre by making it easier for them to work together.[103]

Perhaps the most important effect of the war experience was that both white and Black men of Tulsa gained extensive military training, which they fell back on when unrest began. As discussed below, this likely increased the use of highly lethal wartime tactics during the massacre.

D.   The Massacre

The facts of the massacre, set forth below, are drawn from the Commission Report, survivor accounts, newspaper articles, primary source material, and the many books and scholarly articles describing the massacre. We supplement these relatively well-known accounts with descriptions from a report submitted by Agent T.F. Weiss of the Department of Justice's Bureau of Investigation (a predecessor agency to the FBI).

1.   The Catalyst for the Massacre (May 30, 1921)

The immediate catalyst for the massacre was an allegation that Dick Rowland, a young Black man, had assaulted Sarah Page, a young white woman, in an elevator that Page operated in the Drexel building.[104] According to most accounts, Rowland was a shoe shiner (some accounts identify him as a "delivery boy") who used the bathroom at the Drexel building because it was one of the few public bathrooms designated for use by "colored" Tulsans.[105]   On May 30, 1921, a white clerk in the Drexel

building told police that Rowland had tried to sexually assault Page.[106]

It is not known—and will likely never be known—what happened in the Drexel elevator.

Some maintain that the two were romantically involved and that the clerk had witnessed a lovers'

quarrel (or a lovers' embrace cut short by an unexpected witness).[107]   Others believe Rowland

accidentally bumped into Page or stepped on her foot, perhaps because the Drexel building's unreliable

elevator landed unevenly.[108]   Police Chief John Gustafson told Agent Weiss that Page "bore no

scratches, bruises, or disarranged dress and that she stated the boy made no bad remark of any kind."[109]

This observation is corroborated by the fact that Page declined to pursue charges,[110] which suggests

that she did not perceive Rowland's actions to be criminal.   Although there was no evidence that Page

suffered *any* physical injury, much less that she suffered a sexual assault, police arrested Rowland the

next morning.[111]

2.   **The News Article (May 31, 4:00 p.m. to 6:00 p.m.)**

On the afternoon of Rowland's arrest, the *Tulsa Tribune* ran an article about the incident

entitled, "Nab Negro for Attacking Girl in Elevator."[112]   The article falsely claimed that Page was a

poor orphan and characterized the incident as an "attempt[ed] assault," language that would have

implied to white readers of the time that Rowland tried to rape Page.[113]   The article also falsely

asserted that Page bore scratches and other evidence of a violent attack.[114]

Before their deaths, several survivors reported that, along with the "Nab Negro" article, the

Tulsa Tribune ran an inflammatory editorial expressly encouraging white Tulsans to lynch Rowland.[115]

Copies of the front-page "Nab Negro" article are still accessible, likely because the article was

reprinted in other papers, but no editorial has been located, even though the Oklahoma Commission

offered a reward for anyone with a copy of the editorial.[116]   One historian obtained a microfilm copy of the *Tulsa Tribune*'s May 31, 1921 edition from official newspaper archives and observed that both the front-page article and most of the editorial section had been removed, suggesting an editorial inflammatory enough to be deliberately cut from the paper.[117]

There are several possibilities for the conflict between the survivors' accounts and the lack of a physical copy of the editorial. It is possible that, at a time when newspapers published multiple editions each day, the paper with the editorial had only a limited run and all copies have been lost or destroyed over time. One journalist suggests that there might never have been an editorial, noting that a June 1, 1921 *Tulsa Daily World*'s front page arrest article, similar to the *Tulsa Tribune*'s article from the day before, reported that there was a "movement afoot" to "go to the county courthouse . . . and lynch [Rowland]."[118] The journalist suggests that some readers may have conflated the *Tulsa Daily World*'s lynching statement with the *Tribune*'s non-existent editorial.[119] The journalist further notes that a June 1, 1921 edition of the paper otherwise identical to the May 31 edition was found intact and did not include an inflammatory editorial.[120] But a historian who viewed the microfilm copy of the *Tulsa Tribune* believes an editorial existed and was deliberately excised, perhaps so the *Tulsa Tribune* could avoid blame for the subsequent massacre.[121]

Whether such an editorial existed, separate and apart from a news article, is less important than the fact that the *Tulsa Tribune* ran an inaccurate article suggesting that a Black man had sexually assaulted an innocent young white woman. The editors likely would have known that such an allegation of unwanted sexual contact between a Black man and a white woman would be inflammatory and that, in America at that time, this type of allegation often led to a lynching. Yet, the paper chose to run the article.

Massacre scholars have noted that the newspaper's owner, Richard Lloyd Jones, held racist beliefs;[122] thus, he may have hoped to incite a lynching or may not have cared if one resulted if the article helped to sell papers. One author has suggested that members of the police force who made the arrest deliberately fed the paper inaccurate information because they hoped to incite a lynching and wanted to blame the paper later if their plan succeeded.[123] It is impossible to apportion blame for the article at this date or to determine whether the article was the result of ill intent or recklessness. What is certain is that, by the afternoon, Tulsa was rife with rumors of an imminent lynching.[124]

3. The Standoff at the Courthouse (May 31, 6:00 p.m. to 10:15 p.m.)

By 6:00 p.m. on May 31, police handed Rowland over to the Sheriff's office, which had control of the courthouse jail—perhaps because authorities believed that the jail would be easier to defend from a mob than Tulsa Police Department facilities. Sometime between 6:00 and 7:00 p.m., a crowd of approximately 300 white men gathered at the courthouse, many clamoring to lynch Rowland.[125] Sheriff Willard McCullough refused demands to hand Rowland over to the assembled white crowd. He also took steps to surround Rowland with his deputies and to disable the elevator to make it difficult for any would-be lynchers to reach Rowland.[126]

At about 8:00 p.m., three white men breached the courthouse entrance intending to get to Rowland, but Sheriff McCullough refused to let them get past him.[127] This incident shows how serious some in the crowd were about lynching Rowland. In fact, according to District Judge Redmond S. Cole, one white man in the crowd was a hardened criminal who previously participated in a lynching.[128] In a letter to Bureau Agent Findlay, Judge Cole opined that one of these would-be lynchers was Claud "Yellow Hammer" Cranfield, a suspect in the earlier Belton lynching.[129] If Judge Cole's opinion is correct, then some in the assembled crowd were both serious about the lynching and capable of carrying out their intent. In at least one interview, Sheriff McCullough indicated he thought the lynching threat serious, estimating that of the crowd of 500-600 white men gathered at the courthouse, at least 100 were talking loudly and openly about committing a lynching.[130]

Black residents decided to go to the courthouse to protect Rowland.[131] These men were not confident that Rowland's cell was impervious to mob attack, since this was the same facility that had housed Roy Belton before a mob lynched him.[132] After the massacre, the media[133] as well as the federal report[134] characterized the attempt to lynch Rowland as "half-hearted" and the men at the courthouse as more "curious" than violent.[135] The implication was that the Black men of Greenwood overreacted to an innocuous gathering; this attitude would animate the subsequent state grand jury determination that it was the unnecessary presence of armed Black men that caused the massacre.[136] Yet, as discussed above, it is not now clear—and certainly would not have been clear in 1921—that law enforcement would have protected Rowland if the Black men of Greenwood had remained in Greenwood.

The Black men of Greenwood twice marched to the courthouse. First, a group of approximately 25 Black men arrived at the courthouse shortly after 9:00 p.m.[137] Many of these men were veterans, some dressed in uniform and many openly carrying weapons.[138] This group spoke with members of law enforcement (perhaps to Sheriff McCullough himself or perhaps to a Black officer named Barney Cleaver) who convinced the group of men that there would be no lynching, and so the men returned to Greenwood.[139] The presence of armed Black men, some in uniform, infuriated the white men who had assembled at the courthouse.[140] In response, the white mob began to grow. Alarm spread through the white community as there were reports of incursions of other groups of Black men, some armed, into the white part of Tulsa.[141]

After the first Black men departed, the white crowd grew to approximately 2000 people.[142] Upon learning that the size of the white mob was increasing, another group of approximately 75 Black Greenwood residents marched to the courthouse.[143] Some of these Black men believed that Sheriff McCullough had asked for their aid.[144] Federal reports show that some white men thought so as well.

Police Chief Gustafson told Agent Weiss that he had "heard" that Sheriff McCullough had "called these armed [N]egros by phone" and asked them to protect Rowland.[145] Likewise, a Deputy United States Marshal told Agent Weiss that, while at the courthouse on May 31, he heard a white man accuse Sheriff McCullough of calling in the armed Black men.[146] When the sheriff denied doing so, the unidentified white man called him a liar, stating he had heard Sheriff McCullough make the request.[147]

Sheriff McCullough and Chief Gustafson were political enemies.[148] As a result, Gustafson may have been trying to deflect blame by accusing McCullough of summoning armed Black men to the courthouse (because the presence of the Black men was the excuse the white community gave for the massacre). The federal files, however, suggest it is possible that Sheriff McCullough *did* seek help from the men of Greenwood and certainly that it is possible that the men of Greenwood believed that they had the invitation—or at least the tacit approval—of the sheriff when they assembled at the courthouse.

4. The White Mob Storms the National Armory (May 31, 9:00 p.m. to 10:00 p.m.)

Sometime after the Black men of Greenwood first appeared at the courthouse, white men attempted to break into a federal armory to steal weapons.[149] Major Jas. A. Bell, a member of the National Guard ("Guard") who resided in Tulsa, learned that a white lynch mob had gathered near the courthouse to lynch a prisoner and that Black men were "arming to prevent it."[150] In response, Major Bell ordered guardsmen to assemble at the armory to be ready if called into service.[151] Before he himself could report to the armory, he learned that a white mob he estimated to be "about three or four hundred strong" was attempting to break into the armory.[152] Major Bell ran to the armory and found 300 to 400 white men demanding "rifles and ammunition."[153] He and other guardsmen dispersed the mob.[154]

Timelines[155] indicate that the mob's unsuccessful attempt to storm the armory occurred before the first shots were fired at the courthouse, suggesting it was the mere presence of armed Black men—not any acts of violence they committed—that caused the white men to arm themselves and prepare for violence. The National Guard's after-action reports not only claim that the Guard repelled the white mob[156] but also indicate that the Guard did not distribute any armory weapons to mob members at any time.[157] However, weapons in the armory may well have been provided to the Tulsa contingency of the National Guard, who, as discussed below, participated in the invasion of Greenwood.[158] As some members of the Guard were also police officers,[159] it is also possible that some police officers carried National Guard weapons.

5.   Violence Begins (May 31, between 9:00 p.m. and 10:15 p.m.)

Back at the courthouse, the presence of armed Greenwood men, some in uniform, continued to enrage the assembled white mob, many of whom believed the Black men were "hunting trouble."[160] The most common report of how violence began is that, as the men of Greenwood stood their ground at the courthouse demanding that they be permitted to protect Rowland, a white man, whom some sources identify as E.S. McQueen (or MacQueen),[161] attempted to disarm one of the Greenwood residents—a Great War veteran identified alternatively as Johnny Cole[162] or O.B. Mann.[163] Reportedly, the white man asked the Black veteran what he was doing with his pistol, to which the veteran replied, "I'm going to use it if I need to."[164] The white man objected and tried to disarm the veteran.[165] A shot rang out.[166] At that point, "all hell broke loose."[167]

L.W. Crutcher, a white attorney[168] interviewed by Agent Weiss, gave a different account of the first shot than the one discussed above.[169] According to Crutcher, the Black men who were gathered at the courthouse engaged in "insulting" behavior.[170] Shortly after 9:00 p.m., a white man in the crowd remarked that, "as [perhaps 'if'] he had a gun," he would "show ni**ers about cursing whites" or words to that effect.[171] In response, another white man handed the speaker a firearm, saying, "[t]here is a gun, brother."[172] The first man then fired into the crowd of Greenwood residents, causing them to run back to Greenwood, "shooting aimlessly as they ran."[173] Unlike the more commonly recited account, which suggests that it is unknown whether the first shot came from a Black or white man (or asserts that the first shot was fired by a Black man[174]), Crutcher's account squarely places the blame on a white man trying to teach Black men a lesson.

6.   Overnight Violence (May 31, 9:00 p.m. to June 1, 5:00 a.m.)

Whatever prompted the first shot, other shots followed in quick succession. After the first exchange of gunfire, "more than twenty people, both [B]lacks and whites, lay dead or wounded."[175] The white mob refused to allow an ambulance to pick up one of the first Black casualties, insisting that the drivers attend to white gunshot victims instead.[176]

a.   Chaos

Chaos reigned as gun battles broke out all over downtown Tulsa. Both Black and white men engaged in these attacks.[177] Witnesses remembered men (both Black and white) shooting wildly from moving cars.[178] White residents who had not gathered at the courthouse but who had been out in the evening, engaged in other activities, were surprised and terrified by the sudden violence.[179] One of the residents who participated in the massacre, a Native American named Andre Wilkes who identified as a white Klansman, said he spent the night "running amuck" like all of the other Tulsans who were dashing down towards the Frisco Depot, "wildly shooting" pistols, shotguns, and rifles "at any moving object."[180]

Although there were both white and Black shooting victims, "[B]lack casualties soon outnumbered white ones."[181] The Black men who had marched to the courthouse raced back to their neighborhood pursued by mobs of white men, outnumbered more than twenty-to-one.[182] As the Black men ran north towards the Frisco tracks, which separated white Tulsa from Greenwood, they encountered heavy gunfire two blocks north of the courthouse.[183] A deadlier skirmish broke out a few blocks further north, as the Black men continued to run north from the courthouse towards Greenwood.[184] Afterwards, "the [B]lack men, their numbers seriously reduced, were able to head north across the Frisco tracks."[185] Enraged members of the white mob did not limit their wrath to those Black men who had marched to the courthouse; instead, they shot indiscriminately at Black men in the white section of Tulsa. A pack of white men chased an unarmed Black man through an alley, and when he tried to escape by ducking into the Royal Theater, his pursuers murdered him on stage.[186] Angry white men murdered a white man in an automobile, apparently believing the victim to be Black.[187]

Most of the Greenwood men made it back into their neighborhood and quickly prepared to defend Greenwood from the white men who had pursued them. These Greenwood men spread the word in the Black community, causing other Black men to gather as reinforcements to protect Greenwood.[188] Rumors of a "Negro uprising" that had begun when the first group of armed Black men had arrived at the courthouse spread quickly through the white community.[189]

b.   *Special Deputies*

Allegedly in response to this rumored "uprising," police indiscriminately deputized white men of Tulsa.[190] Police deputized as many as 500 white men in less than 30 minutes,[191] precluding the police from making any kind of assessment as to the character, competency, or even sobriety of the newly deputized men. Many of these men had been drinking.[192] Most were members of the mob that had earlier been demanding Rowland's lynching. In fact, one of the special deputies, whose name appears in records of the post-massacre grand jury investigation of Police Chief Gustafson, is identified as "Cranfield";[193] this man was likely Claud ("Yellow Hammer") Cranfield, the very same man Judge Cole identified as a probable ringleader in the attempt to lynch Rowland.[194]

Several years after the massacre, civil rights advocate Walter White, a light-skinned Black man who could pass for white, wrote that he had been appointed as a special deputy when he arrived in Tulsa to report on the massacre.[195] According to White, he only had to provide his name, age, and address, without any other proof of character, because his skin "was apparently white."[196] He reported he was told by a "villainous-looking man" that he could now "go out and shoot any ni**er you see and the law'll be behind you."[197] Another white witness reported that he was told by police authorities, whose names he did not know, to "get a gun and get busy and try to get a ni**er."[198] Several lawsuits against the city likewise alleged that unidentified city officials instructed white men to "[g]o out and kill you a [damn ni**er]" and that, as a result, the "streets of Tulsa became all agog with a seething, surging sea of humanity, a veritable army of mad men . . . fanned into white heat of racial hate and racial prejudice."[199]

Unable to obtain weapons from the federal armory, many white men of Tulsa, including special deputies, "broke into a hardware store, a pawnshop, and another place where arms were kept, and armed themselves with guns, revolvers, and ammunition."[200] A hardware store owner accused Tulsa Police Captain George Blaine of breaking into the store and "deal[ing] out" arms.[201]

c.   *Fighting at the Frisco Tracks*

Throughout the late night of May 31 and the early morning of June 1, the fiercest fighting occurred at or near the "Frisco tracks," which separated Greenwood from white Tulsa.[202] Black men fought in defense of Greenwood,[203] killing or wounding many white men during the battle. In the words of one scholar, "[v]eterans, replaying the military techniques they had recently learned, bunkered down in buildings along the railroad tracks, they found good vantage points from which to defend Greenwood. Some went to the belfry of the new Mount Zion Baptist Church . . . . Others bunkered down in their homes and businesses. They sought good spots to fire from, like concrete buildings. They put on their uniforms as they prepared to protect their community."[204] From midnight until 1:30 a.m., "scores—perhaps hundreds—of whites and [B]lacks exchanged gunfire across the tracks. At one point during the fighting, an inbound train arrived, its passengers forced to take cover on the floor."[205]

At 1:46 a.m., a telegram, signed by the police chief, the sheriff, and a judge, requested that the Governor J.B.A. Robertson send National Guard troops from across the state to Tulsa.[206] Meanwhile, National Guard members already stationed in Tulsa had offered assistance to the police.[207] Thirty guardsmen, armed with a machine gun as well as with other firearms, positioned themselves along Detroit Avenue between Brady Street and Standpipe Hill, establishing a "skirmish line."[208] In the early morning hours, white men (guardsmen, police, and special deputies) began rounding up Black civilians, whom they handed over—as prisoners—to the police.[209] The National Guard also sent patrols to arrest Black "domestic" workers in the servants' quarters of white homes, lest "bad [N]egroes" set fire to their white employers' homes.[210] In fact, it was the white men who started the fires. Most accounts estimate that the first fires were set in Greenwood around 1:00 a.m. near the Frisco tracks.[211] The fire department responded to the scene, but white men with guns threatened the firemen who tried to douse the flames, telling them to let the Black homes burn.[212]

At about 2:30 a.m., word spread that a trainload of armed Black men from nearby towns were coming to Tulsa to join the "Negro uprising." Guardsmen rushed to the depot, but the train had no Black men on it.[213] During this time, some Black Greenwood residents, including women and children, began to flee from Tulsa, running along the railroad tracks.[214] However, many residents did not appreciate the risk to Greenwood at this time. Some had likely gone to bed and were too soundly asleep or too far away to hear the shooting. Others assumed that the fighting would blow over by daylight.[215] In fact, by the early morning hours, it appeared the effort to save Greenwood had succeeded. Most of the fighting at the Frisco tracks had ended, and some of the men of Greenwood concluded that they had successfully repelled the white men.[216] Greenwood did not know that, in the quiet, what had been a lawless mob was organizing into an invading force.

d.   *White Tulsans Organize*

It was not a wild and disorderly mob,[217] but an organized force that invaded Greenwood.[218] In the early morning of June 1, white Tulsans, many of whom had previous war experience, divided into companies. Although chaos had reigned since 10:15 p.m., it took Tulsa city officials until 1:45 a.m. to summon the National Guard—perhaps because the request to Governor Robertson required the signature of the police chief, the sheriff, and a judge.[219] Because of this delay, it was white men of Tulsa, not professional guardsmen from outside the city, who engaged in "riot control." As explained above, many of these men had initially assembled to watch (or participate in) a lynching and some had been drinking all evening.

The Tulsa Police Department and local members of the National Guard, aided by white veterans of the American Legion, organized these white men into companies.[220] The role of the police and National Guard in organizing the white men was not a secret. The June 1, 1921 edition of the *Tulsa Daily World* reported that "[f]or three hours city officials, under direction of J. F. Adkison, police commissioner, and Charles Daley, inspector of police, with the assistance of part of the Home Guard company, formed armed white men into companies and these companies were marched to advantageous positions."[221] The National Guard's after-action reports corroborate that the National Guard helped to organize the white Tulsans.[222] During these early morning hours, the assembled white men were encouraged to make sure that their weapons and ammunition (some newly obtained from pawnshops and hardware stores) were compatible and to swap with others if they were not.[223]

When police and guardsmen initially divided men into companies, Adkinson, Daley, and the other unidentified officials may have believed they were defending white Tulsa from the "Negro uprising" that whites mistakenly believed was underway. In other words, the original goal may have been to have companies patrol streets and serve as a defensive bulwark against the anticipated incursion by Black men.[224] However, at some point in the early hours of June 1, a different plan evolved. The companies did not merely stand guard to prevent Black men from coming into the white section of Tulsa; instead, they made plans to invade Greenwood. One massacre participant recalled that the plan was to "go in at daybreak."[225] As explained below, a coordinated invasion did occur at "daybreak," heralded by a whistle.

Bureau of Investigation records corroborate the theory that law enforcement participated in planning a raid on Greenwood and that the invasion into the city was not an out-of-control attack of a lawless mob. Agent Weiss recorded a witness account stating that a police officer (identified only as "Rignon" but, as explained below, possibly a law enforcement officer named Jack Rigden or Rigdon) drove to a town outside of Tulsa to recruit white men, "intimating a raid on the [N]egroes."[226] The Bureau's account does not provide the identity of any other law enforcement officer involved in planning a raid.

7.   **The Invasion (June 1, 5:00 a.m. to 12:00 p.m.)**

The invasion of Greenwood differed considerably from the violence of the previous evening. Although there were pockets of resistance, much of the morning's violence was one-sided and directed not only at Black men with firearms but also at women, children, and the elderly.[227] In the words of one witness, "Tuesday night, May 31st, was the riot, and Wednesday morning, by daybreak, was the invasion."[228] Maurice Willows, the white director of Red Cross relief in Tulsa, wrote in his personal memoir, "[t]his was NOT a RIOT, as some of the out of town papers called it in their screaming headlines of the next day. It was a well-planned, diabolical ouster of the innocent [N]egros from their stamping grounds."[229]

a.   *The Whistle*

The invasion began in earnest when a whistle or siren blew a little after 5:00 a.m. on June 1.[230] Although many remember the siren, there is little consensus on what it was.[231] Some claim it was a city signal regularly used for fire[232] or other catastrophes, while others thought it was a factory whistle.[233] At the sound of the whistle, the white men (who had been organized into companies the night before) poured into Greenwood from multiple directions.[234] Although papers claimed that white men surrounded Greenwood, they actually gathered southwest of Greenwood, primarily at three points: (1) behind the Frisco freight depot, (2) at the Frisco and Santa Fe passenger station, and (3) at the Katy passenger depot.[235] According to news accounts, armed white men in automobiles encircled Greenwood, and with the dawn, the "continuous rattlle [sic] of rifle and revolver fire could be heard" as the men began to "range through" Greenwood to "clean it out."[236] At the same time bi-planes flew overhead, some of which may have dropped incendiary material.[237] A machine gun, mounted on a grain elevator, provided cover for those who invaded.[238]

It is unclear how many white Tulsans took part in the invasion of Greenwood. The Commission Report estimates that approximately 10,000 white Tulsans participated in the attack.[239] This is consistent with numbers given by a scholar in 1946, who reported estimates of 8,000 to 10,000 white men were "under arms" during the time of the massacre.[240] The *New York Times* reported that Adjutant General Charles Barrett, the National Guardsman who arrived in Tulsa on June 1 and imposed martial law, estimated that there were "[t]wenty-five thousand whites, armed to the teeth . . .

ranging the city in utter and ruthless defiance of every concept of law and righteousness."[241] Many

believe this to be a misprint (or a misstatement) and that his calculation was actually twenty-five

hundred.[242] An attorney representing Chief Gustafson later argued that police, city officials, business

men, and "every other white man in the town who was awake" armed themselves during the

massacre.[243] Moreover, while participants in this invasion mostly included men, there are reports of

women and boys participating in the events of the massacre, particularly in the looting and arson that

followed.[244] In addition, the number of "white Tulsans" included several Native Americans who

identified as white.[245]

      Once these white Tulsans crossed into Greenwood, they moved efficiently from house to

house, burning the community. The burnings were methodical, which corroborates that they were the

product of a plan rather than spontaneous acts of violence.[246] Survivors later recalled that these white

men systematically destroyed Greenwood neighborhoods, block by block.[247] A journalist who studied

the massacre described the efficiency of the process as follows: "The fires were set systemically, like

this: A team of white men, some of them deputized by police, entered a chosen home, blowing the lock

off the door if necessary."[248] They would then "smash[] the valuables inside, wrench[] open dresser

drawers and tear[] down window drapes."[249] "After gathering the bedding, wooden furniture, and

other flammable items into the center of a room, the men [would] douse[] the objects in kerosene" and

then "li[gh]t a match."[250] As the white men moved north, "they set fire to practically every building in

[Greenwood], including a dozen churches,[251] five hotels, 31 restaurants, four drug stores, eight

doctor's offices, more than two dozen grocery stores, and the [B]lack public library," as well as

"[m]ore than a thousand homes."[252] The fire "bec[ame] so hot that nearby trees and outbuildings also

burst into flame."[253]

The white men prioritized arresting or otherwise incapacitating Black men,[254] which facilitated the burning and looting of Black neighborhoods.[255] The Tulsa white community would later blame a largely unnamed criminal element for these atrocities.[256] But while law enforcement was quick to take every Black man into custody (even those who were not doing anything remotely threatening), law enforcement often ignored white arsonists, looters, or murderers, at least during the height of the massacre.[257]

b.　*The Burning*

Black survivors, many now deceased, have provided vivid accounts of the events that followed the invasion, but most could not identify any particular perpetrator by name. One witness reported that white men entered her home after shooting through the window, a bullet lodging in the couch.[258] Another described white men "kicking in doors, setting houses on fire, crashing, trashing, and burning what they didn't take with them."[259] A survivor who was a child at the time recalled hiding in the attic, smelling smoke, and realizing that his house had been set on fire with him in it.[260] Another child victim recalled hiding under the bed while white men were in his house; when one stepped on his finger, his sister put her hand over his mouth so he would not scream and give away their presence.[261] Another relayed an account of white men kicking in his door and grabbing his mother and sister, ransacking the house, and throwing a Molotov cocktail into his room, lighting it on fire.[262]

As these white men moved northward, word spread from house to house that white people were killing Black people. One survivor remembers her mother urgently waking her and telling her that the family had to leave because white people were killing all the Black people.[263] A Black man from the neighborhood ran from house to house, urging residents to save themselves. Other survivors, who were children at the time of the massacre, similarly remembered being hastily awakened by adults telling them that white Tulsans were killing all the Black people of Greenwood.[264]

Women fled with babies in their arms, leading crying children by the hand.[265] Many had no time to dress; they ran shoeless, wearing only their night-clothes.[266] Bullets were "falling like rain" as young children were "frantically trying to find parents."[267] Women dragged their children along seeking safety, while "white rascals fir[ed] at them as they ran."[268] A woman was killed falling out of a wagon when it made a sharp turn in an effort to get away.[269] White Tulsans in nearby homes looked at the Black people fleeing Greenwood as if they "were animals escaping a forest fire."[270] One survivor was haunted for nearly a century by the memory of her neighbor's stillborn child, whose body she had placed in a shoebox; when the shoebox was lost during the devastation, the mother was inconsolable.[271] Families were separated; one survivor recounted that his adolescent sister was separated from their family, and whatever happened during the separation traumatized her for the rest of her life.[272] Another survivor summed up the ordeal by saying, "[w]hat a pitiful bunch we were. In our night clothes . . . barefoot . . . electric lines falling down around us . . . smouldering [sic] relics of once-beautiful homes . . . the sight and smell of death and destruction all around us."[273]

Several particularly horrifying accounts are well documented. One is the murder of A.C. Jackson, a Black doctor recognized as one of the country's leading surgeons.[274] A white landowner reported going to Greenwood to check on his property and seeing 70-year-old Dr. Jackson walk out of his home with his hands in the air, surrendering to armed white men. The landowner asked these men not to hurt Dr. Jackson, but a young white man wearing a white shirt and cap nonetheless shot Dr. Jackson, who later died from his wounds.[275] Men then looted and burned Dr. Jackson's house while other looters were "dancing a jig and just having a rolic[k]ing easy good time."[276]

One Black survivor described how white men shot his grandfather in front of him as he and his family tried to escape in a wagon. He would later recall, with terror, how he worried that the white men would also kill his mother when she screamed in response to her father's murder.[277] Another survivor recounted how white men shot her husband in the stomach as the two of them ran, leaving him with his intestines "hanging outside" his stomach.[278] White massacre participants committed additional atrocities: They broke into the home of an elderly paralyzed man and ordered him and his wife to "march." When the man protested that he could not do so, white men shot him and forcibly removed his wife from their home.[279] Four white men tied a blind Black double amputee, well-known as someone who begged on the streets of Tulsa, to the bumper of a car and dragged him through the streets to his death.[280] Massacre participants shot an elderly couple living on Greenwood Avenue in the back of their heads while they were praying.[281] One eyewitness saw a Black man attempt to flee a burning building, but was "shot to death as he emerged" and "his body was thrown back into the flames."[282]

c.   *The Looting*

The white men looted homes before burning them. One eyewitness reported that the mob "carried away everything of value, opened safes, destroyed all legal papers and documents, then set fire to the building to hide their crime."[283] Another Greenwood resident reported that, when he returned home after the massacre ended, he saw that his piano and elegant furniture were in the street, money had been stolen from his safe, and his silverware and other items of value had been stolen.[284] Another witness reported seeing members of the Home Guard "break into stores of all kinds and carry out the contents."[285] Another survivor reported seeing trucks back up to homes of Greenwood's Black residents so white men could load "everything moveable and of value."[286] Yet another survivor reported seeing looting, including by "[white] women with shopping bags [who] would come in, open drawers, take every kind of finery from clothing to silverware and jewelry." That same witness saw white men "carrying out the furniture, cursing as they did so, saying, 'these [damn] [N]egroes have better things than lots of white people.'"[287] Another survivor reported coming home to find that his dog had been killed.[288] In addition to looting homes, white Tulsans who captured Black Greenwood residents often searched and robbed them of any possessions they carried.[289]

These survivor accounts are corroborated by accounts that white witnesses gave to Agent Weiss the day after the massacre. Deputy U.S. Marshal Ellis told Agent Weiss that he saw white people "stealing and pillaging in the [N]egro section, which was on fire," describing that they "stole Victrolas, sewing machines, clothes, furs, autos, [and] furniture."[290] Another white witness told Agent Weiss that he saw "hundreds of whites, including white women and white girls," undisturbed by police, "carrying Victrolas, trunks, clothing, furs," and other items "out of [N]egroes' houses before they were burned."[291]

d. The Resistance

Although the nature of the events of June 1 were more of a one-sided slaughter than the previous night's fighting, not all Black men of Greenwood surrendered peacefully. Black men made a stand at Mount Zion Baptist Church, "position[ing] themselves in the belfry . . . whose commanding view of the area just below Standpipe Hill allowed them to temporarily stem the tide of the white invasion."[292] These men were defeated when guardsmen unleashed a machine gun, perhaps with aerial support.[293] At Standpipe Hill, a firefight took place between white Tulsans and a group of Black men, led by the quasi-mythical figure of "Peg Leg" Taylor, who is renowned for "singlehandedly" fighting off "more than a dozen" white men.[294] J.B. Stradford fought to protect his hotel, shooting from the second story; he surrendered only when the men promised not to burn his hotel—a promise they did not keep.[295]

e. The Destruction

The murders, arsons, and looting continued from dawn through the early afternoon of June 1. "By the time that martial law was declared in Tulsa County at 11:29 a.m.," the most violent aspect of the massacre had largely run its course.[296] Fires continued to smolder through the rest of the day.

Photographs were taken of the destruction of Greenwood, some of which were turned into postcards.

One of the most infamous bore the caption, "Run[n]ing the Negro Out of Tulsa."[297]

E.   Examination of the Role of Particular Persons or Organizations

During our review we examined allegations of misconduct of particular groups. Specifically,

we examined the conduct of the Tulsa Police Department, the sheriff, the National Guard, the mayor,

companies that owned and operated airplanes, the Klan and other hate groups, and the white Tulsa

business community and city leaders.

1.   The Tulsa Police Department

We reviewed allegations that members of the Tulsa Police Department engaged in misconduct

during the massacre. We examined the culpability of the Tulsa Police Department as a whole, as well

as the conduct of some individual members (both identified and not identified). A century after the

massacre, we have no evidence that any of these individuals are still alive.

The Tulsa Police Department took few, if any, steps to disperse the white mob when it first

gathered outside the courthouse.[298] Due to a shift change, the Tulsa Police Department was

understaffed when violence broke out. Thus, there were not enough officers either to disperse the

white mob members who initially assembled, nor were there sufficient staff to disarm combatants once

shooting started.[299]

After the first shots, when "all hell broke loose," police deputized hundreds of white Tulsans,

many of whom had been drinking,[300] and most of whom had assembled to (at worst) participate in a

lynching or (at best) to watch one. Police conferred badges quickly with few questions about

suitability. In an interview conducted in 1946, 25 years after the massacre, Police Captain Blaine

indicated that within about 30 minutes, "about five hundred" white men "had been given special commissions."[301] This precluded even a cursory check for fitness or judgment. Adkison, the police commissioner, testified that he "usually" commissioned only men he thought would be cool-headed, but he conceded that some might have lost their heads during the massacre.[302] In the words of a National Guard member, the special deputies became "the most dangerous part of the mob" that invaded Greenwood.[303]

We have found no evidence that, after deputizing the white men, the police took steps to ensure the newly minted deputies acted responsibly. Unabated by police, one of the first things these special deputies did was to break into hardware stores and pawnshops in a search for weapons, setting an example of lawless conduct from the start.[304] A hardware store owner, whose guns were confiscated and given to the mob, later identified Captain Blaine as the Tulsa police officer who had given out the weapons.[305] Moreover, instead of instructing everyone to take steps to preserve life and safety, evidence suggests that at least some (unidentified) members of law enforcement told the newly commissioned deputies to use their guns to "get a ni**er."[306]

Later, the police actively coordinated the invasion of Greenwood. The papers named Police Commissioner Adkison and Inspector Daley as the officials primarily responsible for organizing white men into companies.[307] A witness told Agent Weiss that a Tulsa police officer, identified as "Rignon" (who, as explained more fully below, may be an officer named Jack Rigdon or Rigden) drove to Jenks, Oklahoma, to recruit white men to participate in a raid on Greenwood.[308] Moreover, in the days before cell phones, police were best positioned to communicate and thus to help in the coordination. For example, Police Chief Gustafson testified that, on the night of the massacre, police communicated using the "Gamewell system,"[309] which, despite its modern-sounding name, was a telegraph-based fire and emergency communications alert system patented by John Gamewell.[310]

Thus, there is considerable evidence that police participated in a plan to invade Greenwood and imprison its residents. Although there is less evidence that police were involved in planning the subsequent destruction of Greenwood (or the murder of its inhabitants), *some* evidence exists that this was the plan of at least *some* police officers. The most persuasive evidence of police involvement in a plan to destroy the community comes from sworn testimony in the trial of Chief Gustafson.[311] John A. Oliphant, a white witness referred to as "Judge" Oliphant by the prosecutor,[312] testified about the murder of Dr. A.C. Jackson. Oliphant described Jackson's killer as a "citizen," not a law enforcement officer,[313] but when prosecutors asked if he had seen any police on the scene, he responded that he had: "[t]hey were the chief fellows setting fires."[314]

Oliphant further identified a man named Brown as someone he knew[315] to be a police officer and accused Brown and a civilian named "Cowboy Long" of being the chief arsonists.[316] Significantly, Oliphant testified that these men told him that they were given an "order" to destroy Greenwood, although Oliphant qualified that "destroy" was not the word these men used in describing the instructions they had been given.[317] While certainly not dispositive, the fact that the arsonists used the word "order" suggests complicity by someone in authority who was capable of giving orders. If Brown was in fact a police officer, as Oliphant testified, then the implication is that police gave an order. This suggests, though certainly does not conclusively prove, that arsons were not a spontaneous act of crazed mob members.

This evidence of police complicity in a plan to destroy Greenwood is corroborated by evidence that police directly participated in arsons and looting. The Oklahoma Supreme Court cited evidence that many of the men who set fires in Greenwood were "wearing police badges."[318] Some of these were doubtless special deputies,[319] but there is evidence that others were full-time law enforcement officers. A witness named Jack Krueger alleged that a uniformed police officer named William

Mauldin "went home[,] changed his uniform to plainclothes, and went to [the] [N]egro district and lead [sic] a bunch of whites into [N]egro[e]s['] houses, some of the bunch pilfering, never offered to protect men, women or children, or property."[320] Krueger likewise accused Irish Bullard, a Tulsa Police Department motorcycle officer, of "shoot[ing] down all [N]egro[e]s as they showed up."[321] Deputy Sheriff Bostic, identified as a "colored" law enforcement officer, accused Traffic Policeman Pittman of forcing Bostic and his wife and children to leave their home, pouring oil on the floor, and setting the home on fire.[322] News accounts report that a motorcycle officer named Leo Irish "captured" six Black men in Greenwood, "roped them together in single file, and led them running behind his motorcycle to detention at Convention Hall."[323] A white witness reported seeing white officers search Black men, reportedly looking for weapons, only to steal money from them and shoot them if they protested.[324] A white witness named Tom Dyer told Agent Weiss that an officer identified as "Rignon" (who, as explained below, may be an officer named Jack Rigdon or Rigden) bragged of personally killing four Black men.[325]

Even in 1921, many Tulsans, both white and Black, blamed police for the massacre.[326] A grand jury charged Gustafson with failing to intercept or prevent men and boys "of both white and colored race" from traveling, armed, on the streets of Tulsa to "set fire to and burn many buildings [and to] . . . with impunity and without molestation commit the crimes of murder, arson, burglary and grand larceny," permitting "the law abiding citizens of the city of Tulsa and their property for many hours to be and remain at the mercy of armed men."[327] This wording, of course, suggests a theory of failure-to-protect more than a theory that police were directly involved in the massacre. Private lawsuits against the city, however, alleged that police had planned Greenwood's destruction with members of the mob.[328]

2.   The Sheriff

We have reviewed allegations that Sheriff William McCullough engaged in misconduct during the massacre. When the white lynch mob initially assembled, Sheriff McCullough refused to hand Rowland over to mob members, even when three men breached the courthouse and demanded that he do so. This was, of course, no more than should be expected from a lawman but, at a time when officials often gave into demands of lynchers (some enthusiastically participating in a lynching; others agreeing reluctantly, to protect their own popularity), Sheriff McCullough's resistance to mob pressure is significant.

Sheriff McCullough, however, took no other steps to prevent violence. At some point when the mob assembled, he ordered the white crowd to disband, but "he apparently did not attempt to enforce his order."[329] After initial violence broke out at the courthouse, Sheriff McCullough became myopic, focusing only on Rowland while ignoring the chaos erupting around him. In fact, while he spent the night guarding Rowland at the courthouse, he admitted sleeping through the massacre, paying no attention when he heard shots.[330] Not only did Sheriff McCullough remain in the courthouse, but he also barricaded his deputies in there so that they were unavailable to help prevent further violence. In fact, it was difficult for guardsmen to reach him so that he could execute a telegram (which by law he had to sign) requesting assistance from the National Guard.[331] Had National Guard troops from Oklahoma City arrived earlier, they might have prevented at least some of the destruction and death. McCullough apparently testified in a lawsuit filed by J.B. Stradford to recover insurance proceeds that, at some point on the morning of the massacre, he drove to Greenwood and tried to stop the burning. We did not find any corroboration for this assertion and, even if true, it was too little, too late.[332]

3.   **The National Guard**

We reviewed allegations that the National Guard engaged in misconduct during the massacre. To examine the role of the National Guard, we must first define terms. National Guard troops from outside of Tulsa did not arrive until after 9:00 a.m. on the morning of June 1 and were not fully activated until two hours later, when the worst of the massacre had ended. There were, however, members of the National Guard who resided in Tulsa and who participated directly in the events of the massacre. Some of these guardsmen, like Major Daley, were also members of the Tulsa Police Department, leaving it unclear the capacity in which each had acted.

In addition, many Black witnesses condemned atrocities committed by the "Home Guard," while the National Guard reports discuss the actions of the American Legion. These organizations (the Home Guard and the American Legion) differed from each other and from the National Guard, although there was likely considerable overlap in membership, and some witnesses may have used the terms interchangeably.[333] As discussed above, the Home Guard consisted of men who had volunteered to protect Tulsa during the Great War and who had drilled together and acted as enforcers for the domestic council, which set itself up as something of a morality police. The American Legion consisted of Great War veterans with military experience.

a.   Members of the Tulsa National Guard

Members of the Tulsa contingency of the National Guard played a major role in the events of the massacre. In May 1921, the Oklahoma National Guard had three Federally recognized units stationed in Tulsa: (1) Company "B," a rifle company; (2) the Service Company, a supply unit; and (3) a Sanitary Detachment of surgeons and field medics.[334] Company "B" had access to more advanced weapons, including six Browning Automatic Rifles.[335] Guardsmen operated at least one machine gun during the massacre.[336] White Tulsans involved in the attack possessed at least two machine guns, and one scholar who interviewed various massacre participants for a 1946 article asserted that the Tulsa contingency of the National Guard provided both of them.[337] Guardsmen, however, insisted that these machine guns were *not* from the National Armory, but admitted possession of one during the time, claiming it had either been "dug up" by the Tulsa police or a war relic, and insisting it was barely operable.[338] The credibility of such statements cannot now be evaluated,[339] and it may be that one of the machine guns was the property of the American Legion.[340] The (allegedly defective) machine gun used by the National Guard is visible in photographs, later turned into postcards, of guardsmen on a truck bed with a machine gun.[341]

As explained above, at the outbreak of the violence, Major Bell and other guardsmen kept firearms out of the hands of an angry white mob that stormed their armory. Once initial shots were fired, the Tulsa guardsmen worked closely with police, establishing their headquarters at the police station and placing themselves under the authority of Chief Gustafson and Commissioner Adkison.[342] Governor Robertson had not activated the Guard at this point, so it could not act independently. But the effect of the Guard submitting to police authority was that some of the best trained and best armed men in the city were under the command of the Tulsa police, who, as noted above, engaged in acts of violence and arson.[343] Initially, the Tulsa guardsmen were deployed downtown, tasked with patrolling the streets.[344] Later in the evening, guardsmen assisted police in forming companies of white men and, by their own admission, they played a direct role in entering Greenwood and rounding up Black residents.[345]

There are some credible accounts of guardsmen trying to disarm white men attacking Greenwood. Indeed, white massacre participants assaulted one veteran who was traveling with the National Guard (operating its machine gun), because the Guard had tried to "disarm a white rioter."[346] Major Daley, who was both a guardsman and a Tulsa police officer, reportedly tried for hours to hold off enraged white mob members seeking to attack Greenwood before dawn.[347] However, the Guard did not disarm white and Black men equally.[348]

Although there are reports (like those described above) that members of the Tulsa National Guard protected Black people and property, by their own admission there were many other incidents in which guardsmen fired upon Black men in Greenwood.[349] A group of guardsmen fired "at will" at a group of Black men.[350] According to a guardsman named Captain McCurn, these Black men had been firing at white people's homes; thus, it is possible that they believed they were acting in defense of those being fired upon.[351] After-action reports stress that guardsmen followed instructions not to fire unless fired upon.[352] However, there are allegations that the guardsmen often unquestioningly joined in with the white Tulsans who were attacking Greenwood, instead of playing a more impartial role by trying to neutralize all combatants.[353] Since guardsmen possessed a machine gun and superior rifles, they seriously outgunned any Black men they encountered.[354]

The primary role of the National Guard in the massacre was to subdue and capture Black men and take them into custody.[355] This had the effect, intended or not, of facilitating the burning and looting of unprotected Black homes. By his own admission, guardsman (and police officer) Major Daley ordered the arrest of Black people living in "servants['] quarters,"[356] a reference to people (mostly women) working as domestic workers in white homes. If a Black individual was physically located in a white person's home, that individual was clearly not participating in the violence taking place outside on the streets. Yet, Major Daley still authorized their arrests. Captain McCurn reported that he and his men "captured, arrested and disarmed a great many [N]egro men . . . and sent them under guard to the convention hall and other points where they were being concentrated."[357]

Although it is clear the Guard played a significant role in the mass arrests of Black residents, it is less clear what motivated the guardsmen. At least one guardsman referred to Black residents as the "enemy,"[358] and it is possible that many in the all-white Guard harbored racial beliefs similar to those of the white mob that originally gathered at the courthouse. However, other accounts identify additional motivations. According to a treatise describing the role of the Oklahoma National Guard in the massacre, the Guard received "rules of engagement" from Governor Robertson before he declared martial law.[359] Relying solely on an account provided by interviewee Sergeant T. J. Essley, the treatise maintains that these rules included an order to take Black people in Greenwood into custody and transport them to Convention Hall for internment and safeguarding.[360] The treatise's author viewed this as equivalent to placing Black residents into protective custody, essentially asserting that they were arrested for their own protection.[361] There is not, however, a field order discussing "protective custody."[362] Major Daley's after-action report confirms that the Guard, along with veterans and other white men, took Black people into custody.[363] But it is not clear whether they did so in order to protect the Black detainees, to "safeguard" against a suspected uprising, or with the purpose of harming those taken into custody. While the treatise (and the Essley interview) suggest that some guardsmen (and those working with them) may have believed that they were seizing the residents of Greenwood to protect, not punish them, other reports seem to contradict that motive—in particular, reports that guardsmen turned a blind eye to acts of looting by white Tulsans.[364] Moreover, photographs of some of the Black men apprehended by guardsmen are more consistent with the treatment of criminal suspects than protected victims.[365]

In sum, the arrest of the Black men of Greenwood was a leading reason that acts of arson and looting were subsequently able to occur. It is difficult to assess the reason why guardsmen took Black residents of Greenwood into custody. Some guardsmen may have thought they were taking residents into protective custody or that the arrests were an appropriate means of preventing an "uprising." Others may have understood that their actions were inappropriate but, nonetheless, still chose to engage in misconduct. We have not uncovered any evidence that any of the guardsmen (including those identified by name in after-action reports and those whose names are unknown) are still living.

b.   Guard Members from Elsewhere in Oklahoma

Governor Robertson officially activated National Guard troops after he received the 1:45 a.m. telegram signed by Sheriff McCullough, Police Chief Gustafson, and a judge. A contingency of guardsmen arrived by train at approximately 9:15 a.m. on the morning of June 1.[366] Because the Guard first had to report to local authorities, whom they had to find in the fighting, they did not take immediate action to stop the burning and looting.[367] Some report that the guardsmen dawdled, eating breakfast;[368] one photograph depicts guardsmen standing around watching Tulsa burn.[369] Black residents writing at the time, however, praised the Oklahoma contingency of the National Guard.[370] While these non-Tulsan guardsman did make efforts to prevent looting,[371] critics contend that, had the guardsmen taken action as soon as they arrived, they could have saved houses on Detroit Avenue from burning.[372]

When Governor Robertson finally activated the Guard, guardsmen assisted in taking Black men into "protective custody," confining them to internment camps.[373] One witness recalled guardsmen shooting at the feet of women they escorted to detention camps if the women did not move fast enough.[374] The Guard arrested some white residents for looting but did not confine any white resident to the camps. Thus, these troops did not protect Black and white Tulsa equally.

4.   The Mayor

We have also examined the potential culpability of Mayor T.D. Evans, whose role in the massacre is best defined by his absence. In the words of a journalist who has written about the massacre, Mayor Evans "all but abdicated during the crisis. . . . Despite warnings from whites and [B]lacks that trouble was brewing, he remained mostly silent and entirely invisible."[375] However, several lawsuits naming Mayor Evans as a defendant allege that he bore more direct responsibility than being absent.[376] Specifically, these lawsuits assert that Evans (and other city officials) directed special deputies to "go and kill a d[amn ni**er]."[377] Some lawsuits also alleged that Mayor Evans gave an order to "burn every Black house 'as far north as Haskell street.'"[378] The pleadings do not cite any witness testimony, affidavits, or other evidence to support these contentions, and the lawsuits were dismissed before depositions were taken. It is possible that the plaintiffs were suing Mayor Evans on a theory of *respondeat superior* (i.e., asking that he be held responsible for the actions of those who worked for him), and that they were not planning to show that he personally made such statements. It may be that litigants inferred that Mayor Evans engaged in this conduct *during* the massacre from statements he made *after* the massacre, congratulating the National Guard and police and intimating that he was glad that Greenwood had been destroyed.[379] It remains possible, however, that these litigants had access to information that is now lost to us. We have not uncovered any evidence beyond these barebones allegations that Mayor Evans instructed anyone to kill Black residents or that he directed the burning of Greenwood.

5.   Airplane Owners and Operators

We have examined allegations that men in airplanes dropped incendiary material and fired guns into Greenwood (and on those fleeing Greenwood). News accounts of the day, published by white papers, asserted that airplanes provided support for the invasion.[380] The planes involved in the massacre were likely Curtis JN-4 "Jenny" biplanes,[381] which were small aircraft made of spruce and covered in cloth,[382] and likely came from the nearby Curtiss-Southwest Airfield.[383] Curtiss Southwest likely owned some of the planes, and Sinclair Oil likely owned others.[384] It is undisputed that, during the massacre, planes kept tabs on Black Greenwood residents and informed law enforcement of the movements of Black people.[385]

What is hotly disputed is whether, and to what extent, airplanes dropped incendiary material such as turpentine balls, nitroglycerin, bombs, dynamite, or kerosene on Greenwood buildings, and to what extent the pilots or passengers shot at those fleeing the devastation. Many survivors reported seeing incendiary material fall from the planes.[386] While some massacre scholars have dismissed such claims, they are extremely prevalent.[387] Some of these reports come from older adults recalling events of their childhood, but these recollections are corroborated by accounts written shortly after the massacre by prominent adult members of the Black community. For example, well-respected Black attorney B.C. Franklin, an eyewitness to the massacre, described seeing turpentine bombs in an account dated a decade after the massacre.[388]

Black newspapers of the day reported that airplanes dropped nitroglycerin on buildings to set them on fire.[389] Multiple lawsuits filed in 1923 by plaintiffs (who presumably knew they would have to prove their allegations in court to recover) included assertions that planes had dropped incendiary materials.[390] In addition, a witness told the Oklahoma Commission that, in the fifties, he had heard an unidentified white man brag that he had dropped dynamite on fleeing refugees.[391] There were also contemporaneous reports of weapons fired from planes.[392] Journalist Mary Jones Parrish, writing in the wake of the massacre, reported passing the airfield and seeing men with high-powered rifles board airplanes.[393]

Some believe these memories are inaccurate, stressing how easily a wooden Jenny could catch fire and citing the difficulty of lighting flammables in an open cockpit.[394] One journalist concluded that such an attempt would have been foolhardy, while conceding that "foolhardiness ruled the day."[395] Another journalist noted that pilots had successfully transported nitroglycerin and that doing so would, thus, not be impossible.[396]

Accounts from an incident in 1919 may shed light on the plausibility of these allegations. For one day in May 1919, Tulsa officials employed three pilots to protect Tulsa from feared "May Day" radicals.[397] A news report suggests that the May Day planes primarily engaged in surveillance and does not indicate that the planes dropped bombs or flammables.[398] Interestingly, however, the papers reported that the pilots were "heavily armed" and carried "signal rockets."[399] This suggests that the May Day pilots may have been prepared to shoot radicals from the air. Although this is certainly not conclusive evidence of what equipment pilots carried two years later, this report at least suggests that pilots of the time were prepared to shoot from the air.

The fact that the May Day pilots carried signal rockets may likewise suggest that the massacre pilots did as well,[400] although we have not found direct evidence that any pilot had such a rocket in 1921 (and, if so, how many signal rockets any pilot might have). But, if pilots regularly used such equipment during this period, and if pilots had the ability to fire these rockets from the air, it is possible that victims interpreted the rockets, which emitted a colored flare,[401] as incendiary devices.[402] It is also possible that the signal rockets were aimed at massacre victims, either as weapons, or for their intimidation value. This theory would not, of course, explain the turpentine balls observed by B.C. Franklin, nor the allegations of survivors who claimed buildings caught fire from the top.

In addition to alleging that planes dropped incendiary devices, lawsuits also claimed that police officers directly participated in the aerial attack. Several lawsuits alleged that Tulsa Police Captain George H. Blaine directly took part in the aerial assault on Greenwood.[403] Captain Blaine did undertake a scouting trip by air several days after the massacre, apparently to see whether there was unrest in outlying counties.[404] It is possible that this gave rise to the allegations that he was also in a plane during the massacre itself. We have not uncovered any other evidence suggesting Blaine was present in a plane during the massacre, but it remains possible that litigants had access to evidence now

lost to us.

At this time, we cannot draw firm conclusions about whether planes dropped incendiary

materials during the massacre, or whether or how often planes fired shots. It does not appear that any

pilots testified before the grand jury or in any civil deposition. We observe only that, had there been a

criminal trial in the immediate aftermath of the massacre, prosecutors could have called multiple

eyewitnesses who would have testified that they saw incendiary materials fall from planes and

witnessed shots being fired at victims from the air.

6.   **Hate Groups (The Klan and Similar Groups)**

We have also examined the role of the Ku Klux Klan and pre-Klan white supremacy

organizations. In the 1920s, many white men of Tulsa supported white supremacy groups like the

Klan, which enjoyed a huge resurgence across the country after the 1915 film *Birth of a Nation*.[405]

Scholars have estimated that hundreds of members of the Klan worked for the City of Tulsa during the

1920s.[406] Klan rolls show that in 1928, seven years after the massacre, nearly 60 persons who

identified themselves as members of law enforcement were Klan members.[407] Many of the experts we

spoke with believe that the Klan, while active in other parts of Oklahoma, was not well organized in

Tulsa in May 1921.[408] They maintain that the massacre was a catalyst for Klan membership, not a

result of it.[409] Others disagree. William O'Brien, who wrote a white perspective of the massacre

called *Who Speaks for Us*, declared that groups like the Klan were involved in the massacre, viewing it

as "an opportunity" for such groups to "actively practice their racial, ethnic, and religious hatred under

the immunity of police authority."[410] O'Brien also asserted that many members of the white mob and

of the Tulsa police shared the "common bond" of Klan membership.[411] In 1924, an anti-Klan reformer

lectured that "[a]bout four years ago the Ku Klux Klan stole silently into Oklahoma . . . Six months later it had developed the velocity of a hurricane and the madness of a maniac. By the spring of 1921, no man's business, no man's employment, no man's life was safe unless he belonged to the Invisible Empire."[412] A white massacre participant, who identified himself as a former Klansman, claimed that the Klan had formed in Tulsa in 1918 or 1919.[413] None of this is conclusive evidence of Klan responsibility for the massacre. The Klan did not publicly take credit for the massacre (or for putting down a "Negro uprising"), which could be because it was not, in fact, responsible, or because it was, as it billed itself, an "invisible" empire that did not want to publish its deeds.

Even if the Klan did not yet have a firm foothold in Tulsa before the massacre, Klan sentiment certainly did. Groups like the Confederate Veterans had a strong presence in Tulsa.[414] So too did the Knights of Liberty, a vigilante group formed as an enforcement wing of the Council of Defense, an organization with white supremacist leanings formed during the Great War.[415]

7. Other City Officials and Tulsa Business Interests (Conspiracy Theories)

We have examined allegations that the massacre was the result of a pre-planned conspiracy by the city of Tulsa, city leaders, and/or leading businessmen. Many in the Greenwood community, when speaking with us, opined that the massacre was planned long before May 31, 1921. As explained more fully below, in the weeks following the massacre, city leaders (like Mayor Evans) and businessmen (like Tate Brady and Merritt Glass) immediately attempted to capitalize on the destruction. For example, city leaders planned to acquire the burned land for industrial use.[416] This would move the Greenwood community farther from white Tulsa (satisfying segregationist impulses) and enrich business interests. Under a *quo bono* (who benefits) theory, some have speculated that the men who stood to benefit from Greenwood's destruction must have planned the massacre.[417] Some suggest that the plan was to invade Greenwood the next time there was news of misconduct by a Black person, and that once Rowland's arrest appeared in the paper, the conspirators sprang into action. Others have gone so far as to suggest that the elevator incident was staged to provide a pretext for the invasion.[418] We have found much speculation, but little direct evidence, of such a longstanding plan.

The evidence most often cited to support the existence of a longstanding conspiracy comes from statements made to the NAACP by individuals identified as "refugees" from Oklahoma.[419] According to *The Crisis*, these refugees told the NAACP that flyers of some sort appeared in the months before the massacre, warning Black people to "leave Oklahoma" by June 1.[420] The refugees were from the nearby town of Okmulgee, not Tulsa, and said the warning was to leave "Oklahoma," not Tulsa specifically. We have not found any copies of the posters, and neither Mary Jones Parrish, writing after the massacre, nor any of the survivors whose accounts are included in her book, mentioned flyers. People who sued the city and their insurance companies, claiming that the massacre was not a "riot" but an action for which the city was responsible, did not mention any flyers. One survivor questioned by a massacre historian about whether he had seen posters or "handbills" warning of the massacre denied it.[421]

The other evidence cited for a longstanding conspiracy (by the city or business interests) is the statement of a survivor that her mother's white employer brought her and her family to the employer's home in advance of the massacre, implying that the employer had foreknowledge of the massacre and wanted to keep her own Black employees safe.[422] The recorded interview of this survivor does not suggest that the requests came weeks (or even days) in advance, however. Instead, it appears that the white employer invited her Black employee to stay with her at about the time rumors of a lynching circulated,[423] which could have disrupted the city enough to warrant white employers suggesting their Black employees avoid Greenwood.

A journalist who has written about the massacre notes that it began with chaos and running gun battles on the streets of white Tulsa, which killed or injured many white residents.[424] He persuasively argues that, if the massacre was the result of longstanding planning, it likely would have been undertaken in a manner that avoided such danger and destruction.[425] In addition, it was white indignation about Black men gathering at the courthouse that prompted the mob to swell.[426] Given racial attitudes of the day, it would seem unlikely that white city leaders would institute a plan that depended upon bringing armed Black men into the white section of the city.

That said, even if there was no longstanding plan to acquire Greenwood through murder, arson, and pillage, it is possible that businessmen were contemplating ways to obtain the land before the massacre and were, thus, quick to turn the massacre to their advantage. It well may be, as some scholars have suggested, that before dawn on June 1 (when white Tulsans were organizing for invasion), men with property interests (or their representatives) participated in planning the invasion of Greenwood with the goal of acquiring land.[427]

F.   The Aftermath

1.   Internment Camps and Tent Cities

On June 1, 1921, at 11:30 a.m., Governor Robertson declared martial law in Tulsa and placed Adjutant General Barrett of the National Guard in command.[428] Barrett lifted martial law at 5:00 p.m. on June 3, and the Guard left the next day on June 4.[429] Police ordered that the city remain in a "semi-military state" after the Guard left.[430] Approximately one hundred "extra officers" drawn from the American Legion and Veterans of Foreign War, which were comprised of men who had taken part in the massacre, remained on duty.[431]

During and after the massacre, law enforcement officers and special deputies arrested Black residents of Greenwood and confined them to internment or "concentration" camps.[432] While some Black men were later charged with "inciting" the "riot,"[433] authorities confined residents regardless of whether they were suspected of committing acts of violence (or were even physically capable of doing so). In other words, detention was not based on probable cause or even reasonable suspicion that Greenwood residents had committed crimes.

Camps were set up in three locations: the Convention Hall, McNulty Park, and the Tulsa fairgrounds.[434] Armed men guarded the camps to prevent escape.[435] Some detainees reported that their white captors taunted them, "rejoic[ing]" over their condition.[436] One Black leader described "trembly, weak, tired, hungry . . .bodies, compelled to be in the stalls of the fair grounds under a heavy, cruel guard of home-guards—guards who greet them with harsh orders and vulgar language."[437] At their fullest, there were between 4,000 and 6,000 people living in the camps.[438] Some Greenwood residents stayed at the camp only for a few days and others for as long as two weeks.[439] At least in some camps, sanitary conditions were horrible and the food was inadequate.[440]

Authorities required Black residents to show special identification cards to leave the camp.[441] A Black detainee needed the sponsorship of a white person to obtain a card.[442] Those working in white homes and businesses were given permanent green passes[443] while unemployed Black workers had red travel ("permit for passage") cards that were valid for only one day.[444] Anyone without a card, or with an expired card, would be re-arrested and forced back to camp.[445] Even having work and the backing of a white employer did not always save Black men from detention. On June 14, 1921, the *Tulsa Tribune* announced that Black men working as porters in "questionable" hotels would be arrested, taken to the fairgrounds, and forced to work on the streets until they found "honest occupation," "whether or not" the porters had been issued "green tags."[446] This identification system was used for at least a month after the massacre.[447] Those forced to live under it found it humiliating, likening it to being treated "as though they [were] dogs."[448]

Officials ordered detainees without other employment to clean up the city, which included burying the bodies and clearing debris.[449] The day after the massacre, the commander of the National

Guard issued a field order directing that "all able bodied [N]egro men remaining in the detention camp at the fairgrounds and other places in the city of Tulsa" will be "required to render such service and perform such labor as is required by the military commission and the Red Cross in making the proper sanitary provisions for the care of the refugees."[450] According to Red Cross records, Black men conscripted into service were paid up to 25 cents an hour for work.[451] This was, however, the only way these men could get money for food; most Black men had to pay 20 cents for meals.[452] The Red Cross, which had been put in charge of relief operations upon order of Mayor Evans, [453] was not allowed to give "able bodied men" money or goods. Instead, the Red Cross provided assistance (characterized as "relief") by giving these men work and then paying them for the work they performed.[454] This was viewed as a form of charity since, without a city or civic organization providing work, the men would have no money. Some scholars assert that at least some conscripted men were entirely uncompensated.[455] Guards confiscated weapons of all Black men (and many Black women), and Black people were not allowed to possess or purchase firearms for several weeks after the massacre.[456]

Even after Black residents were allowed to move about more freely, many were forced to live for more than a year in tents and other makeshift shelters provided by the Red Cross.[457] Because many of the tents did not have floors, some occupants were forced to sleep on the cold ground.[458] Conditions were unsanitary.[459] Booker T. Washington High School was converted into a makeshift hospital,[460] but many of the dispossessed of Greenwood nevertheless got sick and some died.[461] Volunteers from across the country and from the community worked with the Red Cross to provide food, temporary shelter, clothing, and medicine,[462] and despite the conditions in the tent city, members of the Black community would later refer to the Red Cross as Angels of Mercy.[463]

2. The Dead and Injured

The massacre killed as many as 300 Tulsans,[464] perhaps even more. Although efforts to find bodies of additional victims continue, consensus on an accurate death toll may never be reached due to the haphazard disposal of bodies in the Arkansas River, on flatbed rail cars, and in unmarked mass graves.[465] Additionally, many surviving residents fled the city and never returned. Thus, it is difficult to determine whether post-massacre accounts of missing neighbors refer to those who died or to those who permanently relocated. In addition to the deceased, the Red Cross estimated another 700 victims were injured. According to the Red Cross, 163 operations were performed the week after the massacre.[466] Mary Jones Parrish recalled seeing victims in hospitals with amputated limbs, burned faces, and bandaged heads.[467]

3. Property Loss

In the immediate aftermath of the massacre, the "burned district" looked like "the devastation left in the wake of a conquering and pillaging army."[468] The Red Cross estimated that white Tulsans burned more than 1256 houses, looted another 215 houses, and burned and looted businesses.[469] In his report to the Federal Bureau Chief, Agent Weiss stated that a "real estate and insurance firm estimated the total loss at $1,500,000.00," and noted that witnesses told him there was more than $250,000 in lost merchandise alone.[470] After inspecting the burned area, Agent Weiss characterized these estimates as "conservative" for an area approximately "two miles long and from two to six blocks wide."[471] A researcher working for the Oklahoma Commission estimated the damage to be $1.8 million in 1921 dollars and $16,752,600 in 1999 dollars.[472] The Bureau of Labor Statistics CPI inflation calculator computes this amount as $32,266,329.55 in December 2024 dollars.[473]

Interference with mail was a federal crime in 1921, and one of the buildings burned during the massacre was a federal post office.[474] Postal authorities reported that "monetary loss at the substation was slight" and that "[n]o mail bags were at the station when it burned."[475] News accounts also

indicated that the building was not owned by the government but was private property.[476]

4. The State Grand Jury Investigation and Attitude of White Community

The state quickly summoned a grand jury that subpoenaed almost 200 witnesses.[477] The grand

jury returned indictments against about 70 men, including many Black leaders of Greenwood, whom

the grand jury accused of inciting the "riot."[478] Most cases were eventually dismissed, including the

assault case against Dick Rowland that had served as the initial catalyst of the massacre.[479] Some

white men were accused of looting, but ultimately none were ever sent to prison.[480] On June 26, 1921,

after finishing its investigation, the grand jury issued a report which the *Tulsa Daily World* ran under

the headline, "Grand Jury Blames Negroes for Inciting Race Rioting: Whites Clearly Exonerated."[481]

The grand jury cited the conduct of the Black men (who had gathered at the courthouse to protect

Rowland) as a "direct cause" of the "riot," implying these Black men had overreacted to a group of

curious spectators.[482] The grand jury also identified two "indirect causes" of the "riot" as "agitation

among the [N]egroes of social equality" and the "laxity of law enforcement."[483] The grand jury

charged Police Chief Gustafson with dereliction of duty and with other corruption alleged to have

occurred before the massacre.[484] Gustafson was subsequently convicted and removed from his

position.[485]

White Tulsans largely expressed the same opinion as the grand jurors: Black men of

Greenwood were responsible for the destruction of their neighborhood.[486] A white bishop blamed

national Black "radicals," like civil rights leader W.E.B. Du Bois, for stirring up trouble.[487] The

attitude of white Tulsans to the plight of the people of Greenwood is perhaps best captured in a news

article published three days after the massacre on June 4, 1921, when men and women who had lost

their homes, possessions, and often their loved ones were living in camps under guard. The article's author stated that there were "white mourners in Tulsa as well as colored ones," and explained that the source of the white community's grief was the loss of their clothing, since "[n]early all who had their family washing in the destroyed [N]egro huts lost their clothes."[488]

5.   The Unfulfilled Promises of Reparations

The day after the massacre, Tulsa's Chamber of Commerce Director characterized the destruction of Greenwood as "the greatest wound Tulsa's pride has ever received," assuring the community that "every right thinking man and woman" was "doing everything possible to heal."[489] He announced that Tulsa's business leaders were organizing a movement "not only for the succor, protection and alleviation of the sufferings of the [N]egroes, but to formulate a plan of reparation in order that homes may be rebuilt and families . . . rehabilitated."[490]

The city initially took steps to follow through on this goal, setting up a Public Welfare Board to "temporarily take charge of the appalling situation."[491] The newly appointed Board chairman publicly emphasized that the city and county were liable for all damages.[492] The Board began collecting money, which it used for food and clothing; however, it set nothing aside for building or compensation, perhaps assuming more money would follow.[493]

The all-white Board also enacted a resolution rejecting aid from outside of Tulsa.[494] The Board even sent back a $1,000 check from the Chicago Tribune intended to assist the residents of Greenwood.[495] It is unclear if the Board rejected these proffered funds because Board members genuinely believed that the Tulsa business community would step forward and provide for Greenwood; if the return of money was part of a public relations campaign designed to let the rest of the country know that Tulsa was capable of taking care of itself; or if the Board rejected the monetary contribution for the very purpose of depriving Greenwood residents of financial assistance. From the beginning, money from white Tulsa was slow to come in. In the words of one journalist, white Tulsans were not willing to give their Black neighbors much more than "old clothes and a meal or two" along with some financial aid to a few individuals "deemed deserving."[496]

Working with city landowners, Mayor Evans soon replaced this Public Welfare Board with a "Reconstruction Committee." Mayor Evans announced the appointment of the new committee during the same speech in which he blamed the massacre on the Black men of Greenwood.[497] In that speech, he took the opportunity to opine that the land Greenwood occupied was "better adapted" for industrial, rather than residential, purposes, declaring "[l]et the [N]egro settlement be placed farther to the north and east."[498] Mayor Evans's new Reconstruction Committee included Tate Brady, a wealthy white landowner and civic leader who was also later identified as a Klansman.[499] The main goal of the Reconstruction Committee seemed to be to appropriate the land for industrial purposes and to move Greenwood further away from the white community. The Reconstruction Committee raised no significant funds and provided no reparations.

6.   **The Fire Ordinance and Attempts to Displace Greenwood**

On June 7, 1921, a week after the massacre, the city enacted Fire Ordinance No. 2156, placing most of Greenwood within official fire limits of the city of Tulsa.[500] All buildings on land covered by the ordinance had to be made "of concrete, brick, or steel and had to be at least two stories high."[501] The effect of this ordinance was to make rebuilding in most of Greenwood prohibitively expensive.[502] This was not an unintended consequence of a well-intentioned initiative; instead, those who drafted the ordinance planned to drive Black people out of Greenwood. This is clear from the first news article to announce the decision, which asserted that the land would "never again be a [N]egro quarter but will become a wholesale and industrial center," explaining that this result had been accomplished through the ordinance.[503] The article stressed that, "[b]ecause of the building requirements . . . it is believed impossible that the [N]egroes will again build homes there."[504]

Attorney B.C. Franklin, acting with two of his colleagues (I.H. Spears and T.O. Chappelle), set up a tent on Archer Street as a temporary law firm and immediately began to collect information to file lawsuits for recovery and to attack the fire ordinance.[505] In one of the Black community's very few victories during post-massacre litigation, attorneys were able to temporarily halt implementation of the fire ordinance on the grounds of insufficient notice.[506] This was followed by an even greater victory in September 1921, when attorneys obtained a permanent injunction on the grounds that the ordinance amounted to a deprivation of their property rights.[507] Before the ordinance was invalidated, however, many people of Greenwood were arrested during early efforts to rebuild.[508]

7. Early Attempts to Recover Through Insurance Claims and Civil Lawsuits

Many homes and businesses destroyed in the massacre had been insured. Owners tried to collect insurance proceeds so that they had enough money to rebuild. Franklin and his firm filed an estimated 4 million dollars in claims against the city and insurance companies.[509] Insurance companies denied compensation, citing each policy's standard "riot clause," which precluded compensation for any damage caused during a riot.[510] Homeowners and business owners challenged these determinations without success. In 1926, the Oklahoma Supreme Court issued a definitive ruling that precluded suits against insurance companies for damages from the massacre.[511]

Residents also sought legal redress through tort claims against the city, Mayor Evans, the police, and other city officials, as well as against the company that owned the airplanes blamed for causing some of the conflagration.[512] The suits were all dismissed,[513] but we could not locate any opinion setting forth the reason for these dismissals. As a result of these legal decisions, many longtime homeowners could not afford to rebuild.

8. More Recent Attempts to Recover Damages or Achieve Reparations

More recent attempts to recover damages or reparations have likewise been unsuccessful. In 2003, survivors and descendants of the massacre filed suit against the state of Oklahoma and the city of Tulsa in *Alexander v. Oklahoma*. The suit alleged civil rights violations and denial of equal protection, and included state law claims of negligence and promissory estoppel.[514] Specifically, this lawsuit included claims for relief under 42 U.S.C. §§ 1981, 1983, and 1985, the civil analogues of the criminal civil rights statutes discussed elsewhere in this Report.[515] The district court found, and the Tenth Circuit Court of Appeals agreed,[516] that the suit could not go forward because the statute of limitations had expired. In other words, the federal courts held that the plaintiffs filed their claim after the deadline for filing such a suit had passed. The Tenth Circuit rejected the plaintiffs' argument that their two-year deadline for filing suit began in 2001, when the Oklahoma Commission to Study the Tulsa Race Riot of 1921 issued its report, which the plaintiffs claimed first made them aware of the culpability of city and state actors. The Tenth Circuit likewise rejected plaintiffs' arguments for equitable tolling, rejecting their argument that, even if their claims had accrued in 1921, the limitations period should be tolled due to the efforts of the city and its officials to conceal its role in the massacre.[517]

In 2020, another group of plaintiffs filed suit in *Randle v. Tulsa*, suing under Oklahoma state law. The *Randle* plaintiffs alleged that the massacre had been, and continues to be, a public nuisance.[518] These plaintiffs claimed that, as a result of the massacre, they faced racially disparate treatment and city-created barriers to basic human needs.[519] The Oklahoma Supreme Court rejected this argument, holding that, even if it "accep[ted] as true that the Massacre is a continuing blight within all property in the Greenwood community—and that the pall of the Massacre continues to envelop the Greenwood community over one-hundred years later—Plaintiffs' claim does not present a conflict resolvable by way of abatement."[520] The Oklahoma Supreme Court also held that it could not create a new form of liability "wherein both State and non-State actors could be held liable for their predecessors' wrongdoing, in which current actors played no part."[521]

The *Randle* plaintiffs also alleged that the city had engaged in "unjust enrichment" by appropriating the name "Black Wall Street" to use in marketing efforts to promote the city of Tulsa as a tourist attraction, without returning any of those benefits to members of the community. The Oklahoma Supreme Court found that the plaintiffs had not alleged fraud, abuse of confidence, or unconscionable conduct and held that "neither law nor equity prevent Defendants from promoting the Massacre for historical purposes and community improvement."[522]

G.   The 1921 Federal Investigation

Shortly after the massacre, U.S. Attorney General Harry Daugherty announced an "informal" federal investigation to determine whether any federal laws had been violated.[523] A *Tulsa Daily World* article announced that a "Secret Service Officer" was looking into the destruction of a United States post office as a potential federal crime.[524] In fact, the matter was not assigned to a Secret Service officer, but to the Department of Justice's Bureau of Investigation, a precursor to today's Federal Bureau of Investigation. Agent T.F. Weiss, acting under instruction from Agent James G. Findlay, sent a preliminary assessment to the Bureau Chief by telegram on June 2, the day after the massacre.[525] The telegram said that "[n]o Federal violation appears."[526]

Agent Weiss wrote an eight-page report on June 6, 1921, concluding that the incident had not been a "race riot" as it was *not*, in his words, the "result of racial feeling, or agitators."[527] Instead, Agent Weiss claimed that the incident began as just a "small" and "half-hearted" attempt to lynch an innocent man,[528] and that the situation "spontaneously" grew out of control.[529] Agent Weiss blamed Sheriff McCullough for inviting Black veterans and other men of Greenwood to help protect Rowland

and, by implication, blamed the later violence of the white Tulsans on the Black men of Greenwood who came to the courthouse to protect Rowland.[530]

While he claimed that he had talked to over 100 witnesses, both Black and white, Agent Weiss's report summarizes only five interviews, all with white men: (1) William Ellis, the Deputy United States Marshal; (2) Police Chief Gustafson; (3) Gustafson's Secretary, Mr. Hall; (4) a white attorney named L.W. Crutcher; and (5) a white man named Tom Dyer from Jenks, Oklahoma.[531] Although Agent Weiss admitted that these witnesses, whom he stressed "did not condone" the actions of the white mob, were all "a little prejudiced" against the Black community,[532] he did not include accounts from any individual Black witness. Instead, his report cursorily states that all the Black witnesses told the "same story" of "hearing shots, seeing houses set on fire, and fleeing for their lives, some of their members, who had guns, shooting as they fled."[533] Although only a day had passed since the witnesses experienced these events, the report noted that all of the Black witnesses had an "optimistic attitude" about their situation.[534] In fact, Agent Weiss asserted that by June 2, the day after the massacre, white and Black residents of Tulsa were "mingling amicably on the streets of Tulsa,"[535] a virtual impossibility given that the city was under martial law and that most Black residents were in detention or performing manual labor. Agent Weiss assured supervisors that city officials were "distributing blanks" (from context, this appears to reference blank forms) "to the losers" to file claims.[536]

Agent Weiss's report indicates that the Deputy U.S. Marshal did little to stop the massacre; indeed, the Marshal admitted that he and his wife went to the courthouse as spectators to *watch* (not to stop) Rowland's lynching.[537] Significant to the legal analysis later in this Report, Agent Weiss's report indicated that a police officer identified only by the last name of "Rignon" tried to recruit witness Tom Dyer, as well as other white men, to travel from Jenks, Oklahoma to Tulsa on the night of the massacre.[538] According to Dyer, Officer Rignon drove to Jenks asking for help from white men and "intimating a raid on the [N]egroes."[539] Not only did Dyer tell Agent Weiss that Officer Rignon had solicited white men to participate in a raid, but he also told Agent Weiss that Officer Rignon bragged to him the next day about having personally killed four Black men.[540] Agent Weiss's report even stressed that Dyer was "indignant" about this fact.[541] Dyer also told Agent Weiss that the Tulsa police had done nothing to stop the burning and looting.[542] Despite this information, Weiss does not appear to have considered whether the government could prosecute local officials for "color of law" or conspiracy offenses under then-existing civil rights laws (discussed more fully below).

In fact, Agent Weiss, who had been in contact with Police Chief Gustafson (who presumably had access to the names of all Tulsa officers), did not verify that Rignon was a Tulsa police officer or secure Rignon's first name for his report. We could not find any information about an officer named "Rignon"; however, handwritten attorney notes related to the 1921 state grand jury investigation into the "riot" contain the names "Major Rigden," "Rigden," and "Jenks" on the same page.[543] News accounts report that a man named "Jack Rigden" testified before that state grand jury investigating the massacre.[544] Although not identified as a law enforcement officer in this news account, other news articles indicate that Jack Rigden (usually spelled Rigdon) was a law enforcement officer in Tulsa and in nearby Red Fork, Oklahoma.[545]

It is unclear whether Agent Weiss's report was considered by federal prosecutors.[546] In 1921, the Eastern District of Oklahoma had authority to investigate and prosecute federal crimes committed in Tulsa; now, the Northern District of Oklahoma (which did not exist in 1921) has jurisdiction over such offenses.[547] On June 4, 1921, newspapers announced that Frank Lee, then the U.S. Attorney for the Eastern District of Oklahoma, stated that he had not been apprised of any federal investigation and that no violation of federal law had been reported to him.[548] He opined, however, that the reported facts might give rise to two potential federal charges: (1) interference with the United States mail service, caused by delay of passenger trains, and (2) a conspiracy to deny to United States citizens the rights to which they were entitled by federal statutes.[549]

Although we have found Department files with correspondence related to the Tulsa Race Massacre, we have found no evidence that any Department prosecutor (from the United States Attorney's Office or from Main Justice) evaluated Agent Weiss's report. Nonetheless, we cannot discount the possibility that some evaluation or summary exists that has been misfiled or included in unindexed boxes.[550] Nor can we discount the possibility that an evaluation was made and subsequently lost. No federal or Congressional investigation was seriously pursued. President Warren G. Harding condemned the massacre at a speech he gave at Lincoln University, a historically Black college.[551]

H.   Legal Analysis

1.   General Principles of Legal Review

When Assistant Attorney General Kristen Clarke announced that the Department would review the events of the Tulsa Race Massacre, she explained that, in addition to reviewing the facts, the Division would evaluate the actions of those involved under current and then-existing federal civil rights laws.[552] Because a crime must be prosecuted under the law in effect at the time of the offense, the only laws relevant to the actual prosecutability of this matter are the narrowly construed civil rights laws that were in existence in 1921. Today, there are many more tools available to federal civil rights prosecutors, and our analysis explains that, if this conduct were to occur today, the Department could investigate and, where appropriate, prosecute offenders using a wide variety of federal hate crime laws.

Because all but two witnesses of the massacre are deceased, this review necessarily relies on a cold record and inadmissible hearsay. We reviewed recorded interviews of now-deceased witnesses.

Because these interviews were conducted by others, we were unable to ask our own questions and, therefore, could not elicit details about the precise elements the government would need to prove a violation of federal law. Some original accounts (for example, those given during civil litigation) are now unavailable, and the substance of the witnesses' statements are available only through summaries provided in legal briefs.[553] Some survivors provided statements decades after the traumatic events they witnessed (often trauma they experienced when they were quite young); understandably, these survivors often did not have perfect memories, and interviewers did not press for grim and upsetting details. And many relevant witnesses, whom we would have interviewed had we investigated immediately after the massacre, never provided an account (or any account they gave has been lost over time).

This Report examines the legal theories that could have given rise to federal criminal liability in 1921, using the facts we have reviewed. However, there is no way to determine—over a century after the massacre—whether any particular incident could have been proved beyond a reasonable doubt in a federal court. Moreover, the racial attitudes of the day infected federal legal proceedings, as well as state proceedings; thus, there is no guarantee that, even if strong evidence had been elicited, a federal grand jury would have indicted or a petit jury would have convicted. As explained more fully below, federal prosecution is now foreclosed due to the expiration of the statute of limitations for those few federal civil rights statutes that existed in 1921, the death of perpetrators of any offense, and constitutional hurdles imposed by the Confrontation Clause.

2. Hate Crime Analysis

No federal hate crime laws existed at the time of the massacre. Thus, in 1921, the federal government could not have prosecuted *anyone* for committing a federal hate crime offense. Even in the improbable event that a living perpetrator could be identified today, over a century after the massacre, the Constitution forecloses prosecuting anyone for violating a law that did not exist at the time of their wrongful conduct. If contemporary hate crime laws were in effect in 1921, the government could have used a variety of federal statutes to investigate the massacre and prosecute perpetrators. Most readily, prosecutors could have investigated perpetrators for violating the Matthew Shepard and James Byrd, Jr. Hate Crimes Prevention Act ("HCPA"), including its recently enacted anti-lynching provisions, and could also have investigated the destruction of the Greenwood community under the criminal provisions of the Fair Housing Act ("FHA"). Prosecutors could have also used the Church Arson Prevention Act to investigate the intentional destruction of churches.

To prove any hate crime, the government would have to prove that a perpetrator who committed any assault, murder, or act of arson was motivated by bias; that is, the government would have to prove that any crime it prosecuted would not have occurred if the victim had been white. There is ample evidence to show bias motivation on a large scale. Murders, assaults, and destruction of property occurred after white Tulsans invaded a community most referred to as "Little Africa" or "Ni**ertown." Those who invaded the community clearly identified their targets by skin color; there are no reports of white men assaulting other white men, except, as explained above, allegations of an accidental attack of a white man believed to be Black and a few allegations of white men attacked for trying to protect Black men or property. No White homes were looted or burned. No white Tulsans were held in detention camps. When the massacre ended, it was justified in racial terms as being the fault of "bad [N]egroes." White men talked of "hunting ni**ers"[554] and special deputies were told to "get a ni**er."[555] Given these facts, the government would likely be able to establish for most, if not all, incidents that various illegal acts were motivated by race.[556]

a.   *The Matthew Shepard and James Byrd, Jr. Hate Crimes Prevention Act (HCPA) (18 U.S.C. §*
249)

Had it been in effect in 1921, the HCPA, enacted in 2009 and amended in 2022 to include the Emmett Till antilynching provision, would have allowed federal prosecutors to investigate anyone who committed a murder or assault during the massacre or who conspired to do so. To obtain a conviction under the substantive provisions of the HCPA, the federal government would need to prove that a perpetrator willfully caused bodily injury to someone (or attempted to do so with a dangerous weapon) because of race or color.[557] For example, if the HCPA were in effect in 1921, federal prosecutors could have used it to investigate the murder of Dr. Jackson. According to a witness, a young white man shot Dr. Jackson while he had his hands in the air and while his neighbor begged for Dr. Jackson's life. Yet, the white man shot Dr. Jackson and left him to die, while men looted Dr. Jackson's home. As described, a murder like this happening during a racially motivated attack on Greenwood would establish a violation of the HCPA.

Dr. Jackson's murder is the crime for which we have the most details, given that we have a transcript of a witness account of how it happened. But the murder was not an isolated incident. As explained above, witnesses described many similar atrocities, including victims who were shot while fleeing, questioning authority, or not moving quickly enough; a man dragged to his death behind a car; and victims thrown into burning buildings. All these accounts, if proved, would clearly establish violations of the HCPA, were it in effect in 1921.

Had the Emmett Till Antilynching Act Amendments to the HCPA been in effect in 1921, the federal government could have investigated allegations that white Tulsans conspired (agreed) to murder and injure victims because of their race or color. If the federal government proved any person agreed with at least one other person to cause bodily injury to a resident of Greenwood because of a resident's race, and if death or serious bodily injury occurred as a result of that agreement, it could have obtained a jury verdict for the crime of lynching.

b.   *Criminal Provisions of the Fair Housing Act (FHA) (42 U.S.C. § 3631)*

If the criminal provisions of the FHA, enacted in 1968, had been in effect at the time of the massacre, federal prosecutors could have used them to investigate bias-motivated acts of violence that interfered with the people of Greenwood's housing rights.[558] The government could have investigated allegations that white men (1) forcibly removed victims from their homes, (2) burned down homes, or (3) committed murder or assault to interfere with the victim's housing right. The federal government could have prosecuted anyone who did these things intending to interfere with the housing rights of residents of Greenwood because of their race. As explained above, there is ample evidence of racial bias. There is, likewise, evidence that the white men not only acted because of race but also to interfere with housing rights. Most obviously, they destroyed an entire neighborhood, leaving only char and rubble. Perhaps that intent is best captured in the postcard, circulated after the massacre, entitled, "running the [N]egro out of Tulsa."[559]

Had the FHA been in effect in 1921, the federal government could also have used conspiracy law[560] to investigate allegations that, motivated by bias, white Tulsans conspired to interfere with any victim's housing rights. Pursuant to such an investigation, the government would have been able to prosecute anyone who agreed with another to use violent means to "run the [N]egros out of Tulsa" or to interfere with any particular Greenwood resident to peacefully enjoy his or her right to live in Greenwood.

c.   *The Church Arson Prevention Act (18 U.S.C. § 247)*

White Tulsans destroyed many churches during the Tulsa Race Massacre. Had the Church Arson Prevention Act, originally enacted in 1988 and significantly revised in 1996, been in effect in 1921, the federal government could have used it to investigate anyone involved in this destruction. To obtain a conviction, prosecutors would have had to prove beyond a reasonable doubt that the perpetrators intentionally defaced, damaged, or destroyed the church *because* congregants or others associated with the church were Black.[561]

3.   **Official Misconduct**

a.   *Deprivation of Rights Under Color of Law (Section 20 of the Criminal Code of 1909; 28 U.S.C. § 242)*

Currently, the federal government uses 18 U.S.C. § 242 to charge public officials (like police officers) who willfully violate the constitutional rights of others, such as by using excessive force against them. Section 242 applies only to public officials who act "under color of law"; in other words, it applies to those who use or abuse an official position they hold (such as the position of police officer). Section 242, first enacted in the First Enforcement Act of 1866,[562] existed in 1921, codified at § 20 of the Criminal Code of 1909. Section 20 (like its modern counterpart, § 242) prohibited persons acting under color of law from willfully violating the constitutional rights of others.[563] In 1921, however, the government almost never charged officials with violating § 20. As explained more fully below, in 1921, the statute of limitations for prosecuting an offense under § 20 was five years and expired in 1926.

Under current interpretations of the law (not those available in 1921), the federal government could investigate public officials involved in the massacre for a myriad of constitutional violations; the most promising constitutional theories for a modern-day prosecution would be (1) using unreasonable force,[564] (2) arresting residents of Greenwood without probable cause,[565] (3) unreasonably seizing the property of residents,[566] (4) denying residents the right to equal protection of the law,[567] and (5) being deliberately indifferent to a state-created danger.[568]

The federal government may not prosecute officials for willfully violating the Constitution, or conspiring to do so, unless, at the time of their offense, it was clearly established that their conduct was unconstitutional. In 1921, federal courts had not yet developed most of the standards they now use to evaluate whether a particular action of an official violates the Constitution.[569] In other words, while the constitutional amendments themselves existed long before the massacre, many of the court opinions explaining these amendments and recognizing liability when officials violate rights protected by them were decided afterwards. For example, it was not until the 1980s that law developed recognizing that an official can violate the Constitution for being deliberately indifferent to state-created danger.[570] The leading Supreme Court case establishing the standard for evaluating whether an officer used excessive force during an arrest or other seizure was decided in 1989.[571] Because the courts developed these theories of constitutional liability well after the massacre, the government could not have relied upon them in 1921.[572]

That does not mean that federal prosecution was foreclosed in 1921. In 1879, well before the Tulsa Race Massacre, the Supreme Court held that a state official could be criminally charged for "depriv[ing] another of property, life, or liberty, without due process of law" and, likewise, recognized that such an official could be charged with denying another "the equal protection of the laws."[573] The allegations of official misconduct that occurred during the Tulsa Race Massacre were not subtle or premised on sophisticated theories such that they could be appreciated only by consulting case law developed after the massacre.[574] They are allegations of extrajudicial murder, arson, theft, and conspiracy to engage in such actions using official authority.

Thus, in 1921, the federal government could have investigated any police officer, National Guardsman, or other public official who murdered Black residents on the grounds that such an act deprived the victims of life without due process of law.[575] Similarly, the government could have investigated officials who burned and looted homes on the grounds that these officials deprived homeowners of property without due process of law. The government could have investigated those who confined residents of Greenwood to detention camps, without affording them a hearing, on the grounds that they deprived the victims of liberty without due process of law.[576] Finally, the government could have used an equal protection theory to investigate any official who, during and after the massacre, treated Black residents of Greenwood differently than white residents of Tulsa—for example, by disarming and arresting Black men who fired at white people but refusing to disarm or arrest white people who shot at Black people.

Some of those investigated would have had defenses to assert. Anyone who killed a Black person who was, at the time, firing at white individuals, likely would have argued that they acted in self-defense (or defense of others) rather than to willfully deprive the victim of a constitutionally protected right. In addition, in 1909, the Supreme Court held in *Moyer v. Peabody* that the governor has the authority to call out the National Guard to put down an insurrection during serious unrest.[577] The Court further held that, in putting down an insurrection, troops may constitutionally seize individuals "not . . . for punishment," but "by way of precaution, to prevent the exercise of hostile power."[578] The Court held, however, that such precautionary arrests must be "made in good faith and in the honest belief that they are needed in order to head the insurrection off."[579] Many Black residents of Tulsa were seized and taken to detention camps long before martial law was officially declared; thus, they were detained in the absence of any official declaration of a crisis or "insurrection." Nonetheless, *Moyer*'s holding would likely have provided a defense for *some* seizures made by *some* officials. If—based upon rumors of a "[N]egro uprising"—an official had asserted a plausible "good faith" belief that precautionary custody was needed to prevent an insurrection, that official might have argued to a jury that he had not willfully violated the Constitution. Given that virtually every resident of Greenwood was taken into custody, regardless of whether they had participated in any acts of violence, the government may well have been able to prove that many deprivations of liberty were unconstitutional, even under the *Moyer* standard.[580]

These avenues of potential prosecution were not pursued in the last century and are now time-barred by the statute of limitations and other time-related factors.

b.   *Civil Rights Conspiracy (Section 19 of the Criminal Code of 1909; 18 U.S.C. § 241)*

Currently, the federal government charges public officials who conspire to violate the rights of others using the civil rights conspiracy statute, codified at 18 U.S.C. § 241.[581] That statute, first enacted in 1870[582] and often referred to as the Ku Klux Klan Act, existed in 1921, codified at § 19 of the Criminal Code of 1909. This law prohibits conspiring to injure, oppress, threaten, or intimidate a victim "in the free exercise or enjoyment of any right or privilege secured to him by the Constitution or laws of the United States."[583]

As explained more fully below, in 1921, § 19 had a five-year statute of limitations which expired in 1926, making prosecution now impossible.[584] Before June 1926, the federal government could have used § 19 to investigate any public official who agreed with another official to deprive a resident of Greenwood of a recognized constitutional right. The constitutional theories for prosecution would have been more limited in 1921 than they are now, but in 1921, the government could have prosecuted any conspiracy to deprive people of due process and equal protection rights. In fact, Frank Lee, then the U.S. Attorney for the Eastern District of Oklahoma, opined that, although he had not been informed of the results of the pending federal investigation, a potential federal charge might have included a conspiracy to deny the people of Greenwood rights to which they were legally entitled.[585] Thus, in 1921, at least one government attorney believed charges were possible based upon what he knew about the massacre.

Under current interpretation of the law, the government can use § 241 to prosecute both public officials *and* private persons (people not employed by the city or state) who join a conspiracy to violate the constitutional rights of others, as long as those private persons acts jointly with a public official who abuses his own authority.[586] But in 1921, the Supreme Court had interpreted § 19 narrowly, holding that the federal government could prosecute only public officials for violating most constitutional rights.[587] For this reason, the federal government likely could not have successfully prosecuted any white participant in violence who was not a public official. But it is possible the federal government could have used § 19 to prosecute any police officer, sheriff's deputy, National Guardsman, or other Tulsa official who conspired to deprive the people of Greenwood of their life, liberty, or property in the absence of due process of law, or who conspired to deny the people of Tulsa the equal protection of the laws.

Over a century after the massacre, it is difficult to say with certainty when any conspiracy started and what its scope was.[588] There is evidence that, at minimum, police and National Guardsmen conspired in the early morning hours of June 1 to invade Tulsa and to round up and imprison all Black men—including those they did not suspect of taking any part in the violence the evening before—without providing the men an opportunity to challenge that imprisonment. In fact, Major Daley, who was both a police officer and a member of the National Guard, admitted ordering the roundup of Black employees working in the homes of white people. If these Black employees were at the homes of their employers, they could not have taken part in any fighting. As noted above, the Supreme Court had held that, during an insurrection, individuals could be taken into custody provided officials believed in good faith that the action was necessary to prevent an insurrection. Whether this could provide a defense to a conspiracy would depend upon whether the plan was only to round up individuals (mistakenly) deemed potentially threatening or whether the plan encompassed those clearly innocent of any and all wrongdoing. If the latter, anyone who willfully joined this conspiracy could be prosecuted for conspiring to deprive the people of Greenwood of their liberty without due process of law.

As explained above, there is less evidence that police and guardsmen agreed, at an agency level, to destroy Greenwood through arson, murder, and looting. However, as set forth in Sections E(1) to (3), there is some evidence that at least some law enforcement officers participated in such acts and that they may have done so pursuant to an order. Perhaps a more fulsome investigation conducted at the time of the offense could have uncovered more evidence. Certainly, any officer who conspired to burn and loot Greenwood or to murder its residents could be prosecuted for violating § 19. Moreover, although any officer prosecuted for conspiracy to take Black men into custody could attempt to defend such a charge by asserting that the only reason he did so was because he believed (mistakenly) that such men were involved in a dangerous uprising, this belief would provide no justification for theft, arson, or murder.

4.   Other Federal Crimes

Assailants burned a federal post office substation during the massacre.[589] According to news reports, the financial loss was slight, but a few deposited letters and money orders were destroyed. Federal criminal law, codified at 18 U.S.C. §1701, makes it a crime "to knowingly and willfully obstruct[] or retard[]" the delivery of mail punishable by up to six months in prison.[590] The statute existed in 1921.[591] Therefore, the federal government could have used § 1701 to investigate the destruction of the post office and interference with the mail and could likely have successfully prosecuted anyone they could prove willfully obstructed the delivery of the mail. News articles at the time reported that the government did not own the post office and very little mail was affected. It may be that federal prosecutors determined that the government lacked sufficient interest to prosecute interference with the mail.

It has been suggested that the federal government could have prosecuted any homicide that occurred at the substation on the grounds that the federal government has the ability to prosecute murders on federal land. However, the government did not own the building and the fact that it was used for federal purposes does not bring it under the Special Maritime and Territorial Jurisdiction of the United States.[592] Nor have we found any evidence suggesting anyone was, in fact, killed at the postal substation or, if so, who was responsible for the murder.[593]

Some have suggested that the federal government could prosecute people for murders that occurred on Tribal land. The Supreme Court has recognized that much of the land in Oklahoma, including most of the city of Tulsa, is in Indian country.[594] Under the General Crimes Act[595] and the Major Crimes Act,[596] the federal government has the authority to prosecute a murder committed by an Indian against a non-Indian or by a non-Indian against an Indian.[597] States, however, retain jurisdiction when both the defendant and the victim are non-Indian.[598]

As explained above, many Black residents of Greenwood also self-identified as members of native Tribes. In addition, some white residents of Tulsa self-identified as Tribal members. Thus, it is theoretically possible that certain murders that occurred during the massacre (1) occurred in Indian country; (2) were committed by or against an Indigenous person; and (3) are subject to federal prosecution under either the General Crimes Act or the Major Crimes Act. Assuming these criteria are met, and that the offense is punishable by death, the statute of limitations would not have run on such an offense.[599]

Prosecution under either the General Crimes Act or the Major Crimes Act would nonetheless be complicated for several reasons. First, knowing the status of the defendant and the victim is often essential in identifying what court (either state or federal) has jurisdiction over the case.[600] Second, both the defendant's and the victim's status (that is, whether the defendant or victim is an Indian) are essential elements of any crime brought under the General Crimes Act and the Major Crimes Act; as such, the government must prove the defendant's and the victim's status beyond a reasonable doubt.[601] Third, no one has provided, and we have not uncovered, information about a particular murder committed by an Indian against a non-Indian or by a non-Indian against an Indian. Finally, this avenue of prosecution is foreclosed because there are no identified perpetrators to prosecute.

5. Prosecution Is Now Impossible

During our review, several people we spoke to questioned why the federal government had not initiated a grand jury investigation with the goal of indicting a person or entity for their role in the massacre. The federal government cannot now prosecute anyone for committing hate crimes, as there were no federal hate crime statutes in 1921. The statute of limitations has expired for the other civil rights crimes identified above.

Prosecutors typically have five years to bring most federal charges.[602] However, prosecutors may bring charges in capital cases (those punishable by the death penalty) at any time.[603] Section 1701, prohibiting obstruction of the mail, is not now, nor has it ever been, a capital crime. Its statute of limitations expired in 1926. The current versions of §§ 241 and 242 allow imposition of the death penalty for the most serious violations of the statute, principally those resulting in death. Thus, under the current statutory language, willful violations of constitutional rights (and conspiracies to violate such rights) that resulted in death can be prosecuted decades after the commission of the crime (even centuries after, if there is a living person to prosecute). However, §§ 241 and 242 (codified in 1921 at

§§ 19 and 20) did not provide for capital punishment until 1994.[604] Thus, in 1921, the law imposed a five-year deadline for the government to prosecute even the most egregious violations of civil rights statutes, and legally the government must apply the statute of limitations in effect at the time of the offense.[605]

Federal prosecution is also impossible because there is no one alive to prosecute. We did not locate any living perpetrators, and no one we consulted provided information that could lead to the location of a living subject. Anyone old enough to be reasonably held responsible for their acts during the massacre would now be at least 115 or 116 years old, and we have not found any person that old who has any connection to Tulsa.

We have also been asked whether the federal government could prosecute the city for its alleged role in the 1921 massacre or whether we could prosecute corporations that are successors-in-interest to companies that participated in the massacre (for example, we have been asked if the federal government could prosecute the companies that owned the planes used in the massacre). In addition to the expiration of the statute of limitations, any attempt to prosecute such entities would present insurmountable legal barriers.

Current city officials cannot be prosecuted today simply because they hold the same offices as the wrongdoers did during the massacre. Likewise, state actors cannot be held criminally responsible for constitutional violations *solely* based upon the fact that people working for them violated the Constitution. Drawing on cases analyzing the civil counterpart of the criminal civil rights statutes,[606] we believe that to establish criminal responsibility under § 241 and § 242, the federal government would have to show beyond a reasonable doubt that the execution of a government's policy or custom inflicted injury, even assuming that the government could criminally prosecute a city in the first instance—which it has never done under the criminal civil rights laws.[607] Even if the statute of limitations had not expired (which it has), the government simply could not meet this burden, more than a century after the massacre.

Similarly, after passage of a century and the death of all corporate officers and employees, the government could not prove beyond a reasonable doubt that any person who provided or flew a plane during the massacre did so specifically in his role as an employee to benefit a corporate entity.[608] Nor has the government identified, and it is doubtful that it could identify, the employees who provided or flew the planes.

Finally, the Constitution's Confrontation Clause would prove an insurmountable barrier to prosecution. This clause guarantees a criminal defendant the right to confront the witnesses against him.[609] The Federal Rules of Evidence likewise prohibit using statements made *out of court* to prove *in court* the truth of what the speaker said.[610] The government could not prove any person or entity guilty beyond a reasonable doubt without living witnesses who could be subject to cross-examination. The testimony of such witnesses, combined with any evidence admissible under hearsay rules and other rules of evidence, would have to be sufficient to tie the charged defendant to the crime so that a jury could find him (or her) guilty beyond a reasonable doubt. Most of the evidence, discussed above, is from recorded or transcribed accounts of witnesses who are now deceased. The people who provided those statements cannot now be cross-examined. There are only two living witnesses to the massacre, and they were young children at the time it occurred. Although they can now speak with chilling clarity about the horrors of the massacre, neither they nor anyone else can provide the evidence necessary to prove a perpetrator's guilt beyond a reasonable doubt, even if there were someone alive today who could be prosecuted and even if the statute of limitations had not expired.

I.   Conclusion

The events of May 31 and June 1, 1921, were horrific. If they happened today, the federal government would have authority to investigate all participants (those employed by the city and those who were private residents of Tulsa) and to charge anyone who committed or conspired to commit any of the offenses described above. But no federal hate crime laws existed then, and the existing civil rights laws were narrowly construed and rarely charged.

Federal prosecutors did not pursue charges in 1921 under the narrowly construed civil rights statutes that then existed. It may be that federal prosecutors considered filing charges and, after consideration, did not do so for reasons that would be understandable if we had a record of the decision. If the Department did not seriously consider such charges, then its failure to do so is disappointing, particularly in light of the local grand jury exonerating most white participants in the massacre, despite evidence that they had committed crimes. Because the statute of limitations on all federal offenses has expired and because of the death of perpetrators and the limitations imposed by the Confrontation Clause, federal prosecution is not possible in this instance.

That conclusion in no way negates the horror, the depravity, or the bigotry reflected in the massacre. Nor does it impugn the reality and intensity of the trauma that has reverberated across generations or the other enduring effects of extinguishing a thriving community.

That is why, outside the narrow confines of federal criminal law enforcement, the reckoning for this atrocity continues. We hope that this report is useful in that process.

[1] We thank the following organizations, in alphabetical order, for meeting with us and/or providing information: Deep Greenwood; Greenwood Chamber of Commerce; Greenwood Cultural Center; Greenwood Rising Black Wall Street History Center; Helmerich Center for American Research (Gilcrease); Eddie Faye Gates Collection; Historic Vernon AME Church; John Hope Franklin Center for Reconciliation; Justice For Greenwood; National Museum of African American History and Culture (Smithsonian); Oklahoma Department of Libraries, Tulsa Race Massacre Collection; The City of Tulsa (Police Department, Clerk's Office, and Legal Department); The University of Tulsa, College of Law (B.C. Franklin Papers); The University of Tulsa, McFarlin Library, Department of Special Collections and University Archives; Oklahoma State University, Tulsa Campus, Ruth Sigler Avery Collection.

[2] There is a list of those who, as of the year 2000, are known to have died in the massacre. *See* Richard "Dick" Warner, *Computations as to the Deaths from the 1921 Tulsa Race Riot*, Tulsa Historical Society & Museum, Accession No. 2006.126.001. This list does not include C.L. Daniels, who was only this past year determined to be a massacre victim after the city's mass grave investigation discovered his body and tested his DNA. *See* Nicquel Terry Ellis, *A Tulsa Race Massacre victim was recently ID'd as a World War I veteran*, CNN (Nov. 17, 2024). In addition, descendants and survivors are identified in cases filed in federal and state court. *See Randle v. City of Tulsa*, No. CV-2020-1179, 2022 WL 22861061 (Okl. Dist. Sept. 2, 2022); *Alexander v. Oklahoma*, 382 F.3d 1206 (10th Cir. 2004).

[3] Some descendants we met with have questioned the claims of other descendants that their loved ones were, in fact, survivors or victims of the massacre. This Report neither endorses nor disputes any claim that any particular individual is a survivor or victim or the descendant of a survivor or victim.

[4] This Report—and the Bureau Reports and correspondence contained in the appendices—deal with sensitive issues of racial violence. They contain frank descriptions of brutality and describe the use of racial slurs.

[5] This Report will generally refer to those who acted against Black Greenwood residents as "white Tulsans" or "white men." "White men" is the phrase often used in historical accounts, but reports indicate that some women and boys also participated in the events of May 31 and June 1. *See* Scott Ellsworth, *The Tulsa Race Riot*, DANNEY GOBLE ET AL., TULSA RACE RIOT: A REPORT BY THE OKLAHOMA COMMISSION TO STUDY THE TULSA RACE RIOT OF 1921 (Feb. 2001) (hereinafter "THE COMMISSION REPORT"), at 64 (discussing boys sworn in as special deputies) and 76 (discussing a survivor's account of being captured by a group that included boys with guns); *Race War Rages for Hours After Outbreak at Courthouse; Troops and Armed Men Patrol[l]ing Streets*, TULSA DAILY WORLD, June 1, 1921, at 20 (reporting that women, as well as men, "armed with every available weapon" were part of mob).

[6] Mary Jones Parrish, a massacre survivor, referred to Greenwood as "the Negro's Wallstreet" in the report she published in 1923. MARY E. JONES PARRISH, THE NATION MUST AWAKE: MY WITNESS TO THE TULSA RACE MASSACRE OF 1921 (Trinity University Press, 2021) (including Jones' 1923 Publication *Events of the Tulsa Disaster*). The name "Negro Wall Street" may have originated with Booker T. Washington. *See* HANNIBAL B. JOHNSON, TULSA'S HISTORIC GREENWOOD DISTRICT at 9 (Arcadia, 2014) ("Dubbed 'the Negro Wall Street' by Booker T. Washington, it became the talk of the nation."); *The Tulsa Race Massacre*, OKLA. HIST. SOC'Y ("In fact, Booker T. Washington may have given Greenwood its nick-name: Black Wall Street.").

[7] Emmett Till Unsolved Civil Rights Crime Act of 2007, Pub. L. No. 110-344, 122 Stat. 3934 (2008), as amended by its 2016 Reauthorization, Pub. L. No. 114-325, 130 Stat. 1965 (2016).

[8] This Report sets forth citations supporting the information in the Executive Summary in parts C, D, E, and F.

[9] The lack of unbiased investigative rigor displayed in response to the massacre and the derogatory language used within the report by personnel employed by the FBI's predecessor organization, the Bureau of Investigation, are inconsistent with the expectations, core values, and mission of today's FBI.

[10] Deputy Chief Barbara Kay Bosserman led the review, along with Walter Henry, an experienced retired FBI agent who now works as a cold case investigator.

[11] Even before the announcement, we conducted an in-depth interview of two massacre survivors: Viola "Mother" Fletcher, who was 109 at the time of the interview, and Hughes "Uncle Red" Van Ellis, who was 101 at the time of the interview and has since passed away. In addition, we reviewed the deposition and Congressional testimony of these survivors along with the deposition and testimony of Lessie Benningfield Randle ("Mother Randle"), another massacre survivor. We later met with Mother Randle in October 2024 and were able to discuss Mother Randle's account with her granddaughter, LaDonna Penny who had heard the account from Mother Randle on multiple occasions.

[12] Appendix B lists all the descendants we interviewed, redacted pursuant to the Privacy Act.

[13] VIOLA FORD FLETCHER & IKE HOWARD, DON'T LET THEM BURY MY STORY: THE OLDEST LIVING SURVIVOR OF THE TULSA RACE MASSACRE IN HER OWN WORDS (Mocha Media, 2023).

[14] See generally PARRISH, THE NATION MUST AWAKE.

[15] Buck Cobert Franklin, The Tulsa Race Riot and Three of Its Victims (Aug. 22, 1931) (first-hand account of the massacre written ten years after it occurred).

[16] BUCK COLBERT FRANKLIN, MY LIFE AND AN ERA: THE AUTOBIOGRAPHY OF BUCK COLBERT FRANKLIN (John Hope Franklin & John Whittington Franklin, eds., LSU Press, 1997).

[17] These materials include accounts obtained by the Oklahoma Commission in preparing its report; other accounts collected by Eddie Faye Gates and available from the Gilcrease Museum (The Eddie Faye Gates Tulsa Race Massacre Collection - Gilcrease Museum); accounts from the Tulsa Historical Society and Museum Online Collection; accounts from Justice For Greenwood's oral history project, Oral History Project - Justice For Greenwood; 17 accounts collected by Mary Jones Parrish and included in her 1923 publication; and accounts contained in longer oral histories maintained by the Oklahoma Historical Society's oral history collection.

[18] See Reports of Agents T.F. Weiss & James G. Findlay, Bureau of Investigation (June-July 1921), National Archives, College Park, Maryland, Record Group 60 of the Department of Justice General Records, Entry 112-B, Straight Numerical Files, #158260, Boxes 1276-1293 (Jan. 1, 1914-Dec 31, 1949), available on ProQuest (hereinafter "Weiss Reports," with citation to PDF pagination).

[19] See Department of Justice Correspondence File (June 1, 1921–July 31, 1921), Department of Justice Classified Subject Files on Civil Rights (1914–1949), Department of Justice General Records, Entry 112-B, Straight Numerical Files No. 158260, available on ProQuest.

[20] See DANNEY GOBLE ET AL., TULSA RACE RIOT: A REPORT BY THE OKLAHOMA COMMISSION TO STUDY THE TULSA RACE RIOT OF 1921 (Feb. 2001), available here, including the following chapters: Don Ross, Prologue; John Hope Franklin and Scott Ellsworth, History Knows No Fences: An Overview; Scott Ellsworth, The Tulsa Race Riot; Richard Warner, Airplanes and the Riot; Clyde Snow, Confirmed Deaths: A Preliminary Report; Robert Brooks and Alan H. Witten, The Investigation of Potential Mass Grave Locations for the Tulsa Race Riot; Lesley Rankin-Hill and Phoebe Stubblefield, History Uncovered: Skeletal Remains As a Vehicle to the Past; Larry O'Dell, Riot Property Loss; Alfred Brophy, Assessing State and City Culpability: The Riot and the Law; Maxine Horner, Epilogue; and Chronological Maps of the Tulsa Race Riot.

[21] We have listed in Appendix A all primary source material we consulted, whether cited in this Report or used as background.

[22] AMERICAN RED CROSS, REPORT: TULSA RACE RIOT DISASTER RELIEF (Loula Watkins, comp.), Tulsa Historical Society & Museum, Accession No. 1984.002.060 (hereinafter "AMERICAN RED CROSS REPORT"; because the website contains a collection of separately paginated reports, all page numbers refer to PDF pagination of the posted report).

---

[23] This included reports of the following: Major Jas. A. Bell (July 2, 1921); Major M.C. Paul R. Brown (July 1, 1921); Major C. W. Daley (July 6, 1921); Lieut. Roy R. Dunlap (July 1, 1921); Major Byron Kirkpatrick (July 1, 1921); Capt. John W. McCurn B Co 3d Inf. (undated); L.J.F. Rooney, Lieut. Col. 3rd Infantry and Chas. W. Daley, Inspector General's Dept. (June 3, 1921); Lt. Col. L.J.F. Rooney (July 29, 1921); and Frank Van Voorhis, Capt. Com. Service (July 30, 1921). These materials were provided to us by Justice For Greenwood and are also available through McFarlin Library's Special Collections.

[24] These documents, including testimony about the massacre given in the weeks after it occurred, are available through the Oklahoma Department of Libraries. *See Oklahoma v. Gustafson, No. 10537 (Okl. Dist. 1921)*, collected by Okla. Dept. of Libraries, Okla. State Archives Division, Box 25, RG 1-2, Case No. 1062 (cited hereinafter as *Oklahoma v. Gustafson* with reference to the particular document).

[25] The University of Tulsa, McFarlin Library, Department of Special Collections & University Archives.

[26] University of Tulsa College of Law and its dean, Oren Griffin, provided access to materials in its B.C. Franklin Collection. In addition, some of these materials have been collected by the Tulsa Historical Society and Museum, XXXXXX provided information about W.D. Williams (son of John and Loula Williams) and provided Loula Williams' legal papers.

[27] We have identified all books, articles, and other secondary sources we consulted, whether cited in this Report or used as background, in Appendix A.

[28] *Chronological Maps of the Tulsa Race Riot*, THE COMMISSION REPORT; I. Marc Carlson, *Timeline of the Tulsa Race Massacre* (as posted on the John Hope Franklin Center for Reconciliation website); *Timeline: The 1921 Tulsa Race Massacre*, TULSA WORLD (last updated May 29, 2021); *Timeline: The Questions That Remain*, TULSA WORLD (2009).

[29] The primary articles we have consulted (whether cited in this Report or used for background) are identified in Appendix A.

[30] We reviewed the photographs in the Tulsa City-County Library Digital Collection, *1921 Tulsa Race Massacre*, (collection of photographs taken in the days following the massacre) as well as the collection of photographs in Karlos K. Hill's THE 1921 TULSA RACE MASSACRE: A PHOTOGRAPHIC HISTORY (University of Oklahoma Press, 2021).

[31] *See generally* THOMAS E. WRIGHT, ET AL., REPORT OF THE 1898 WILMINGTON RACE RIOT COMMISSION (May 31, 2006); DAVID ZUCCHINO, WILMINGTON'S LIE: THE MURDEROUS COUP OF 1898 AND THE RISE OF WHITE SUPREMACY (Atlantic Monthly Press, 2020).

[32] Allison Keyes, *The East St. Louis Race Riot Left Dozens Dead, Devastating a Community on the Rise*, SMITHSONIAN MAG. (June 30, 2017); *The East St. Louis Riot*, PBS: AM. EXPERIENCE.

[33] *Red Summer: The Race Riots of 1919*, NAT. WWI MUSEUM & MEM'L.

[34] *Id.; see also* DeNeen L. Brown, *Red Summer: When Racist Mobs Ruled*, PBS: AM. EXPERIENCE (Feb. 4, 2021). During the Red Summer, significant attacks occurred in Chicago, Illinois, Washington, D.C., Omaha, Nebraska, and Elaine, Arkansas, while dozens of smaller "riots" occurred elsewhere. *Id.; see also* Jesse J. Holland, *Hundreds of [B]lack deaths during 1919's Red Summer are being remembered*, PBS NEWS (July 23, 2019).

[35] Nicole Chavez, *Rosewood, Florida, marks 100 years since race massacre. Here's what happened*, CNN (Jan. 8, 2023).

[36] *Lynchings: By State and Race, 1882-1968*, ARCHIVES AT TUSKEGEE INSTITUTE (Nov. 2020).

[37] Suzette M. Malveaux, *A Taxonomy of Silencing: The Law's 100 Year Suppression of the Tulsa Race Massacre*, 102 B.U. L. REV. 2173, 2192 (2022) (internal footnote omitted).

[38] VICTOR LUCKERSON, BUILT FROM THE FIRE 49 (Random House, 2023) ("In its pre-statehood days, Oklahoma was an unusually egalitarian place."); HANNIBAL B. JOHNSON, BLACK WALL STREET 100 25-26 (Eakin, 2020); JAMES S. HIRSCH, RIOT AND REMEMBRANCE: THE TULSA RACE MASSACRE AND ITS LEGACY 33 (Second Mariner Books, 2021) ("The region, in short, seemed to be moving toward more racial equality than any other place in America.").

[39] HIRSCH, RIOT AND REMEMBRANCE, at 30-33; JOHNSON, BLACK WALL STREET 100, at 26; *see also* Ellsworth, THE COMMISSION REPORT, at 39-40 ("For many, Oklahoma represented not only a chance to escape the harsher racial realities of life in the former states of the Old South, but was literally a land of hope, a place worth sacrificing for, a place to start anew.").

[40] Archiebald Browne, *Oklahoma's Historic All-Black Towns: Built on Hope, Survived by Pride*, NONDOC.COM (July 25, 2019) ("Between 1856 and 1920, more than 50 all-[B]lack towns were founded in Oklahoma, totaling more than anywhere else in the country and creating a mindset that Oklahoma could be a land of opportunity for [B]lack Americans.").

[41] Ross, THE COMMISSION REPORT, at v-vi (noting that Native American Tribes were forcibly removed from southern states and that "[t]his odyssey, during the 1830s and before, the lives of [B]lacks and Native Americans would be linked on the infamous, cruel 'Trail of Tears.' On long marches under extreme duress and hardship, the trail led to present-day Oklahoma, Kansas and Nebraska. . . . [During the Civil war] many of the [T]ribes officially sided with the Confederacy. Afterward, many former [B]lack slaves, Freemen, were registered as members of the [T]ribes and offered sections of the Indian land allotments"); Michael K. Velchik & Jeffery Y. Zhang, *Restoring Indian Reservation Status: An Empirical Analysis*, 40 YALE J. ON REG. 339, 354 (2023) ("During the Civil War, the Five Civilized Tribes allied and fought for the Confederacy. As a result, the United States forced the Creek Nation to free their slaves and cede the western half of their lands, which were ultimately opened to non-Indian settlement and called Oklahoma Territory."); *see also, generally,* JOHNSON, BLACK WALL STREET 100, at 25-26.

[42] Ryan P. Smith, *How Native American Slaveholders Complicate the Trail of Tears Narrative*, SMITHSONIAN MAG. (March 6, 2018) (quoting museum curator Paul Chaat Smith as stating, "[t]he Five Civilized Tribes were deeply committed to slavery, established their own racialized black codes, immediately reestablished slavery when they arrived in Indian territory, rebuilt their nations with slave labor, crushed slave rebellions, and enthusiastically sided with the Confederacy in the Civil War").

[43] LUCKERSON, BUILT FROM THE FIRE, at 11 (explaining how Congress enacted laws that forced Native Americans to split up community land and distribute it to individuals Tribal members); *United States v. City of McAlester, Okl.*, 604 F.2d 42, 63-64 (10th Cir. 1979); Velchik & Zhang, *Restoring Indian Reservation Status*, at 354-55 ("In 1893, Congress created the Dawes Commission and tasked it with extinguishing the Five Tribes' territory. . . . In 1896, Congress authorized the Commission to survey Indian territory and enroll [T]ribal members in preparation for allotment—a process whereby the [T]ribe's communal land tenure was broken up into individual parcels and distributed to Indians. . . . In 1898, Congress passed the Curtis Act, which abolished [T]ribal courts and directed the Dawes Commission to allot the Five Tribes' land following [T]ribal enrollment. The 1901 Creek Allotment Agreement originally provided that the allotted lands would be alienable within five years, except for forty acres of homestead for each allottee, which remained inalienable for twenty-one years.") (internal footnote omitted); Alina Ball, *Lost in the Fire: Reflections on the Tulsa Race Massacre Centennial*, 49 HASTINGS CONST. L.Q. 216, 231 (2022) ("When communal Cherokee lands were divided into individual allotments, [T]ribal members with treaty rights to land and citizenship (which included members of African descent) were permitted to establish individual land claims in the Cherokee Outlet. The redistribution of Cherokee land created the pathway for what would become the Greenwood District.") (internal footnote omitted); Trevion Freeman, *For Freedmen's Sake: The Story of the Native Blacks of the Muscogee Nation and Their Fight for Citizenship Post-McGirt*, 57 TULSA L. REV. 513, 525-26 (2022) (explaining division of land between Native Americans and Freedmen).

[44] LUCKERSON, BUILT FROM THE FIRE, at 11-12 ("Many freedmen and Native Americans quickly sold their land for little money or lost it as victims of fraudulent schemes. But those who held on to it . . . became fantastically rich. Freedmen were granted about 2 million acres of Oklahoma land, the largest transfer of property wealth to [B]lack people in the history of the United States.").

[45] SCOTT ELLSWORTH, DEATH IN A PROMISED LAND: THE TULSA RACE RIOT OF 1921 9 (LSU Press, 1982) (discussing oil boom).

[46] HIRSCH, RIOT AND REMEMBRANCE, at 33; Walter F. White, _The Eruption of Tulsa_, THE NATION, June 29, 1921, at 909.

[47] HIRSCH, RIOT AND REMEMBRANCE, at 36 ("The state constitution mandated segregated schools but otherwise included no segregation language, lest President Roosevelt, a Republican, refuse to sign it. However, when the state legislature convened for the first time on December 2, 1907, it passed emergency legislation requiring separate railroad coaches and waiting rooms for people of African descent."); LUCKERSON, BUILT FROM THE FIRE, at 52 (explaining that when Oklahoma applied for statehood, "[its] constitution would segregate only schools," but that "legislators had plans to segregate train cars, libraries, even phone booths, just as soon as they were free of federal oversight").

[48] Malveaux, _A Taxonomy of Silencing_, at 2192 (citing _Lynching in America: Racial Terror Lynchings (Map)_, EQUAL JUST. INITIATIVE (entry for Oklahoma)).

[49] _A History of Racial Injustice Calendar_, EQUAL JUST. INITIATIVE (last visited Dec. 8, 2024) (entry for May 24, 1911).

[50] RANDY KREHBIEL, TULSA 1921: REPORTING A MASSACRE (U. Okla. Press, 2021) at 10 (discussing Creek origins of Tulsa); Tulsa City-County Library, _Tulsa-Area FAQs_, "History" ("The first historic Tulsa was a Creek Indian settlement on the Tallapoosa River in what is now Alabama. The name 'Tulsa' (originally spelled Tulsey or Tulsee) is a shortened pronunciation of Tallasi, which is almost certainly a contraction of Tullahassee or Tallahassee, meaning 'Old Town' ('Tulwa,' meaning town, and 'ahassee,' meaning something old) in the Creek language.").

[51] Tulsa City-County Library, _Tulsa-Area FAQs_, "When was the city of Tulsa founded?"

[52] KREHBIEL, TULSA 1921: REPORTING A MASSACRE, at 14 (explaining that Tulsa had "the ambition and foresight to turn itself into a railroad center, to build hotels, to start banks and opera houses, and to tolerate the saloons and gambling dens and bawdy houses where rough, hardworking men found entertainment").

[53] Ellsworth, THE COMMISSION REPORT, at 38 ("By 1910. . . Tulsa had mushroomed into a raucous boomtown of more than 10,000. . . . [B]y 1920, the population of greater Tulsa had skyrocketed to more than 100,000.").

[54] _Id._ at 37 ("Indeed, Tulsa had grown so much and so fast—in a now-you-don't-see-it, now-you-do kind of fashion—that local boosters called it the Magic City.").

[55] LUCKERSON, BUILT FROM THE FIRE, at 47-48 (discussing passage of housing ordinance) and 54 (describing the reaction of hotel entrepreneur and Black community leader J.B. Stradford to housing ordinance).

[56] Ellsworth, THE COMMISSION REPORT, at 50-51 (discussing lynchings in Tulsa prior to the massacre).

[57] LUCKERSON, BUILT FROM THE FIRE, at 71 ("A young white man, Roy Belton, was in the downtown jail, accused of murdering a white taxi driver. In the middle of the night, he was taken from his cell at the top of the courthouse, driven out of town by a caravan of cars, and hanged from a billboard. A mob of dozens ripped the clothes from Belton's body as souvenirs while police officers directed traffic."); Ellsworth, THE COMMISSION REPORT, at 51 (noting that when the cab driver Belton was accused of assaulting died, "hundreds of whites had gathered outside of the courthouse. Soon, a delegation of men carrying rifles and shotguns, some with handkerchiefs covering their faces, entered the building and demanded of [then] Sheriff Woolley that he turn Belton over to them. The sheriff later claimed that he tried to dissuade the intruders, but he appears to have done little to stop them. For a little while later, the men appeared on the courthouse steps

with Roy Belton. 'We got him boys,' they shouted, 'We've got him,'" then describing lynching); Randy Hopkins, *The Plot to Kill "Diamond Dick" Rowland and the Tulsa Race Riot*, 99 CHRON. OF OKLA. 4, 7-8 (Spring 2021) ("Most of the city's police watched the murder, ordered by Gustafson to stand down for fear of harming the audience of thousands, including women and children."); KREHBIEL, TULSA 1921: REPORTING A MASSACRE, at 36-37 (describing lynching).

[58] Hopkins, *The Plot to Kill "Diamond Dick" Rowland and the Tulsa Race Riot*, at 8 (noting that instead of stopping Belton's lynching, "the police helped manage the crowd and control traffic"); LUCKERSON, BUILT FROM THE FIRE, at 71 (explaining that police officers directed traffic during Belton's lynching).

[59] Ellsworth, THE COMMISSION REPORT, at 51-52 ("Among the crowd—estimated to be in the hundreds—were members of the Tulsa police, who had been instructed by Chief Gustafson not to intervene.").

[60] *Id.* at 52; Hopkins, *The Plot to Kill "Diamond Dick" Rowland and the Tulsa Race Riot*, at 8.

[61] Ellsworth, THE COMMISSION REPORT, at 52 (generally discussing effect of Belton's lynching); PARRISH, THE NATION MUST AWAKE, at 8 ("Since the lynching of a [w]hite boy in Tulsa, the confidence in the ability of the city official to protect its prisoner had decreased.").

[62] *Mobs Lynch White Boy at Tulsa and a Colored at Oklahoma City*, TULSA STAR, Sept. 4, 1920, at 1 ("Belton was held in the county jail on top floor of Court House, only accessible by elevator, but owing to the Sheriff to take proper precautions [for] his protection, the mob easily overpowered the Sheriff, siezed [sic] Belton and . . . hanged him.") and 4 ("The lynching of Roy Belton explodes the theory that a prisoner is safe on top of the Court House from mob violence."); *see also* Ellsworth, THE COMMISSION REPORT, at 52 (citing *Mobs Lynch White Boy at Tulsa and a Colored at Oklahoma City*, TULSA STAR, Sept. 4, 1920, at 1, 4).

[63] PARRISH, THE NATION MUST AWAKE, at 7-8 ("On leaving the Frisco station, going north to Archer St. one could see nothing but Negro business places . . . [o]n Greenwood one could find a variety of business places which would be a credit to any section of the town. In the residential section there were homes of beauty and splendor which would please the most critical eye the schools and many churches were well attended.").

[64] JOHNSON, BLACK WALL STREET 100, at 27.

[65] *See generally*, JOHNSON, TULSA'S HISTORIC GREENWOOD DISTRICT; HIRSCH, RIOT AND REMEMBRANCE, at 42-43.

[66] PARRISH, THE NATION MUST AWAKE, at 64.

[67] Virtual interview by Cold Case Team with XXXXXX (Nov. 7, 2024) and live interview with XXXXXX in Tulsa, Oklahoma (Nov. 15, 2024) (recalling businesses). The Dreamland Theater had 750 seats and "offered live musical and theatrical revues as well as silent movies accompanied by a piano." Ellsworth, THE COMMISSION REPORT, at 41.

[68] Ellsworth, THE COMMISSION REPORT, at 42 (noting that Stradford was "a highly successful owner of rental property" and noting that the Stradford hotel, opened in 1918, was a "modern fifty-four room structure" that became "not only one of the true jewels of Green wood Avenue, but . . . also one of the largest [B]lack-owned businesses in Oklahoma.").

[69] Interview by Cold Case Team with XXXXXX, in Tulsa, Okla. (Nov. 15, 2024) (recalling the shoe store, as well as a record store that sold "Black Swan records," the first major [B]lack-owned record label in the U.S.); *see also* PARRISH, THE NATION MUST AWAKE, at 99; Nellie Gilles & Mycah Hazel, *Radio Diaries: Harry Pace and the Rise and Fall of Black Swan Records*, NPR: ALL THINGS CONSIDERED (July 1, 2021).

[70] Ellsworth, THE COMMISSION REPORT, at 42 ("All told, there were more than a dozen African American churches in Tulsa at the time of the [massacre], including First Baptist, Vernon A.M.E., Brown's Chapel, Morning Star, Bethel Seventh Day Adventist, and Paradise Baptist, as well as Church of God, Nazarene, and Church of God in Christ

congregations. Most impressive from an architectural standpoint, perhaps, was the beautiful, brand-new home of Mount Zion Baptist Church, which was dedicated on April 10, 1921.").

[71] HIRSCH, RIOT AND REMEMBRANCE, at 47-48 (describing Detroit Avenue).

[72] Ellsworth, THE COMMISSION REPORT, at 40-43 (describing businesses in Greenwood).

[73] Deposition of Viola Ford Fletcher at 31:8-24, *Randle v. City of Tulsa*, No. CV-2020-1179 (Okl. Dist.) (Oct. 16, 2020) (hereinafter "Fletcher Deposition"); *Tulsa Greenwood Race Riot Accountability Act of 2007: Hearing Before the Subcomm. on the Const., Civil Rights, and Civil Liberties of the H.R. Comm. on the Judiciary*, 110th Cong. 32 (2007) (testimony of Olivia Hooker).

[74] Fletcher Deposition at 10:20-13:17; *Continuing Injustice: The Centennial of the Tulsa-Greenwood Race Massacre Before the H. Subcomm. on the Const., Civil Rights, and Civil Liberties*, 117th Cong. (2021) (hereafter "*2021 Committee Testimony*") (statement of Mother Fletcher).

[75] Fletcher Deposition at 12:22-13:24; *2021 Committee Testimony* (statement of Mother Randle).

[76] Fletcher Deposition at 12:18-13:02; *2021 Committee Testimony* (statements of Mother Fletcher and Mother Randle).

[77] FLETCHER, DON'T LET THEM BURY MY STORY, at 17-18.

[78] *Survivors' Stories*, Interview by Eddie Faye Gates with Georgia Walker Hill and Samuel Walker, Tulsa Massacre Survivors, in Kansas City, Missouri (June 26, 1999), The Eddie Faye Gates Tulsa Race Massacre Collection (Gilcrease Museum).

[79] Interview with Beatrice Campbell-Webster, *Guide to the 1921 Tulsa Race Massacre Oral History Collection, 2004-2007*, NAT. MUSEUM OF AFRICAN AM. HIST. & CULTURE, SMITHSONIAN INST.

[80] Account of Kinney I Booker, Tulsa Race Massacre Survivor, available at Tulsa Reparations Coalition, *Meet the Survivors: Oral History Accounts of the Tulsa Race Riot of 1921 by Black Survivors*.

[81] *Tulsa Greenwood Race Riot Accountability Act of 2007: Hearing Before the Subcomm. on the Const., Civil Rights, and Civil Liberties of the H.R. Comm. on the Judiciary*, 110th Cong. 31-32 (2007) (testimony of Olivia Hooker).

[82] Interview of William D. Williams by Ruth Sigler Avery (Nov. 29, 1970), Oklahoma State University – Tulsa Library Ruth Sigler Avery Collection, Box 7, Folder 6 ("[My father] was the first [B]lack man in Tulsa to own an automobile. He had an automobile when there weren't 50 cars in Tulsa.").

[83] KREHBIEL, TULSA 1921: REPORTING A MASSACRE, at 24; Loren Gill, *The Tulsa Race Riot* (Master's Thesis, University of Tulsa) (1946), at 8 ("The city built up the white part of town and left the Negroes to do the best they could. The [Black] section had no sewers, and inadequate water mains for fire prevention purposes ran through the area."). Writing shortly after the massacre, a Black official with the YMCA, describing Greenwood as it existed before the massacre, said the community was "constantly handicapped as to public utilities, which were managed and controlled by the white man. They constantly prayed him to extend and furnish the same. Procrastination, political promises and hope deferred was the final result. The colored section of Tulsa was insufficiently lighted." G.A. Gregg, *Tulsa Then and Now*, Oklahoma YMCA (undated, but included in letter to Department of Justice dated June 9, 1921).

[84] JOHNSON, BLACK WALL STREET 100, at 32.

[85] Interview by Cold Case Team with Michael Eugene Penny, in Tulsa, Okla. (Oct. 16, 2024) (recalling from his grandparents that, on Saturday nights, people from outlying areas would come to Greenwood for supplies and entertainment).

[86] *See* ELLSWORTH, DEATH IN A PROMISED LAND, at 16 (describing how, in Greenwood, "one would also find [B]lack Tulsa's share of prostitution houses, speakeasies, and 'choc' joints"); Ellsworth, THE COMMISSION REPORT, at 50 ("Illegal drugs were also present. Morphine, cocaine, and opium could all be purchased in Tulsa, apparently without much difficulty.") and 55 ("[N]ot only did racial issues suddenly come to the foreground, but more importantly, they did so in a manner that featured the highly explosive subject of relations between [B]lack men and white women."); Greta Katherine Smith, *"The Battling Ground": Memory, Violence, and Resistance in Greenwood, North Tulsa, Oklahoma, 1907-1980* (2018) (Master's Thesis, Portland State University) at 31 ("Greenwood, like its bordering areas on the outer edges of Downtown Tulsa, had problems of vice including gambling, sex work, and the production and sale of illegal drugs and alcohol.").

[87] *See* ALFRED L. BROPHY, RECONSTRUCTING THE DREAMLAND: THE TULSA RACE RIOT OF 1921 – RACE, REPARATIONS, AND RECONCILIATION (Oxford University Press, 2002) at 73 ("[W]hite Tulsans saw the cultural openness of Greenwood as dangerous. Jazz and alcohol were part of the vibrant culture of Greenwood, the ways that it operated at the cultural margins. Yet they also symbolized for whites the dangers of Greenwood. Just days before the riot, a Tulsa paper reprinted a story from Chicago called, '*Jazz the Evil Spirit of Music, Incites Hysteria.*'").

[88] KREHBIEL, TULSA 1921: REPORTING A MASSACRE, at 7 ("Much more disturbing, to at least some white Tulsans, was the perceived erosion of social and moral standards exemplified by the mixing of races in dance halls, speakeasies, and hotels along First Street and in the '[N]egro quarter.'"); Ellsworth, THE COMMISSION REPORT, at 55 ("[N]ot only did racial issues suddenly come to the foreground, but more importantly, they did so in a manner that featured the highly explosive subject of relations between [B]lack men and white women."); *30 Witnesses on Stand in Probe*, TULSA DAILY WORLD, May 21, 1921, at 17 (describing a "[N]egro joint" outside town where "a [N]egro was playing a piano and where several white girls were drunk and dancing").

[89] *Make Tulsa Decent*, TULSA TRIB., May 13, 1921, at 24 (editorial claiming that "[p]rostitution, bootlegging and gambling, with all their degrading influences, have run pretty much unmolested, both by the city and county authorities"); *see also* Hopkins, *The Plot to Kill "Diamond Dick" Rowland and the Tulsa Race Riot*, at 10 & n.57 (citing article).

[90] *See, e.g., Whites Advancing into 'Little Africa'; Negro Death List is About 15*, TULSA DAILY WORLD, June 1, 1921, at 1; *It Must Not Be Again*, TULSA TRIB., June 4, 1921, at 8; *see also* Ellsworth, THE COMMISSION REPORT, at 39 ("Some whites disparagingly referred to it as 'Little Africa,' or worse.").

[91] *See* PARRISH, THE NATION MUST AWAKE, at 38 (account of E.A. Loupe) (blaming "yellow journalism" for increasing racial hatred of "Negro porters" blamed for the presence of "white women" in Black "rooming houses").

[92] PARRISH, THE NATION MUST AWAKE, at 7.

[93] Interview by Cold Case Team with XXXXXX, in Tulsa, Okla. (Nov. 15, 2024).

[94] Ellsworth, THE COMMISSION REPORT, at 45 ("World War I had done much to clarify their thinking. In the name of democracy, African Americans had solidly supported the war effort. Black soldiers—who were placed in segregated units—had fought gallantly in France, winning the respect not only of Allied commanders, but also of their German foes."). In fact, a massacre victim whose body was recently discovered has been identified as a Great War veteran. *See* Sarah Dewberry, *Victim of 1921 Tulsa Race Massacre identified through DNA genealogy as WWI veteran*, CNN (July 12, 2024).

[95] The French Army awarded the Croix de Guerre, the French war medal, to over 170 Black soldiers for acts of valor including bravery during the Second Battle of the Marne and the Meuse-Argonne Offensive. *See* Deborah Savage, *African American Soldiers in World War One*, LA. PUB. LIBR.: LAPL BLOG (Feb. 27, 2024); *see also* Jami L. Bryan, *Fighting For Respect: African-American Soldiers in WWI*, ARMY HIST. FOUND.; *see also, generally*, LUCKERSON, BUILT FROM THE FIRE, at 63-64.

[96] LUCKERSON, BUILT FROM THE FIRE, at 68 ("After risking their lives and losing their innocence, [B]lack soldiers returning home bore no more patience for Jim Crow discrimination and violent white coercion."); Ellsworth, THE COMMISSION REPORT, at 45; RUDIA M. HALLIBURTON, JR., THE TULSA RACE WAR OF 1921 (San Francisco: R and E Research Associates, 1975), at ix ("[B]lacks who served in the United States armed forces overseas, although they suffered discrimination on the part of their own government and military organizations, experienced considerable acceptance by Europeans. Upon their return home, [B]lack veterans thought that they had earned full citizenship, acceptance and partnership in American society."). In *The Crisis*, W.E.B Du Bois had urged Black veterans to seek racial equality. *See* W.E.B. Du Bois, *Returning Soldiers*, 18 CRISIS: A RECORD OF THE DARKER RACES 7, 13-14 (May 1919).

[97] Du Bois, *Returning Soldiers*, at 13-14.

[98] Ellsworth, THE COMMISSION REPORT, at 52-54 (describing attitude of Black men of Greenwood toward attempted lynchings and lynching); LUCKERSON, BUILT FROM THE FIRE, at 40-41 (describing A.J. Smitherman's strong stand against lynching); *see also Mob Rule and the Law*, TULSA STAR, March 6, 1920, at 8 (Smitherman editorial describing a thwarted lynching and stating that "the Colored men of Shawnee who, it is alleged, stole an auto, armed themselves and went to protect the prisoner. . . are the heroes of the story").

[99] KREHBIEL, TULSA 1921: REPORTING A MASSACRE, at 16 (explaining that the Home Guard was "a one-thousand-member paramilitary force ostensibly created to replace National Guard units called to duty in Europe, but that acted more as an enforcement arm" of the Tulsa County Council); ELLSWORTH, DEATH IN A PROMISED LAND, at 131, n.13 (explaining that the proper usage of the term "Home Guards" referred to "a civilian defense organization organized in Tulsa—and elsewhere—in 1917 in response to the American entry into World War 1").

[100] KREHBIEL, TULSA 1921: REPORTING A MASSACRE, at 16; *Tulsa Home Guards Are Imposing Company of Fighters*, TULSA DAILY WORLD, Feb. 17, 1918, at 42 (explaining that Tulsa Home Guard was established pursuant to a bill enacted by Congress, "authorizing the establishment of troops to replace the national guard units that were to be mustered into federal service"); *War Council to Get Behind Home Guards*, OKLA. WEEKLY WORLD, Sept. 6, 1917, at 1 (explaining that Home Guards were to be equipped to protect against riots, labor trouble, or other disturbances).

[101] LUCKERSON, BUILT FROM THE FIRE, at 67 ("Ostensibly, the councils were supposed to maintain domestic morale and run savings bond campaigns; in reality, they used censorship, coercion, and carefully orchestrated acts of violence to enact their will, often for ends that had nothing to do with the war effort. Council members openly advocated the lynching of their political enemies in the pages of the *Tulsa World*. A vigilante offshoot of the council known as the Knights of Liberty, once tarred and feathered a group of oil industry unionists that they deemed to be meddlesome, forcing their victims to flee Tulsa forever."); *see also id.* at 118 (noting that "Tulsa already had experience developing vigilante networks among the city's business elite through the World War I Council of Defense, the Home Guard, and rogue groups like the Knights of Liberty that often worked closely with police"); KREHBIEL, TULSA 1921: REPORTING A MASSACRE, at 15-16 ("[V]igilantism began shortly after America's entry into the Great War, with the creation in Tulsa and throughout the state and nation of local councils of defense charged with monitoring everything from profiteers to draft resisters to Sunday sermons. In theory, Oklahoma's councils had limited legal authority, but that did not prevent them from imposing almost absolute rule. The Tulsa County Council, while accomplishing much in furthering the war effort, also exhibited little regard for the rights of individual citizens."); *Grand Ball New Year's Eve Is Planned by Tulsa Home Guards to Raise Funds*, TULSA DAILY WORLD, Dec. 14, 1917, at 7 (explaining that the Home Guard was organized "for the purpose of guarding the lives and property of the people of the city" and praising the "manner in which they went about their work," including a "tar and feather party").

[102] LUCKERSON, BUILT FROM THE FIRE, at 118 (noting that, at the time of the massacre, "Tulsa already had experience developing vigilante networks among the city's business elite through the World War I Council of Defense, the Home Guard, and rogue groups like the Knights of Liberty that often worked closely with police. The violence these groups organized was about politics and economics as much as it was about enforcing a white supremacist, puritanically Christian social order.").

[103] *Id.* at 67-68; *see also* KREHBIEL, TULSA 1921: REPORTING A MASSACRE, at 16.

---

[104] Ellsworth, THE COMMISSION REPORT, at 56-57.

[105] ELLSWORTH, DEATH IN A PROMISED LAND, at 45-46; HIRSCH, RIOT AND REMEMBRANCE, at 78.

[106] HIRSCH, RIOT AND REMEMBRANCE, at 78-79.

[107] *Id.* at 78-80; BROPHY, RECONSTRUCTING THE DREAMLAND, at 24; *see also* GATES, RIOT ON GREENWOOD, at 97 (account of Veniece Dunn Sims that "[i]t was common knowledge in the [B]lack community that [Sarah Page and Dick Rowland] were lovers").

[108] FRANKLIN, MY LIFE AND AN ERA: THE AUTOBIOGRAPHY OF BUCK COLBERT FRANKLIN, at 199 (stating that Rowland stepped on Page's foot); ELLSWORTH, DEATH IN A PROMISED LAND, at 46 (explaining that the most common explanation of the elevator incident is that "Rowland accidentally stepped on Page's foot in the elevator, causing her to lurch back, and when he grabbed her arm to keep from falling, she screamed"); KREHBIEL, TULSA 1921: REPORTING A MASSACRE, at 32 (noting the Drexel Building elevator was reportedly "notoriously difficult to operate, shaking and shuddering and often leaving an uneven step at the threshold that caused passengers to trip as they exited").

[109] Weiss Reports at 6 (Appendix C).

[110] Brophy, THE COMMISSION REPORT, at 167 (noting that the district attorney dismissed Dick Rowland's case when Sarah Page "failed to appear as the complaining witness").

[111] HIRSCH, RIOT AND REMEMBRANCE, at 78-80. Gustafson himself claimed that Rowland was arrested on May 30. Gustafson Testimony at 6-7, *Oklahoma v. Gustafson*; *see also* Hopkins, *The Plot to Kill "Diamond Dick" Rowland and the Tulsa Race Riot*, at 13.

[112] Ellsworth, THE COMMISSION REPORT, at 58.

[113] HILL, THE 1921 TULSA RACE MASSACRE: A PHOTOGRAPHIC HISTORY, at 3 & n.6 (explaining paper insinuated that Page had been raped); Ellsworth, THE COMMISSION REPORT, at 44-45 ("[D]uring the post-World War I era, and for many years before and after, perhaps no crime was viewed as more egregious by many whites than the rape, or attempted rape, of a white woman by a [B]lack male.").

[114] Ellsworth, THE COMMISSION REPORT, at 58.

[115] *See, e.g.*, Interview by Jean Pittman with Robert L. Fairchild, Jr. (April 18, 1976), Oklahoma State University – Tulsa Library Ruth Sigler Avery Collection Box 2 Folder 12; Interview by Jan Jennings Sparks with William Danforth Williams, Tulsa Massacre survivor (Mar. 29, 1977), [1977.072.001], Oral History Collection, Tulsa Historical Society & Museum (recalling an article headlined "to lynch a [N]egro tonight").

[116] Interview by Cold Case Team of Jimmie White, Vivian Clark Adams, and Jim Lloyd, Commissioners, Oklahoma Commission to Study the Tulsa Race Riot of 1921, in Tulsa, Okla. (Oct. 16, 2024) (stating that the Commission offered a reward of $1000 for anyone to produce article but that no one had come forward).

[117] Ellsworth, THE COMMISSION REPORT, at 58 (explaining that bound version for the *Tulsa Tribune* for that time period is lost but that "[a] microfilm version is, however, available, but before the actual microfilming was done some years later, someone had deliberately torn out of the May 31, 1921 city edition both a front-page article and, in addition, nearly all of the editorial page").

[118] KREHBIEL, TULSA 1921: REPORTING A MASSACRE, at 35 (citing *Race War Start Came in Arrest of Young Negro*, TULSA DAILY WORLD, June 1, 1921, at 1).

[119] *Id.* at 34-35 ("In the confusion of that day and the days that followed, the *World*'s after-the-fact reporting could have become conflated with the *Tribune*'s earlier story into a single, cold-blooded call for Dick Rowland's murder.").

[120] *Id.*

[121] SCOTT ELLSWORTH, THE GROUND BREAKING: THE TULSA RACE MASSACRE AND AN AMERICAN CITY'S SEARCH FOR JUSTICE 85 (Dutton, 2022).

[122] HIRSCH, RIOT AND REMEMBRANCE, at 73 ("If Jones embodied the cosmopolitan aspiration of the city's elite, he also reflected its deplorable attitude on race. He did not write much about racial issues, but his editorials revealed his xenophobic and white supremacist attitudes.") and 125 (citing a post-massacre editorial by Jones condemning Greenwood and noting that massacre scholars cite the editorial to "capture the visceral bigotry" of white Tulsa); *see also* TIM MADIGAN, THE BURNING (St. Martin's Griffin, 100th Anniversary Ed., 2021) at 37-39 (discussing Jones' racism); *see also generally*, Russell Cobb, *'No apology': Richard Lloyd Jones and the 1921 Race Massacre*, TULSAPEOPLE (Feb. 20, 2019).

[123] Hopkins, *The Plot to Kill "Diamond Dick" Rowland and the Tulsa Race Riot*, at 15 ("The prime suspect in the peddling of bad information was the Tulsa Police Department itself. It was the police, and only the police, who handled the investigation, knew what was alleged and what was not, handled the arrest, and filed municipal court charges. The police were identified as the source and their representations would have been accepted not only by some starry-eyed young reporter, but also by the 'old hands' back at the Tribune Building."). Hopkins suggests that police wanted to send a message to the Black community by lynching Rowland and were setting the paper up to take the fall if they were blamed for the lynching. *Id.* at 15-16.

[124] Weiss Reports at 7 (Appendix C); White, *The Eruption of Tulsa*, at 910 ("Chief of Police John A. Gustafson, Captain Wilkerson of the Police Department, Edwin F. Barnett, managing editor of the *Tulsa Tribune*, and numerous other citizens all stated that there was talk Tuesday of lynching the boy.").

[125] ELLSWORTH, THE GROUND BREAKING at 19 (stating that by 7:00 p.m. more than 300 white men had gathered at the courthouse); ELLSWORTH, DEATH IN A PROMISED LAND, at 49 ("Between 6:00 and 7:00 PM, a crowd of whites began to form outside the courthouse where Roland was being held. It has been reported that there were some 300 whites outside the courthouse by 7:30 PM and that this crowd grew to 400 by 9:00.").

[126] Ellsworth, THE COMMISSION REPORT, at 60 ("McCullough positioned six of his men, armed with rifles and shotguns, on the roof of the courthouse. He also disabled the building's elevator, and had his remaining men barricade themselves at the top of the stairs with orders to shoot any intruders on sight."); *First Detailed Story of How the Tulsa Race Riot Started: Statements by Chief of Police and Sheriff of Happenings After Arrest of Negro Tuesday*, ST. LOUIS POST DISPATCH, June 3, 1921, at 21 (Sheriff McCullough quoted as saying that "by running the elevator to the top" and with his deputies he "could hold that against any mob"; McCullough instructed his deputies to "run the elevator to the top of the building, to get behind the barred door, and not to open it under any circumstances").

[127] *First Detailed Story of How the Tulsa Race Riot Started: Statements by Chief of Police and Sheriff of Happenings After Arrest of Negro Tuesday*, ST. LOUIS POST DISPATCH, June 3, 1921, at 21 (reporting Sheriff McCullough's statement that three men breached courthouse between 8:00 and 8:30 in the evening); Ellsworth, THE COMMISSION REPORT, at 60 ("At approximately 8:20 p.m., . . . three white men entered the courthouse and demanded that the sheriff turn over Rowland, but were angrily turned away."); Hopkins, *The Plot to Kill "Diamond Dick" Rowland and the Tulsa Race Riot*, at 22-23.

[128] Letter of Redmond S. Cole to U.S. Department of Justice Official J.G. Findlay (June 6, 1921), M290, Folder 1, Box 12, Redmond S. Cole Collection, Western History Collections, University of Oklahoma (hereafter cited as "Cole to Findlay Letter") (We thank Randall Hopkins for providing this letter to us; although it is addressed to Bureau Agent Findlay, it is absent from the Bureau files we have located). Cole was then serving as District Judge of the 21st Judicial District of Oklahoma. He had previously served as Assistant U.S. District Attorney (what would now be Assistant United States Attorney) for the Western District of Oklahoma and wrote the letter when he read that the Department of Justice was

investigating the matter. *See id.*; *see also* _Biography of Redmond S. Cole_, University Libraries of the University of Oklahoma.

[129] Cole to Findlay Letter at 1 (noting that perpetrators were likely "the same group of rough necks and hoodlums who mobbed Belton" and identifying Cranfield as the leader of the "Belton mob"); Hopkins, *The Plot to Kill "Diamond Dick" Rowland and the Tulsa Race Riot*, at 23.

[130] *First Detailed Story of How the Tulsa Race Riot Started: Statements by Chief of Police and Sheriff of Happenings After Arrest of Negro*, ST. LOUIS POST DISPATCH, June 3, 1921, at 21 ("The crowd in front of the courthouse increased rapidly. They were all white people. There were about 100 who were talking loudly, and possibly 400 or 500 who seemed to be merely spectators, waiting to see if anything would happen.").

[131] Ellsworth, THE COMMISSION REPORT, at 61 ("[A]t about 9:00 p.m. a group of approximately twenty-five African American men decided to cast their lot not only with an endangered fellow member of the race, but also, literally, upon the side of justice. Leaving Greenwood by automobile, they drove down to the courthouse, where the white mob had gathered. Armed with rifles and shotguns, the men . . . marched to the courthouse steps. Their purpose, they announced to the no doubt stunned authorities, was to offer their services toward the defense of the jail."); *see also* Interview by Cold Case Team with Michael Eugene Penny, in Tulsa, Okla. (Oct. 16, 2024) (explaining that when rumors of lynching began, Greenwood leaders approached people with military experience who put on their uniforms and went to the courthouse to protect Rowland).

[132] LUCKERSON, BUILT FROM THE FIRE, at 71 ("A young white man, Roy Belton, was in the downtown jail, accused of murdering a white taxi driver. In the middle of the night, he was taken from his cell at the top of the courthouse, driven out of town by a caravan of cars, and hanged from a billboard. A mob of dozens ripped the clothes from Belton's body as souvenirs while police officers directed traffic.").

[133] *Inefficiency of Police Is Denied*, TULSA DAILY WORLD, July 29, 1921, at 1 (Police Commissioner J.M. Adkison testified regarding the white crowd in front of the courthouse that, "[s]o far as I was able to learn, they were there purely out of curiosity" after hearing the "rumor of a mob"). However, Adkison's opinion seems to be belied by the fact that he also testified that he received a phone call threatening to lynch Rowland. *Id.*

[134] Weiss Reports at 8 (Appendix C) (noting witness statement that "the white mob did not seem to be seriously intending to lynch anybody"); *id.* at 13 ("It began in a small half-hearted attempt to lynch a [N]egro youth . . . .").

[135] KREHBIEL, TULSA 1921: REPORTING A MASSACRE, at 38-39 (characterizing the initial crowd as "more curious than violent").

[136] *Grand Jury Blames Negroes for Inciting Race Rioting; Whites Clearly Exonerated*, TULSA DAILY WORLD, June 26, 1921, at 1 (grand jury report states that there was no "organized attempt" to lynch Rowland and that the crowd assembled about the courthouse were "purely spectators" and "curiosity seekers").

[137] Tulsa Race Riot Map 1, THE COMMISSION REPORT ("At nine o'clock, a group of twenty-five armed [B]lack men traveled by automobile to the courthouse."); ELLSWORTH, DEATH IN A PROMISED LAND, at 50 (putting time at shortly after 9:15 p.m.); HIRSCH, RIOT AND REMEMBRANCE, at 86 (Black men arrived at the courthouse around 9:15 p.m.).

[138] Ellsworth, THE COMMISSION REPORT, at 61 (discussing meeting by veterans and Black leaders planning to protect Rowland, noting that first group of Black men were "[a]rmed with rifles and shotguns" and explaining that "[t]he visit of the African American veterans had an electrifying effect").

[139] White, _The Eruption of Tulsa_, (stating sheriff spoke with Black men who first assembled); BROPHY, RECONSTRUCTING THE DREAMLAND, at 29-30 (stating Black men spoke to Cleaver and that McCullough was present); ELLSWORTH, DEATH IN A PROMISED LAND, at 50 (stating information conveyed by police at the scene).

[140] Ellsworth, THE COMMISSION REPORT, at 61 ("The visit of the African American veterans had an electrifying effect, however, on the white mob, now estimated to be more than one thousand strong. . . . The visit of the [B]lack veterans had not at all been foreseen. Shocked, and then outraged, some members of the mob began to go home to fetch their guns.").

[141] *Id.* at 62 ("Hopping into cars, small groups of armed African American men began to make brief forays into downtown, their guns visible to passersby."). Commissioner Adkison later testified that he encountered an armed group of Black men at Third and Boulder before the courthouse shooting, stating that he convinced them to go back to Greenwood. *Inefficiency of Police Is Denied*, TULSA DAILY WORLD, July 19, 1921, at 1. Another news account states that, prior to the courthouse violence, a group of Black men threatened to lynch a white police officer who was saved by the intervention of a Black preacher. *Race War Rages for Hours After Outbreak at Courthouse; Troops and Armed Men Patrol[l]ing Streets*, TULSA DAILY WORLD, June 1, 1921, at 1. At least one account, written from a white perspective, insists that a white man was killed by a Black incursion from Greenwood. WILLIAM O'BRIEN, WHO SPEAKS FOR US? III-5 (2002). News accounts, however, pinpoint the beginning of the shooting to the shot fired at the courthouse. *See, e.g., Race War Rages for Hours After Outbreak at Courthouse; Troops and Armed Men Patrol[l]ing Streets*, TULSA DAILY WORLD, June 1, 1921, at 1 (stating firing took place all over the city following the "first outbreak at the courthouse about 10:15 [p.m.]").

[142] Ellsworth, THE COMMISSION REPORT, at 62 ("By 9:30 p.m., the white mob outside the courthouse had swollen to nearly two-thousand persons."); HALLIBURTON, THE TULSA RACE WAR OF 1921, at 6 (describing that, after the first group of Black men left, "[t]he white crowd was evolving into a mob of two thousand persons").

[143] Ellsworth, THE COMMISSION REPORT, at 63 ("[M]oments after 10:00 p.m., a second contingent of armed African American men, perhaps seventy-five in number this time, decided to make a second visit to the courthouse."); HALLIBURTON, THE TULSA RACE WAR OF 1921, at 6 (describing that, after the white crowd had grown to 2,000, Black people arrived in cars, and "seventy-five Negroes left the autos and crossed the street to the courthouse and mingled with the white mob"); BROPHY, RECONSTRUCTING THE DREAMLAND, at 32 (identifying prominent Black veterans who were part of the second group to come to the courthouse); Tulsa Race Riot Map 2, THE COMMISSION REPORT; Ellsworth, THE COMMISSION REPORT, at 72.

[144] *See* Statement of O. W. Gurley at 1, *Oklahoma v. Gustafson* (testimony from Gurley that when he told the Black men of Greenwood that there would be no lynching, "one fellow said, ['] that is a dam[n] lie, Mr. McCullough just called for us[']"); *see also* Ellsworth, THE COMMISSION REPORT, at 63, particularly endnote 105; ELLSWORTH, DEATH IN A PROMISED LAND, at 50; Ross, THE COMMISSION REPORT, at vii (quoting J. B. Stradford).

[145] Weiss Reports at 7 (Appendix C).

[146] *Id.* at 8.

[147] *Id.* (noting witness account that "when the [N]egroes came back a second time, a large, tall white man stepped up to McCULLOUGH, and said: 'Bill, why did you called those armed ni**ers up here?'; that McCULLOUGH replied, 'I didn't call them,' and the white man said, 'You are a God damned liar, for I heard you do it'").

[148] *See, e.g.,* Attorney Notes of Witness Testimony (Part 1) at 2, *Oklahoma v. Gustafson* (noting that Sheriff McCullough did "not want to testify for the reason that he remonstrated over the appointment of Gustaffsen [sic] as Chief of Police, explaining to the Commissioners and the mayor that Gustaffsen [sic] had all his life been connected with detective agencies and with the underworld, and knew nothing about working with anybody but snitches and crooks, and that he would have no other kind of men on his force, and that such a police force would be a menace to the City of Tulsa"); *see also* HIRSCH, RIOT AND REMEMBRANCE, at 70 (noting that McCullough had complained to city commissioners about Gustafson's ties to the criminal underworld); Hopkins, *The Plot to Kill "Diamond Dick" Rowland and the Tulsa Race Riot*, at 5-6 & n.18.

[149] *See* Tulsa Race Riot Map 1, THE COMMISSION REPORT; Carlson, *Timeline of the Tulsa Race Massacre*, at 2 (estimating that around 9:00 p.m., "Bell is alerted by a runner that a mob is trying to break into the Armory"); KREHBIEL, TULSA 1921: REPORTING A MASSACRE, at 236 (chronology) (estimating the time as before 10:00 p.m.).

[150] Report of Major Jas. A. Bell (July 2, 1921) at 81.

[151] Id.

[152] Id. at 82.

[153] Id.

[154] Id.

[155] Tulsa Race Riot Maps 1-2, THE COMMISSION REPORT; Carlson, *Timeline of the Tulsa Race Massacre*, at 2.

[156] Tulsa Race Riot Maps 1-2, THE COMMISSION REPORT.

[157] Id.

[158] Report of Capt. John W. McCurn B Co 3d Inf. (undated) ("None of my guns or ammunition had been issued or were afterwards issued to any person other than National Guardsman. Major Bell ordered me to report with 20 of my men who had come in, to Col. Rooney's headquarters at police station. These men were fully uniformed, armed and equipped for riot duty.").

[159] Brophy, THE COMMISSION REPORT, at 161-62 (identifying Daley as a National Guardsman and an officer and noting close ties between police and National Guard); Report of L.J.F. Rooney, Lieut. Col. 3rd Infantry and Chas. W. Daley, Inspector General's Dept. (June 3, 1921) (stating Guardsman Daley was also a police officer).

[160] WILLIAM "CHOC" PHILLIPS, MURDER IN THE STREETS: A WHITE CHOCTAW WITNESS TO THE 1921 TULSA RACE MASSACRE 47 (Eakin Press, 2021).

[161] *See* Cole to Findlay Letter at 1 ("I understand [MacQueen] is the man that fired the first shot."); *Seven Battles Rage During War of Races*, TULSA TRIB., June 1, 1921, at 5 (noting that "E.S. MacQueen, detective, attempted to intervene" in a verbal altercation between the men of Greenwood and the white Tulsans); *see also* KREHBIEL, TULSA 1921: REPORTING A MASSACRE, at 42, nn.87-89.

[162] KREHBIEL, TULSA 1921: REPORTING A MASSACRE, at 42.

[163] MADIGAN, THE BURNING, at 117-18; *Negro Tells How Others Mobilized*, TULSA TRIB., June 4, 1921, at 1.

[164] ELLSWORTH, DEATH IN A PROMISED LAND at 52; HIRSCH, RIOT AND REMEMBRANCE, at 89; BROPHY, RECONSTRUCTING THE DREAMLAND, at 33 & n. 29.

[165] Ellsworth, THE COMMISSION REPORT, at 63.

[166] Id.

[167] White, *The Eruption of Tulsa*, at 910 (attributing words to sheriff); Brief of Plaintiff in Error at 48, *Redfearn v. Am. Cent. Ins. Co.*, 243 P. 929, 929 (Okla. 1926) (No. 15,851) (summarizing the testimony of O.W. Gurley that soon after the confrontation at the courthouse, Plaintiff Redfearn asked him what was going on and he responded, "Hell has broke [sic] loose"). This brief is reproduced as an appendix to Alfred L. Brophy, *The Tulsa Race Riot of 1921 in the Oklahoma Supreme Court*, 54 OKLA. L. REV. 67 (2001), and is hereinafter cited as "Plaintiff's Brief, *Redfearn*."

[168] Weiss Reports at 12 (Appendix C) ("All of the above named [witnesses] are w[hi]tes.").

[169] Id. at 9-10.

[170] *Id.*

[171] *Id.*

[172] *Id.* at 10.

[173] *Id.*

[174] *See, e.g., Public Welfare Board Vacated by Commission: Mayor in Statement on Race Trouble,* TULSA TRIB., June 14, 1921, at 2 (address by Mayor Evans stating that the first shot was fired by a "fool [B]lack person").

[175] Tulsa Race Riot Map 3, THE COMMISSION REPORT; Ellsworth, THE COMMISSION REPORT, at 63 ("The initial gunplay lasted only a few seconds, but when it was over, an unknown number of people—perhaps as many as a dozen—both [B]lack and white, lay dead or wounded.") (citing *Final Edition,* TULSA DAILY WORLD, June 1, 1921, at 1).

[176] PHILLIPS, MURDER IN THE STREETS, at 37 (describing how, when ambulance personnel sought to place injured Black man on stretcher, an armed white man stopped him, stating, "[h]old it. Don't touch him. There are a lot of people who have been hurt and need you. Go find some of them," and how, when the armed man "jabbed a rifle into his stomach"); HALLIBURTON, THE TULSA RACE WAR OF 1921, at 9 (noting that ambulance attendants and the crowd "stood by and watched him die"); Ellsworth, THE COMMISSION REPORT, at 63 (describing ambulance personnel being turned away from aiding Black casualty).

[177] LUCKERSON, BUILT FROM THE FIRE, at 88 ("Cars of young men of both races drove through the dark streets, firing indiscriminately at buildings and forcing people to cower behind whatever protection they could find."); Ellsworth, THE COMMISSION REPORT, at 65 ("Not all of the victims of the violence that broke out downtown were white. Evidence suggests that after the fighting broke out at the courthouse, carloads of [B]lack Tulsans may have exchanged gun fire with whites on streets downtown, possibly resulting in casualties on both sides."); Interview by Pen Woods with John Zink Sr., white witness, Tulsa Historical Society & Museum Oral History Collection (Jan. 29, 1971) (describing Black men shooting out of cars); Interview by Ruth Sigler Avery with James Leighton Avery, white witness (Dec. 2, 1980), Oklahoma State University – Tulsa Library Ruth Sigler Avery Collection Box 1, Folder 10 (noting that he told his father that "there is a lot of shooting taking place, and everything seems out of control"); Interview by Ruth Sigler Avery with Andre Wilkes and Margaret Wilsey, Native American and Former Klansman and his sister-in-law (July 8, 1972), Oklahoma State University – Tulsa Library Ruth Sigler Avery Collection, Box 7 Folder 3 at 33 ("Men were wildly shooting their pistols, shotguns, and rifles at any moving object. They were darting in-and-out among the bushes and trees of nearby residences, behind stores, parked cars, and up-and-down alleyways."); Interview with Zink, Sr., Tulsa Historical Society & Museum Oral History Collection (stating he was awakened to hearing Black men scream, "kill the god damn whites" and saw bullets coming in windows and cars dashing by).

[178] *See, e.g.,* Interview by Ruth Sigler Avery with Helen Donohue Ingraham (Apr. 10, 1980), Oklahoma State University – Tulsa Library Ruth Sigler Avery Collection, Box 3 Folder 6, at 1 ("We could hear shooting in the background, and were frightened, for some had shot out the street lights along Main Street by the time we paid for our food and were . . . rushing out of the drug store. Shots were fired from open touring cars with their tops down by both Black and white men driving in their separate cars, all racing up and down Main Street.").

[179] Interview with Ingraham, Oklahoma State University – Tulsa Library Ruth Sigler Avery Collection, Box 3 Folder 6, note 156 at 3 ("I'll never forget the terror I felt that night.").

[180] Interview with Wilkes and Wilsey, Oklahoma State University – Tulsa Library Ruth Sigler Avery Collection, Box 7 Folder 3 at 32-33.

[181] LUCKERSON, BUILT FROM THE FIRE, at 88.

[182] Tulsa Race Riot Map 3, THE COMMISSION REPORT; Ellsworth, THE COMMISSION REPORT, at 63 ("Outnumbered more than twenty-to-one, the [B]lack men began a retreating fight toward the African American district.").

[183] Tulsa Race Riot Map 3, THE COMMISSION REPORT; Ellsworth, THE COMMISSION REPORT, at 63 ("With armed whites in close pursuit, heavy gun fire erupted again along Fourth Street, two blocks north of the courthouse.").

[184] Tulsa Race Riot Map 3, THE COMMISSION REPORT; Ellsworth, THE COMMISSION REPORT, at 63 ("A short while later, a second, deadlier, skirmish broke out at Second and Cincinnati.").

[185] Tulsa Race Riot Map 3, THE COMMISSION REPORT.

[186] Id.

[187] Id.

[188] Ellsworth, THE COMMISSION REPORT, at 68.

[189] LUCKERSON, BUILT FROM THE FIRE, at 89 (noting that white crowds increased as word spread, "Get your guns! Get your guns! The ni**ers are coming!"); Interview by Ruth Sigler Avery with W.R. Holway (July 1996), Oklahoma State University – Tulsa Library Ruth Sigler Avery Collection, Box 14 Folder 24.

[190] Ellsworth, THE COMMISSION REPORT, at 64.

[191] Brophy, THE COMMISSION REPORT, at 159 ("The police chief had deputized perhaps 500 men to help put down the riot."); Gill, The Tulsa Race Riot, at 28 (citing Gill's 1946 interview with police captain George Henry Blaine for proposition that "within thirty minutes about five hundred [white men] had been given special commissions"); HALLIBURTON, THE TULSA RACE WAR OF 1921, at 10 ("About five hundred of these volunteers were given 'special commissions.' Many of these special officers['] names were not even recorded."). Gustafson maintained that it was half this number, or 250. See LUCKERSON, BUILT FROM THE FIRE, at 91 (quoting Gustafson's deposition, 29-30, in Stradford v. American Central Ins. Co., Cook County Superior Court, No. 370274 (1921) that "[w]e armed during the night probably two hundred fifty citizens who assisted the police department," but that "[t]here were many [more] men than that were armed"). Police Commissioner Adkison "placed the number of deputized men higher, at about four hundred." Id.

[192] Snow, THE COMMISSION REPORT, at 119 (discussing white individuals killed during the massacre and noting "[s]ince boot-legging was a busy cottage industry in Tulsa, it is possible that at least some of them had high blood-alcohol levels by the time the trouble began"); PHILLIPS, MURDER IN THE STREETS, at 47 ("Drinking increased steadily through the night."); id. at 42 ("A great many of those people lining the sidewalks were holding a rifle or shotgun in one hand and grasping the neck of a liquor bottle with the other."); see also Ellsworth, THE COMMISSION REPORT, at 64 (citing Phillips). In addition to the fact that intoxication can generally cloud judgment, Tulsa was a dry city, so even men who were not wholly intoxicated were, if drinking, lawbreakers. Id. at 49 ("During the Prohibition era, both Oklahoma and the nation were supposedly dry, although one would not know it from a visit to Tulsa.").

[193] Police Officer Notepad (Part I) at 15, Oklahoma v. Gustafson (name appearing on a police notepad as a "special officer").

[194] Cole to Findlay Letter at 1 (noting that perpetrators were likely "the same group of rough necks and hoodlums who mobbed Belton" and identifying Cranfield as the leader of the "Belton mob").

[195] Walter F. White, I Investigate Lynchings, 16 AM. MERCURY 77, 82 (Jan. 1929) ("From [a commercial photographer] I learned that special deputy sheriffs were being sworn in to guard the town from a rumored counterattack by the Negroes. It occurred to me that I could get myself sworn in as one of these deputies."). This anecdote did not appear in his earlier article, The Eruption of Tulsa, published in The Nation in June 1921. It is possible White was made a special officer in the days following the massacre, when police recruited white citizens to patrol the streets. See KREHBIEL, TULSA 1921:

REPORTING A MASSACRE, at 153 (discussing the American legion squads' operation post-massacre and noting that "[t]he American Legionnaires organized as special deputies . . . [and] Walter White, the NAACP's light-skinned investigator, seems to have talked his way onto this squad despite being a total stranger to town.").

[196] White, *I Investigate Lynchings*, at 82; KREHBIEL, TULSA 1921: REPORTING A MASSACRE, at 153.

[197] White, *I Investigate Lynchings*, at 82.

[198] *See, e.g.,* Witness Testimony of Laurel Buck at 2, *Oklahoma v. Gustafson*.

[199] Petition at 2, *M. J. and Ellie Lathon v. T.D. Evans, et al.,* No. 23,393 (Tulsa Cty. Dist. Ct. May 31, 1923); *see also, e.g.,* Petition at 2, *P.S. Thompson v. T.D. Evans et. al.,* No. 23,375 (Tulsa Cty. Dist. Ct. May 31, 1923) (same); Petition at 2, *E.R. Brown v. T.D. Evans* et.al., No. 23,415 (Tulsa Cty. Dist. Ct. May 31, 1923) (same); Petition at 2, *Mittie Robinson v. T.D. Evans et. al,* No. 23,399 (Tulsa Cty. Dist. Ct. May 31, 1923) (same).

[200] *Redfearn v. Am. Cent. Ins. Co.,* 243 P. 929, 292 (1926); *see also* Weiss Reports at 9 (Appendix C) (reporting that Chief Gustafson informed him that "from midnight on," white men, whom Gustafson characterized as "crooks and transients," broke into "hardware stores, pawn shots, and sporting good shops" where they stole "hundreds of guns and a lot of ammunition"); Ellsworth, THE COMMISSION REPORT, at 64 (noting that "whites began breaking into downtown sporting goods stores, pawn shops, and hardware stores, stealing—or 'borrowing' as some would later claim—guns and ammunition"; one of the stores police allowed to be looted was "located literally across the street from police headquarters").

[201] Attorney Notes of Witness Testimony (Part 1) at 10, *Oklahoma v. Gustafson*.

[202] MADIGAN, THE BURNING, at 2, 117-18; HALLIBURTON, THE TULSA RACE WAR OF 1921, at 11 ("By midnight the [B]lacks and whites were drawn up in opposing lines along the railroad tracks that separated 'Little Africa' from white Tulsa.").

[203] PARRISH, THE NATION MUST AWAKE, at 10 (describing white Tulsans as "mad bulls" and "thirsty wolves," but stressing that "these brave boys of ours fought gamely and held back the enemy for hours").

[204] BROPHY, RECONSTRUCTING THE DREAMLAND, at 41-42.

[205] Tulsa Race Riot Map 4, THE COMMISSION REPORT.

[206] Ellsworth, THE COMMISSION REPORT, at 71.

[207] Report of Major Jas. A. Bell (July 2, 1921) at 83 ("About 10:30 o'clock, I think it was, I had a call from the Adjt. General asking about the situation. I explained that it looked pretty bad. He directed that we continue to use every effort to get the men in so that if a call came we would be ready. I think it was only a few minutes after this, another call from Adjt. General directed that 'B' Co., the Sanitary Det. and the Service Co. be mobilized at once and to render any assistance to the civil authorities we could in the maintenance of law and order and the protection of life and property. I think this was about 10:40 o'clock and while talking to the General [Lt. L.J.F. Rooney] appeared and assumed command."); Ellsworth, THE COMMISSION REPORT, at 66 (quoting Bell).

[208] Tulsa Race Riot Map 4, THE COMMISSION REPORT; *see also* Report of Capt. John W. McCurn B Co 3d Inf. (undated) (stating Col. Rooney of the National Guard (in Tulsa) ordered him to "post[] guards to keep people from entering 2nd street" and that, after getting shot at by some Negroes, "we fell back to Detroit Ave in order to establish a base line and await reinforcements from the Armory. We formed a skirmish line on Detroit Ave. We executed a flank march to the right at this point and halted with our right flank at Archer St").

[209] Report of Capt. John W. McCurn B Co 3d Inf. (undated) ("While patrolling Detroit Ave a large number of [N]egro prisoners were taken by us from the houses on Detroit Ave, Elgin Ave, Cameron St and the rear out-houses of this area, and these [N]egroes were turned over to the police department."); *see also* Gill, *The Tulsa Race Riot*, at 31 ("The newly commissioned deputies and the regular patrolmen began bringing in disarmed Negro prisoners about eleven o'clock.").

[210] Report of Major C. W. Daley (July 6, 1921) at 86 (stating he gave instructions "to pick up all [N]egroes on the streets and to go to servants['] quarters and gather them in, for I thought some of the bad [N]egroes may set fire to homes of white people causing a lot of destruction to property and a possible loss of life").

[211] *See, e.g.*, Ellsworth, THE COMMISSION REPORT, at 66 ("It appears that the first fires set by whites in [B]lack neighborhoods began at about 1:00 a.m.); Tulsa Race Riot Map 4, THE COMMISSION REPORT ("By 1:00 a.m., whites also had set the first fires in black neighborhoods."); *but see* Plaintiff's Brief, *Redfearn*, at 51-52 (summarizing the testimony of Officer H.C. Pack, a Black police officer, testifying in connection with an insurance claim that he saw a fire as early as 10:00 p.m.).

[212] Tulsa Race Riot Map 4, THE COMMISSION REPORT; Ellsworth, THE COMMISSION REPORT, at 66 ("It appears that the first fires set by whites in [B]lack neighborhoods began at about 1:00 a.m. African American homes and businesses along Archer were the earliest targets, and when an engine crew from the Tulsa Fire Department arrived and prepared to douse the flames, white rioters forced the fire men away at gunpoint. By 4:00 a.m., more than two-dozen [B]lack-owned businesses, including the Midway Hotel, had been torched."); PARRISH, THE NATION MUST AWAKE, at 10 (stating that at about 1:30 a.m. she heard someone say, "[l]ook, they are burning Cincinnati," and saw columns of smoke); BROPHY, RECONSTRUCTING THE DREAMLAND, at 36-37; *Redfearn*, 243 P. at 929 (noting, as part of the "undisputed evidence," that "[t]he fire department, in attempting to respond to calls coming in from the [N]egro section, found the streets full of armed white men who, with pointed guns, refused to permit the firemen to connect the hose, and forced them to return to the fire stations without rendering any service in extinguishing the fires. After a few attempts to reach the fire, the chief of the fire department directed the men to respond to no more calls until morning").

[213] Ellsworth, THE COMMISSION REPORT, at 69.

[214] *See id.* at 68 ("In the early hours of June 1, a steady stream of [B]lack Tulsans began to leave the city, hoping to find safety in the surrounding country side."); HILL, THE 1921 TULSA RACE MASSACRE: A PHOTOGRAPHIC HISTORY, at 266 ("While many Black men and women began taking steps to protect their homes and businesses, others sat tight, hoping that daybreak would bring an end to the violence. A few others began to leave town. Some . . . were killed as they fled Tulsa.").

[215] HILL, THE 1921 TULSA RACE MASSACRE: A PHOTOGRAPHIC HISTORY, at 266 ("While many Black men and women began taking steps to protect their homes and businesses, others sat tight, hoping that daybreak would bring an end to the violence.").

[216] Ellsworth, THE COMMISSION REPORT, at 69 ("At approximately 2:00 a.m., the fierce fighting along the Frisco railroad yards had ended. The white would-be invaders still south of the tracks. As a result, some Greenwood's defenders not only concluded that they had 'won' the fight, but also that the riot was over.").

[217] Reports after the massacre placed the blame on hoodlums and criminals. Weiss Reports at 10 (Appendix C) (noting that a witness named Crutcher stated that "the burning was mostly by the criminal white element of Tulsa"); *World's Sunday Sermon: Tulsa's Race Riot and the Teachings of Jesus*, TULSA DAILY WORLD, July 17, 1921, at C7 (claiming the "riot" was due to a lawless class of crooks and criminals of both races who were responsible for burning, looting, and killing).

[218] Writing shortly after the massacre, Mary Jones Parrish stated, "it then dawned upon us that the enemy had organized in the night and was invading our district the same as the Germans invaded France and Belgium." PARRISH, THE NATION MUST AWAKE, at 11.

[219] Ellsworth, THE COMMISSION REPORT, at 71 (explaining that Governor Robertson instructed Major Byron Kirkpatrick, a Tulsa guard officer, that in order to send in the Guard, state law required Kirkpatrick to send a telegram signed by the chief of police, the county sheriff, and a local judge).

[220] *Race War Rages for Hours After Outbreak at Courthouse; Troops and Armed Men Patrol[l]ing Street*, TULSA DAILY WORLD, June 1, 1921, at 1 (explaining that Commissioner Adkison and Charles Daley, a police officer who was also a member of the National Guard, organized men into companies with the assistance of the Home Guard); Report of Major Byron Kirkpatrick (July 1, 1921) (stating that after the incident at the courthouse, Kirkpatrick "assumed charge of a body of armed volunteers," whom he understood were "Legion men" (likely veterans belonging to the American Legion), divided them into two groups and gave them orders).

[221] *Race War Rages for Hours After Outbreak at Courthouse; Troops and Armed Men Patrol[l]ing Street*, TULSA DAILY WORLD, June 1, 1921, at 1.

[222] Report of Major Byron Kirkpatrick (July 1, 1921) (stating that after the incident at the courthouse, Kirkpatrick "assumed charge of a body of armed volunteers," whom he understood were "Legion men" (likely veterans belonging to the American Legion), divided them into two groups and gave them orders); Report of Major C. W. Daley (July 6, 1921) ("Col. Rooney and myself ... assembled a company of Legion men . . . and placed them in charge of Mr. Kinney a member of the American Legion . . . . I then informed Mr. Kinney to take his men and use them to the best of advantage in maintaining order throughout the City.").

[223] PHILLIPS, MURDER IN THE STREETS, at 46 (discussing preparation in the early morning and quoting a white man, standing on a car, as saying, "[i]f any of you have more ammunition than you need, or if what you have doesn't fit your gun, sing out, there will be somebody here that has the right caliber. Get busy and exchange shells until everybody has the right size. Then have every gun loaded and ready to shoot at daylight"); *see also* HIRSCH, RIOT AND REMEMBRANCE, at 97.

[224] Colonel Rooney of the National Guard initially tried to cordon off Greenwood by forming a perimeter around it to separate the races and keep them apart. Robert D. Norris Jr., *The Oklahoma National Guard and the Tulsa Race Riot of 1921: A Historical, Tactical and Legal Analysis* 149-50 (2001) (available through the McFarlin Library Special Collections). Guardsmen reported that their initial duties were in the nature of patrol. *See* Report of Capt. John W. McCurn B Co 3d Inf. (undated) at 1 (stating that after 11:00 p.m. he reported to the police station and Col. Rooney assigned him to "posting guards to keep people from entering 2nd street between Main and Boulder Ave."); Report of Major Byron Kirkpatrick (July 1, 1921) at 78 (explaining that, under the direction of Lt. Col Rooney, "sentinels were established [on downtown streets] for the purpose of holding back crowds" and that he had "assumed charge of a body of armed volunteers, whom [he] understood were Legion men"; these men were "divided into two groups" and "ordered to patrol the business section and court-house"); *Races at War in Tulsa*, THE KANSAS CITY STAR, June 1, 1921, at 1 (reporting that guardsmen "patrolled the downtown streets in order to protect as much property as possible" and were "thrown about the court house, preventing an attack there").

[225] PHILLIPS, MURDER IN THE STREETS, at 43-46, especially 46 (describing being in a crowded restaurant in the white section of Tulsa after patrolling the streets and learning that there would be a meeting to explain "plans," and being told, "Men, we are going in at daylight!" and "Be ready at daybreak!").

[226] Weiss Reports at 11 (Appendix C) (reflecting that a man named Tom Dyer told police that Tulsa officer Rignon drove to Jenks to recruit him to "raid" the Negro section of Tulsa). Dyer stated he declined to participate but that another white man from Jenks, Robert Hanskon, did. *Id.*

[227] AMERICAN RED CROSS REPORT at 43-44 ("The elements of race rioting were present from all evidences on the night of May 31st, but the wholesale destruction of property—life and limb, in that section of the city occupied by [N]egroes on June 1st between the hours of daylight and noon, testifies to a one-sided battle.").

[228] PARRISH, THE NATION MUST AWAKE, at 54.

[229] Maurice Williams, *Personal Account of the 1921 Tulsa Race Riot*, reprinted in ROBERT N. HOWER, 1921 RACE RIOT AND THE AMERICAN RED CROSS: ANGELS OF MERCY 115 (Homestead Press 1993).

[230] PARRISH, THE NATION MUST AWAKE, at 27 (account of James T.A. West) ("About 5 o'clock it's a very peculiar whistle blew. This seemed to have been a signal for a concerted attack by the whites, for immediately a terrible gun fire began."); Dr. R.T. Bridgewater, *id.* at 35 (stating that he and his wife decided to flee and that "[s]hortly after we left a whistle blew. The shots rang from a machine gun located on the Stand Pipe Hill near my residence and aeroplanes began to fly over us in, some instances very low to the ground"); J.C. Latimer, *id.* at 48 ("[B]etween 5 and 6 AM a 'Riot Call' was given; that is, the city whistle gave one long blow and then looking through the windows I could see the [w]hites, armed with high power rifles, coming from the hill and surrounding the colored district."); A.H., *id.* at 51 ("[A]s daylight approached, they (the [w]hites) were given a signal by a whistle, and the dirty, cowardly outrage took place."); Petition at 1, *Virgil Rowe v. City of Tulsa, A Corp.*, No. 23,286 (Tulsa Cty. Dist. Ct. May 29, 1923) (alleging that, at about 5:00 a.m. on June 1 he was disturbed by the sound of a whistle that usually signaled a fire alarm, followed by the heavy discharging of firearms upon the Black section of town by the white people); Summary of Testimony of C.F. Gabe, Plaintiff's Brief, *Redfearn*, at 39 ("[H]e was awakened next morning about five o'clock by the blow of a whistle," and "when the whistle blew shooting began everywhere in town"); Summary of Testimony of Barney Cleaver, Plaintiff's Brief, *Redfearn*, at 43 ("[A]t about five o'clock the whistle blew, and that shooting started."); Summary of Testimony of Green E. Smith, Plaintiff's Brief, *Redfearn*, at 54 ("[A] whistle blew, about five o'clock, and that after the whistle blew he . . . heard a lot of shooting."); Summary of testimony of C. W. Kern, Plaintiff's Brief, *Redfearn*, at 66 ("That shortly thereafter a whistle blew and at about the same time shooting began down toward the Frisco tracks, then shooting all around, and the witness states that he could see smoke soon afterwards."); Interview of Williams, Oklahoma State University – Tulsa Library Ruth Sigler Avery Collection, Box 7 Folder 6; Account of J.W. Hughes, collected by the Red Cross and reprinted in HOWER, ANGELS OF MERCY, at 211-12.

[231] *See generally* KREHBIEL, TULSA 1921: REPORTING A MASSACRE, at 66-67.

[232] According to a 1917 news article, the city had been "work[ing] out" a plan to use an alarm to summon citizens, bearing firearms, to stop any criminal from escaping the city. *Signal to Call Tulsa for Duty*, TULSA DAILY WORLD, Nov. 18, 1917 ("Tulsa will soon be in a position to become a bristling arsenal upon a moment[']s notice."). One student of the massacre has noted that, during the Great War, there were plans to use a "peculiar signal of the fire whistle at the Public Service plant" to rouse the citizenry in an emergency. Hopkins, *The Plot to Kill "Diamond Dick" Rowland and the Tulsa Race Riot*, at 28. We found no evidence that this signaling system had been implemented or used between the time it was proposed and the time of the massacre. It may, however, indicate that the city's fire alarm was capable of emitting a signal different from the normal fire alarm signal, corroborating those who characterized the sound as "peculiar." PARRISH, THE NATION MUST AWAKE, at 27 (account of James T.A. West) ("About 5 o'clock it's a very peculiar whistle blew.").

[233] Interview of Williams, Oklahoma State University – Tulsa Library Ruth Sigler Avery Collection, Box 7, Folder 6 at 4 ("There used to be as plant around here that blew whistles at noon. I don't know whether it was the plant or a steam engine.").

[234] Plaintiff's Brief, *Redfearn*, at 91 ("The testimony produced by the defendant discloses that these people were organized, wearing police badges and were officers of some character, some of them dressed in soldier uniform; one witness testifying for the defendant that all of them had on police badges.").

[235] Ellsworth, THE COMMISSION REPORT, at 71.

[236] *Whites Advancing into 'Little Africa'; Negro Death List is About 15*, TULSA DAILY WORLD, June 1, 1921, at 1 ("With the coming of dawn this morning, following a night of race rioting and death, hundreds of armed white men in motor cars formed a circle of steel about 'Little Africa,' and a continuous rattlle [sic] of rifle and revolver fire could be heard. Sixty or seventy automobiles filled with armed men were in the line drawn about the black belt and there were many reports to the effect that they planned to range through the [N]egro settlement and 'clean it out.'"); *Race Riot Drama, Wild West Scenes in U.S. City*, THE NORTH STAR, June 2, 1921, at 1 ("Dawn found 70 motor cars, containing armed white men, circling round

the Negro section of Tulsa. Half a dozen aeroplanes are hovering overhead, and a party of white riflemen are reported to be shooting at all [N]egroes, and also firing into [their] houses.").

[237] PARRISH, THE NATION MUST AWAKE, at 28 (account of James T.A. West).

[238] Ellsworth, THE COMMISSION REPORT, at 72 ("While the machine gun in the grain elevator opened fire, crowds of armed whites poured across the Frisco tracks, headed straight for the African American commercial district.").

[239] Tulsa Race Riot Map 6, THE COMMISSION REPORT ("All told, the white rioters may have numbered as many as 10,000."); Ellsworth, THE COMMISSION REPORT, at 71 ("[S]ome contemporary observers estimated the total number of armed whites who had gathered as high as five or ten thousand.").

[240] Gill, The Tulsa Race Riot, at 35. Gill also asserted that 3,000-5,000 Black men were "under arms." Id.

[241] Tulsa in Remorse to Rebuild Homes; Dead Now Put at 30, N.Y. TIMES, June 3, 1921, at 1, 3 (quote on p. 3).

[242] See Norris, The Oklahoma National Guard, at 274. The Sapulpa Herald attributed this lower number (2,500) to General Barrett. See Guard Chief Leaves Riot Scene Today, SAPULPA HERALD, June 2, 1921, at 1 (quoting Barrett as saying that "[w]hen the guard entered this city at 9 a.m. Wednesday I found 2500 armed men roaming the streets").

[243] State Elects to Try Gustafson First on Riot Action Charge, TULSA DAILY WORLD, July 14, 1921, at 2 (argument of counsel defending against charges against Gustafson for dereliction of duty). One author skeptically cited a report that the attack involved 34% of the white population of Tulsa. O'BRIEN, WHO SPEAKS FOR US? at VII-3.

[244] See Ellsworth, THE COMMISSION REPORT, at 64 (discussing boys sworn in as special deputies) and 76 (discussing a survivor's account of being captured by a group that included boys with guns); Race War Rages for Hours After Outbreak at Courthouse; Troops and Armed Men Patrol[l]ing Streets, TULSA DAILY WORLD, June 1, 1921, at 1 (reporting that "several hundred women, and men, armed with every available weapon" were part of the mob).

[245] See generally PHILLIPS, MURDER IN THE STREETS (account of a white Choctaw who participated in some of the events of the massacre); Interview with Wilkes and Wilsey, Oklahoma State University – Tulsa Library Ruth Sigler Avery Collection, Box 7 Folder 3 at 32-33 (account of individual identified by interviewer as a Native American member of the Ku Klux Klan).

[246] Gill, The Tulsa Race Riot, at 34 ("Thirty-five city blocks were looted systematically, then burned to cinders.").

[247] See, e.g., Survivor Olivia J. Hooker recalls the 1921 Tulsa race riots, USA TODAY (June 11, 2020).

[248] LUCKERSON, BUILT FROM THE FIRE, at 97.

[249] Id. at 97-98.

[250] Id. at 98; see also Gill, The Tulsa Race Riot, at 35 ("All evidences showed that most of the men followed the same general procedure in destroying property. Working in small groups, one of them would go up to a door, put a gun against the lock and blow it off. Once inside the cabin everything breakable was smashed, trunks and bureau drawers torn open and pictures and telephones wrenched from the walls and trampled on. Then all the bedding, furniture and other inflammable material was piled together, a little kerosene was scattered and matches applied.").

[251] One of the churches serving the Black community before the massacre was Vernon African Methodist Episcopal Church. Historic Vernon AME still serves the Greenwood community. XXXXXX XXXXXX and XXXXXX XXXXXX welcomed us into the church. XXXXXX XXXXXX gave us a tour, telling us how the church basement survived the massacre and showing us damage caused by the fires that ravaged Greenwood. See documentation of visit by Cold Case

Team, Tulsa, Okla. (Nov. 13, 2024). XXXXXX informed us that many Black Greenwood residents hid in the basement and thus survived the massacre.

252 Tulsa Race Riot Map 8, THE COMMISSION REPORT.

253 *Id.*

254 PARRISH, THE NATION MUST AWAKE, at 33 (account of P.S. Thompson) ("If [the Negro] submitted without question, he was taken to jail, but if he dared to question the intruder, he was shot."); Tulsa Race Riot Map 7, THE COMMISSION REPORT ("Black attempts to defend their homes and businesses were undercut by the actions of both the Tulsa police and the local National Guard units, who, rather than disarming and arresting the white rioters, instead began imprisoning [B]lack citizens.").

255 PARRISH, THE NATION MUST AWAKE, at 33 (account of P.S. Thompson).

256 Weiss Reports at 10 (Appendix C) (stating that a witness named Crutcher told him that "the burning was mostly by the criminal white element of Tulsa"); *World's Sunday Sermon: Tulsa's Race Riot and the Teachings of Jesus*, TULSA DAILY WORLD, July 17, 1921, at C7 (claiming the destruction was due to a lawless class of crooks and criminals of both races who were responsible for burning, looting, and killing).

257 Interview of Williams, Oklahoma State University – Tulsa Library Ruth Sigler Avery Collection, Box 7 Folder 6, at 8 (describing how the white men who apprehended Black men made them hold their hands up while marching them to detention centers and "didn't both[er] [the white] looters").

258 *Survivors' Stories*, Interview by Eddie Faye Gates with Genevieve Elizabeth Tillman Jackson, Willie Mae Thompson, and Julia Bonton Jones, Tulsa Massacre Survivors (Sept. 9-10, 1999), The Eddie Faye Gates Tulsa Race Massacre Collection (Gilcrease Museum).

259 EDDIE FAYE GATES, RIOT ON GREENWOOD: THE TOTAL DESTRUCTION OF BLACK WALL STREET (Eakin Press, 2003), at 74 (account of Madeleine Haynes).

260 *Survivors' Stories 3*, Interview by Eddie Faye Gates with Kinney Booker, Tulsa Massacre Survivor (Sept. 28, 1999), The Eddie Faye Gates Tulsa Race Massacre Collection (Gilcrease Museum) (stating he was told to hide in the attic because there was a race riot).

261 Interview by Eddie Faye Gates with George Monroe, Tulsa Massacre Survivor (June 1, 1999), Oklahoma Historical Society Audio Archives (recalling seeing men with torches and being told by his mother to get under the bed).

262 Interview by Cold Case Team with XXXXXX and XXXXXX, relating account of massacre survivor Wes H. Young, Sr., in Tulsa, Okla. (Oct. 17, 2024).

263 FLETCHER, DON'T LET THEM BURY MY STORY, at 8.

264 *Survivors' Stories 3*, Interview by Eddie Faye Gates with Eldoris McCondichie, Tulsa Massacre Survivor, (Sept. 28, 1999), The Eddie Faye Gates Tulsa Race Massacre Collection (Gilcrease Museum) (including eight interviews of Tulsa Race Massacre survivors and heirs conducted for the Oklahoma Commission to Study the Tulsa Race Riot of 1921; McCondichie states that she was awakened by her mother who told her that white people were killing colored people. She thought that meant that Black people were being lined up and shot, execution style); Interview with Thompson, The Eddie Faye Gates Tulsa Race Massacre Collection (Gilcrease Museum) (stating that she was awakened by a shot coming through the window and lodging in a couch), Interview with Booker, The Eddie Faye Gates Tulsa Race Massacre Collection (Gilcrease Museum) (stating he was told to hide in the attic because there was a race riot); Interview with George Monroe, Oklahoma Historical Society Audio Archives (recalling seeing men with torches and being told by his mother to get under the bed); Interview with Jimmie Lily Franklin, *Guide to the 1921 Tulsa Race Massacre Oral History Collection, 2004-*

2007, NAT. MUSEUM OF AFRICAN AM. HIST. AND CULTURE, SMITHSONIAN INST. (stating she was awakened by pounding on door and told to dress quickly); Interview with Webster, *Guide to the 1921 Tulsa Race Massacre Oral History Collection* (stating that, "on the night of the riots, there was a man who was screaming in the middle of the street, saying 'get up and get out, because they are on their way to kill us'").

[265] PARRISH, THE NATION MUST AWAKE, at 12.

[266] *Survivors' Stories*, Interview with Jackson, The Eddie Faye Gates Tulsa Race Massacre Collection (Gilcrease Museum); *Survivors' Stories 3*, Interview with McCondichie, The Eddie Faye Gates Tulsa Race Massacre Collection (Gilcrease Museum) (recounting seeing people in head rags and old gowns).

[267] PARRISH, THE NATION MUST AWAKE, at 58 (account of Dimple L. Bush).

[268] MARY E. JONES PARRISH, EVENTS OF THE TULSA DISASTER 48 (1922) ("'Negro men, women and children were killed in great numbers as they ran, trying to flee to safety,' one unidentified informant later told Mary Jones Parrish, '. . . the most horrible scenes of this occurrence was to see women dragging their children while running to safety, and the dirty white rascals firing at them as they ran.'").

[269] GATES, RIOT ON GREENWOOD, at 56 (account of Juanita Smith Booker).

[270] PARRISH, THE NATION MUST AWAKE, at 13.

[271] Margarett Zulpo, *Remembering When the Sky Rained Death // 95-Year-Old Wom[a]n Recalls 1921 Riot*, TULSA DAILY WORLD, May 18, 1994 (account of Rosa Davis-Skinner) ("One of my friends put her baby in a shoe box. A dead baby. They put it there because they had no place else to keep it safe during the shuffle. They lost it. I never did hear if they ever found it. It was just gone."); *see also* Interview by Cold Case Team with XXXXXX and XXXXXX, in Tulsa, Okla. (Oct. 17, 2024) (recounting, based on accounts survivors gave to them, that a survivor who was a child at the time of the massacre saw white men stomp on a shoebox that held a baby and saying that he did not know if the baby was alive or dead when they did so).

[272] Interview by Cold Case Team with XXXXXX and XXXXXX, relating account of massacre survivor Wes H. Young, Sr., in Tulsa, Okla. (Oct. 17, 2024).

[273] GATES, RIOT ON GREENWOOD, at 56-57 (account of Kinney I. Booker).

[274] Franklin & Ellsworth, THE COMMISSION REPORT, at 23-24.

[275] Witness Testimony of John Oliphant at 5-6, *Oklahoma v. Gustafson*.

[276] *Id.* at 9 (describing that "there were quite a large number of people looting the houses and taking out everything . . . Some were signing [sic], some were playing pianos that were taken out of the buildings, some were running victrolas, some dancing a jig and just having a rolicing [sic] easy good time").

[277] *Survivor Stories 1*, Interview by Eddie Faye Gates with Elwood Lett, Tulsa Massacre Survivor (1999-2000), The Eddie Faye Gates Tulsa Race Massacre Collection (Gilcrease Museum) (includes interviews of Tulsa Race Massacre survivors conducted for the Oklahoma Commission to Study the Tulsa Race Riot of 1921).

[278] GATES, RIOT ON GREENWOOD, at 61 (account of Rosella Carter). Despite the horrific injury, Carter lived for more than 10 years, but always suffered painful complications. *Id.*

[279] MADIGAN, THE BURNING, at 172.

[280] *Id.* at 168-69; *see also* Kweku Larry Crowe & Thabiti Lewis, *The 1921 Tulsa Massacre: What Happened to Black Wall Street*, MAG. OF THE NAT. ENDOWMENT FOR THE HUMANITIES (Winter 2021) ("Several Black people were tied to cars and dragged through the streets.").

[281] White, *The Eruption of Tulsa*, at 910.

[282] *Id.; see also* Ellsworth, THE COMMISSION REPORT, at 77.

[283] PARRISH, THE NATION MUST AWAKE, at 33 (account of P.S. Thompson).

[284] *Id.* at 37 (account of Dr. R.T. Bridgewater).

[285] *Id.* at 47 (account of M.D. Russel).

[286] *Id.* at 68.

[287] *Id.* at 44 (account of "name withheld").

[288] GATES, RIOT ON GREENWOOD, at 91-92 (account of Almadge Newkirk).

[289] Ellsworth, THE COMMISSION REPORT, at 76 (recounting report of white visitor from Kansas who reported seeing white officers search Black men "while their hands were up, and not finding weapons, extracted what money they found on them").

[290] Weiss Reports at 8 (Appendix C).

[291] *Id.* at 11.

[292] Ellsworth, THE COMMISSION REPORT, at 75; *see also* Interview with Jobie Elizabeth Holderness, Tulsa Race Massacre Survivor, Oklahoma Historical Society Audio Archives (June 1, 1999) (stating that her husband told her he had fought at Mt. Zion); Interview by Eddie Faye Gates of Binkley Wright, Tulsa Race Massacre Survivor (Feb. 2000), available at Tulsa Reparations Coalition, *Meet the Survivors: Oral History Accounts of the Tulsa Race Riot of 1921 by Black Survivors*; GATES, RIOT ON GREENWOOD, at 110 (account of Binkley Wright) (Wright recalled that the "Holderness boys" helped the "protective brigade" by going "high up into the church" to get a vantage point to kill the "white mobsters").

[293] ELLSWORTH, THE GROUND BREAKING at 32-33 (relying on account of Mable Little); GATES, RIOT ON GREENWOOD, at 110 (account of Binkley Wright) ("[M]any [B]lack men who were defending Greenwood from Mt. Zion Church were killed when . . . airplanes flew over, dropping bombs or something that exploded and burned everything they touched."); Interview of Wright, Tulsa Reparations Commission (describing Black resistance and noting "the shotguns and rifles those [B]lack men had could not compete with those machine guns").

[294] Ellsworth, THE COMMISSION REPORT, at 77 ("In the final burst of fighting off of Standpipe Hill that morning, a deadly firefight erupted at the site of an old clay pit, where several African American defenders were said to have gone to their deaths fighting off the white invaders. Stories also have been passed down over the years regarding the exploits of Peg Leg Taylor, a legendary [B]lack defender who is said to have singlehandedly fought off more than a dozen white rioters. Along the northern face of Sunset Hill, the white guardsmen posted there found themselves, at least for a while, under attack."); Tulsa Race Riot Map 6, THE COMMISSION REPORT ("Particularly fierce fighting broke out along Standpipe Hill, where 40 to 50 National Guard soldiers traded fire with African American riflemen, who had set up defensive lines off of Elgin and Elgin Place. On Sunset Hill, the white guardsmen opened fire on [B]lack neighborhoods to the east, using both their standard issue 30-caliber 1906 Springfield rifles, as well as the semi-defective machine gun given them by the Tulsa Police Department.").

[295] HIRSCH, RIOT AND REMEMBRANCE, at 152-54; LUCKERSON, BUILT FROM THE FIRE, at 99.

---

[296] Ellsworth, THE COMMISSION REPORT, at 84.

[297] HILL, THE 1921 TULSA RACE MASSACRE: A PHOTOGRAPHIC HISTORY, at 59 (image of postcard); Karlos K. Hill, _Where Did Images of the Tulsa Race Massacre Come From?_, PBS: AM. EXPERIENCE (May 27, 2021).

[298] Weiss Reports at 9 (Appendix C) (reporting that Hall, a secretary to the chief of police, had been present at the county jail "from start to finish," and that "no effort was made by any county or city peace officer, to disarm the members of the mob"); HALLIBURTON, THE TULSA RACE WAR OF 1921, at 6 (characterizing police attempt to confiscate weapons as "feeble").

[299] _See_ Gustafson Testimony at 10-12, _Oklahoma v. Gustafson_ (testimony of Gustafson that "the traffic men were on their corners at that time, and the regular patrolmen were on their beats, but on account of the shifts, all the beats were not covered that night" and explaining that the shift change was "on account of the last of the month, when we switch from day to night"); _see also_ Hopkins, _The Plot to Kill "Diamond Dick" Rowland and the Tulsa Race Riot_, at 18 ("It also happened to be the exact moment of the police department's monthly shift change, where police officers working the day shift moved to night and vice versa. As a result, from 3 p.m. to 11 p.m. on Tulsa's most fateful Tuesday, the Tulsa Police Department was materially understaffed."). It may be that this was purely coincidental; but some believe that the police, believing there would be a lynching, intended to help facilitate it by their absence. _See id._ at 15, 20-21 (discussing evidence of possible involvement of some police in plan to lynch Rowland); _id._ at 17-18 (suggesting shift change would facilitate lynching).

[300] Snow, THE COMMISSION REPORT, at 119 (discussing white individuals killed during the massacre and noting "[s]ince boot-legging was a busy cottage industry in Tulsa, it is possible that at least some of them had high blood-alcohol levels by the time the trouble began"); PHILLIPS, MURDER IN THE STREETS, at 47 ("Drinking increased steadily through the night.") & 42 ("A great many of the people lining the sidewalks were holding a rifle or shotgun in one hand and grasping the neck of a liquor bottle with the other."); _see also_ Ellsworth, THE COMMISSION REPORT, at 64 (citing Phillips).

[301] Gill, _The Tulsa Race Riot_, at 28.

[302] Alfred L. Brophy, _The Tulsa Race Riot of 1921 in the Oklahoma Supreme Court_, 54 OKLA. L. REV. 67, 88 (2001).

[303] BROPHY, RECONSTRUCTING THE DREAMLAND, at 59 & n.128 (quoting CHARLES F. BARRETT, OKLAHOMA AFTER FIFTY YEARS: A HISTORY OF THE SOONER STATE, AND ITS PEOPLE, 1889-1941 at 209 (1941)).

[304] _Redfearn v. Am. Cent. Ins. Co._, 243 P. 929, 929 (1926); _see also_ Weiss Reports at 9 (Appendix C) (reporting that Chief Gustafson informed him that "from midnight on," white men, whom Gustafson characterized as "crooks and transients," broke into "hardware stores, pawn shots, and sporting good shops" where they stole "hundreds of guns and a lot of ammunition"); Ellsworth, THE COMMISSION REPORT, at 64 (noting that "whites began breaking into downtown sporting goods stores, pawnshops, and hardware stores, stealing—or 'borrowing' as some would later claim—guns and ammunition," and that one of the stores police allowed to be looted was "located literally across the street from police headquarters").

[305] Attorney Notes of Witness Testimony (Part 1) at 10, _Oklahoma v. Gustafson_; _see also_ LUCKERSON, BUILT FROM THE FIRE, at 88.

[306] Witness Testimony of Laurel Buck at 2, _Oklahoma v. Gustafson_; Ellsworth, THE COMMISSION REPORT, at 64.

[307] _Race War Rages for Hours After Outbreak at Courthouse; Troops and Armed Men Patrol[l]ing Stre_et, TULSA DAILY WORLD, June 1, 1921, at 1.

[308] Weiss Reports at 11 (Appendix C).

[309] Gustafson Testimony at 18, *Oklahoma v. Gustafson* (Q: "What means had you of calling your men in or of getting them to the station?" A: "Signalling [sic] over the Gamewell system.").

[310] David Hedrick, *Early American Fire Alarm Systems*, FFAM (Sept. 17, 2022).

[311] The evidence is particularly persuasive because, unlike other reports, this testimony was subject to cross-examination. *See* Witness Testimony of John Oliphant at 13-16, *Oklahoma v. Gustafson*.

[312] One journalist identifies Oliphant as a Republican poll watcher and former police commissioner. KREHBIEL, TULSA 1921: REPORTING A MASSACRE, at 26.

[313] Witness Testimony of John Oliphant at 5, *Oklahoma v. Gustafson* (describing the shooter and his companions as "citizens, with guns").

[314] *Id.* at 8.

[315] Oliphant initially testified that he "knew" Brown, a red-complected man, was a police officer. Witness Testimony of John Oliphant at 8, *Oklahoma v. Gustafson* ("They had stars, they had badges on; just one man, they called him Brown, I believe, a red complected fellow, I knew him as a policeman."). Oliphant later said, however, that Brown "had been" a police officer," which was perhaps his manner of speaking or perhaps implied that Brown was a former (not current) officer. *Id.* at 9 (Q: "[I]n the party where you saw one man you called Brown, you knew he was a policeman[?]" A: "Yes, he had been.").

[316] *Id.* at 8.

[317] *Id.* at 10 (stating that the men doing the burning and looting told him that had been "ordered to destroy—that ain't the word they used. I don't remember the word he used but it was to the effect that they was going to make the destruction complete").

[318] *Redfearn*, 243 P. at 929-30 ("A number of witnesses testified that these groups of white men, many of them wearing police badges and badges indicating that they were deputy sheriffs, after removing the [N]egroes from buildings, went inside the buildings, and, after they left, fires broke out inside the buildings.")

[319] Police Commissioner Adkinson later testified that police distributed old police stars to many of the men commissioned that night. Brophy, *The Tulsa Race Riot of 1921 in the Oklahoma Supreme Court*, at 88.

[320] Miscellaneous Witness List (June 8, 1921) at 2, *Oklahoma v. Gustafson*.

[321] *Id.*

[322] *Id.*

[323] HALLIBURTON, THE TULSA RACE WAR OF 1921, at 20; *Blacks Tied Together*, THE BLACK DISPATCH, June 3, 1921, at 5 ("Six [B]lacks, roped together in a line, were hauled into Convention [H]all early this morning by Leo Irish, motorcycle officer, who held up and corralled the band on the outskirts of the North Greenwood district. He tied them together with a line and led them a hot pace behind his motorcycle on the return trip.").

[324] Ellsworth, THE COMMISSION REPORT, at 76 (recounting report of white visitor from Kansas who reported seeing white officers search Black men "while their hands were up, and not finding weapons, extracted what money they found on them").

[325] Weiss Reports at 11 (Appendix C).

[326] See, for example, the following statements *from Oklahoma v. Gustafson*: Affidavit of Barney Cleaver (a Black law enforcement officer) at 1 ("[A]ffiant states that if the officers of the city of Tulsa, Oklahoma had done their duty there would have been no riot or burning; that he failed to see or discover any effort that the city officials put forward in order to avert the great burning and calamity that occurred in the city of Tulsa, Oklahoma, on above mentioned date"); Statement of C. R. Ingersoll at 1 ("Affiant states that it is his knowledge and belief that the cause of said fire and the attending destruction was due [to] the gross negligence of the city officials of the city of Tulsa, Oklahoma; that in his judgement the said city officials could have prevented said destructions but that said officials made no effort to do so; that said city officials failed and refused to use its police powers for the purpose of quelling said riot or to stop the property from being burned.").

[327] Instruction of the Court at 2-3, *Oklahoma v. Gustafson*.

[328] *See, e.g.*, Petition at 2, *E J. H. Bryant v. City of Tulsa, et al.*, No. 23,297 (Tulsa Cty. Dist. Ct. May 31, 1923) (alleging that on May 30, the city through its agents and employees and police forces "did wrongfully conspire, acquiesce in, and assist certain persons and persons to this plaintiff unknown, in the wrongful and felonious endeavors to burn, pillage and destroy certain property in the vicinity of" the plaintiff's property); *see also* Petition at 1, *P.S. Thompson v. T.D. Evans et. al.*, No. 23,375 (Tulsa Cty. Dist. Ct. May 31, 1923) (accusing the city defendants of meeting with sundry unknown persons and of "corruptly, willfully, maliciously, and premeditatively" forming a conspiracy against the "property, liberty, and life" of the plaintiff and other Black residents); Petition at 1, *Ruth Calhoun v. City of Tulsa, et al.*, No. 23,311 (Tulsa Cty. Dist. Ct. May 31, 1923) (same); Petition at 1, *Stalie Webb v. City of Tulsa, et al.*, No. 23,313 (Tulsa Cty. Dist. Ct. May 31,1923) (same); Petition at 1, *Mary E. Titus v. T. D. Evans et al.*, No. 23,316 (Tulsa Cty. Dist. Ct. May 31, 1923) (same); Petition at 1, *Emmett Johnson v. The City of Tulsa et al.*, No. 23,317 (Tulsa Cty. Dist. Ct. May 31, 1923) (same); Petition at 1, *Rev. J. R. McClain v. City of Tulsa et al.*, No. 23,319 (Tulsa Cty. Dist. Ct. May 31, 1923) (same); Petition at 1, *E. I. Saddler v. City of Tulsa*, et al., No. 23,321 (Tulsa Cty. Dist. Ct. May 31, 1923) (same); Petition at 1, *N. L. Gilliam v. T. D. Evans, et al.*, No. 23,312 (Tulsa Cty. Dist. Ct. May 31, 1923) (same); Petition at 1, *J. S. Gish v. T. D. Evans, et al.*, No. 23,315, (Tulsa Cty. Dist. Ct. May 31, 1923) (same).

[329] ELLSWORTH, DEATH IN A PROMISED LAND, at 49.

[330] *M'Cullough to Face Charges Freeing Hints*, TULSA TRIB., July 23, 1921, at 1 (explaining that Sheriff McCullough had admitted on the witness stand during the trial of Police Chief Gustafson, that he "slept through the night of the riot"); *Sheriff Sleeps Through Big Riot at Tulsa*, DURANT DAILY DEMOCRAT, July 15, 1921, at 3 ("The sheriff slept serenely in an upper story of the courthouse while the battle raged about it, he said, and only woke up long enough to sign a telegram, the contents of which he did not read."); HALLIBURTON, THE TULSA RACE WAR OF 1921, at 31 (explaining that Sheriff McCullough had testified he went to sleep after refusing to give Rowland to the white mob and stated he "didn't know there had been a riot until I read the papers the next morning at 8' o'clock"); Gill, *The Tulsa Race Riot*, at 99 ("[T]he sheriff, by his own admission, slept all night on the third floor of the county jail and knew nothing of the disturbance until eight o'clock the next morning. He testified that he heard shots during the night but paid no attention to them.").

[331] Ellsworth, THE COMMISSION REPORT, at 71.

[332] BROPHY, RECONSTRUCTING THE DREAMLAND, at 55 (quoting McCullough Deposition in *J. B. Stradford v. American Central Ins. Co.*, Cook County Superior Court, No.370.274 (1921), at 24).

[333] For example, Lieutenant Colonel Rooney, a National Guard member who wrote an after-action report and led National Guardsmen during the events of the massacre, commanded Tulsa's Home Guard during World War I. *See Home Guard Chooses Rooney for Captain*, TULSA TRIB., June 19, 1918, at 6 ("L.F.J. Rooney was elected captain of the Tulsa Home Guard . . . The vote was unanimous.").

[334] Norris, *The Oklahoma National Guard*, at 99.

[335] *Id.* at 101, 133.

[336] *Id.* at 168 ("The National Guard in Tulsa was presented with one such [machine] gun. . . .").

[337] Gill, *The Tulsa Race Riot*, at 32 ("Guardsmen under the command of Captain Edward L. Wheeler took two machine guns to the scene, one in an automobile and one in a truck.").

[338] Report of Capt. John W. McCurn B Co 3d Inf. (undated) at 2 ("It was an old machine gun that I understood some ex-service officer had brought from Germany as a souvenir."); Report of L.J.F. Rooney, Lieut. Col. 3rd Infantry and Chas. W. Daley, Inspector General's Dept. (June 3, 1921) (Rooney "asked Major Daley where [the machine gun] came from and he said 'we dug it up' and [Rooney] inferred that he meant it was the property of the Police Department of which Major Daley is an officer").

[339] One group set up one of the machine guns on the Middle States Milling Company's grain elevator to fire to the north of Greenwood Avenue. Ellsworth, THE COMMISSION REPORT, at 71. That gun was not in the official possession of guardsmen when it was fired; it was operated by special deputies and other white Tulsans. There is speculation that there may have been more than two machine guns, brought back as war trophies, from the Great War. Norris, *The Oklahoma National Guard*, at 167-69.

[340] ELLSWORTH, THE GROUND BREAKING, at 27.

[341] HILL, THE 1921 TULSA RACE MASSACRE: A PHOTOGRAPHIC HISTORY, at 41-42.

[342] Brophy, THE COMMISSION REPORT, at 161-62 ("The close connection between the local units of the National Guard and the police department is not surprising. Major Daley, for instance, was also a police officer. The Guard established its headquarters at the police station.") (internal footnotes omitted); Report of Major Jas. A. Bell (July 2, 1921) at 83 ("About 10:30 o'clock, I think it was, I had a call from the Adjt. General asking about the situation. I explained that it looked pretty bad. He directed that we continue to use every effort to get the men in so that if a call came we would be ready. I think it was only a few minutes after this, another call from Adjt. General directed that 'B' Co., the Sanitary Det. and the Service Co. be mobilized at once and render any assistance to the civil authorities we could in the maintenance of law and order and the protection of life and property. I think this was about 10:40 o'clock and while talking to the General [Lt. L.J.F. Rooney] appeared and assumed command."); Ellsworth, THE COMMISSION REPORT, at 66 (quoting Bell).

[343] Hopkins, *The Plot to Kill "Diamond Dick" Rowland and the Tulsa Race Riot*, at 26.

[344] Report of Capt. John W. McCurn B Co 3d Inf. (undated) (stating that after 11:00 p.m. he reported to the police station and Col. Rooney assigned him to "posting guards to keep people from entering 2nd street between Main and Boulder Ave."); Report of Major Byron Kirkpatrick (July 1, 1921) (explaining that, under the direction of Lt. Col Rooney, "sentinels were established [on downtown streets] for the purpose of holding back crowds" and that he had "assumed charge of a body of armed volunteers, whom [he] understood were Legion men"; these men were "divided into two groups" and "ordered to patrol the business section and court-house"; *Races at War in Tulsa*, THE KANSAS CITY STAR, June 1, 1921, at 1 (reporting that guardsmen "patrolled the downtown streets in order to protect as much property as possible" and were "thrown about the court house, preventing an attack there").

[345] *Race War Rages for Hours After Outbreak at Courthouse; Troops and Armed Men Patrol[l]ing Streets*, TULSA DAILY WORLD, June 1, 1921, at 1; *see also* Report of Major C. W. Daley (July 6, 1921) at 86-87 (discussing his organization of patrols at about 2:30 in the morning).

[346] KREHBIEL, TULSA 1921: REPORTING A MASSACRE, at 54, 56.

[347] LUCKERSON, BUILT FROM THE FIRE, at 94; *Mob Held Back by Major Daley for Two Hours*, TULSA TRIB., June 5, 1921, at 7 ("In many places during the past three days there has been mentioned the acts performed by Major Charles W Daley, police inspector, who held back a crowd of nearly 400 persons single-handed for nearly two hours when they were being incited to shoot up and burn the colored district."); Report of Major C. W. Daley (July 6, 1921) at 87-88 (upon seeing white

men shooting into Greenwood, Daley "called for volunteer guards to handle this crowd and to prevent further shooting" and that "[a]bout twenty men with rifles stepped forward").

[348] ELLSWORTH, DEATH IN A PROMISED LAND, at 101 (noting that much of Greenwood might have been saved if law enforcement, including the National Guard, had "been geared toward disarming and dispersing the white rioters, rather than disarming and interning [B]lacks").

[349] Report of Capt. John W. McCurn B Co 3d Inf. (undated) at 2 ("[S]ome [N]egroes who had barricaded themselves in houses refused to stop firing and had to be killed.").

[350] Brophy, THE COMMISSION REPORT, at 162 ("The guardsmen fired at will for nearly half an hour. . . ."); Report of Capt. John W. McCurn B Co 3d Inf. (undated).

[351] Report of Capt. John W. McCurn B Co 3d Inf. (undated) at 2 (describing how National Guard members "moved north to Sunset Hill to stop [N]egroes from firing into white peoples' homes on Sunset Hill from the Negro settlement further northeast" and subsequently spent 20 minutes firing "at will" on the "armed groups of [B]lacks").

[352] Id. ("At all times I warned them not to fire until fired upon as we had been ordered by Col. Rooney to fire only when absolutely necessary to defend our lives."); Report of Frank Van Voorhis, Capt. Com. Service (July 30, 1921) ("My orders from Lt. Col. Rooney were not to fire unless fired upon.").

[353] Ellsworth, THE COMMISSION REPORT, at 78 (explaining how when guardsmen came upon a group of Black men barricaded in a store, exchanging fire with armed white Tulsans, the guard "joined in on the attack" rather than attempting to "get the white invaders and the [B]lack defenders to disengage").

[354] Gill, The Tulsa Race Riot, at 32 (discussing how "[g]uardsmen under the command of Captain Edward L. Wheeler took two machine guns to the scene" and how "at least one of the machine guns had poured lead on the Negroes who sought refuge behind the buildings") (internal footnote omitted); Report of L.J.F. Rooney, Lieut. Col. 3rd Infantry and Chas. W. Daley, Inspector General's Dept. (June 3, 1921) (explaining that volunteers requested rifles because machine gun was inoperable and provided little firepower).

[355] See Alexander v. Oklahoma, 382 F.3d 1206, 1212 (10th Cir. 2004) (stating that National Guardsmen, often acting in conjunction with the white mob, disarmed the African American men who were defending their community and placed them in "protective custody").

[356] Report of Major C. W. Daley (July 6, 1921) at 86.

[357] Report of Capt. John W. McCurn B Co 3d Inf. (undated).

[358] Report of L.J.F. Rooney, Lieut. Col. 3rd Infantry and Chas. W. Daley, Inspector General's Dept. (June 3, 1921) at 72 (referring to "enemy shots"); see also Ellsworth, THE COMMISSION REPORT, at 67 ("At least one National Guard officer went even further, using the term 'enemy' in reference to African Americans.").

[359] Norris, The Oklahoma National Guard, at 170-71.

[360] Id. at 171 & n.580 (relying on interview with Essley) and 114 n.373 (identifying information as coming from the author's interview with Essley conducted in 1987).

[361] Id. at 171.

[362] Id. (discussing orders from Governor Robertson).

---

[363] Report of Major C. W. Daley (July 6, 1921) at 85-88 ("[T]here was a mob of 150 walking up the street in a column of squads . . . [t]hey were split up at this time and placed in groups of from 12 to 20 in charge of an ex-service man, with instructions to preserve order and to watch for snipers from the tops of buildings and to assist in gathering up all [N]egroes bringing same to station and that no one was to fire a shot unless it was to protect life after all other methods had failed.").

[364] There are reports that members of the Home Guard, which may or may not have referred to the Tulsa National Guard, engaged directly in acts of looting and arson. *See, e.g., Personal Experiences of Those Who Came Out from the Shambles of Loot, Arson and Murder*, THE BLACK DISPATCH, June 10, 1921, at 8 (reporting that the "home guards" took one survivor, Dr. S. P. Thompson, into custody and that while he was in the presence of those uniformed men who arrested him, looters wielding crowbars broke into his safe and stole over $400,000); Ross, THE COMMISSION REPORT, at viii ("In his memoirs Stradford recalled the guards acted like wild men. 'The militia had been ordered to take charge, but instead they joined the rioter.'").

[365] HILL, THE 1921 TULSA RACE MASSACRE: A PHOTOGRAPHIC HISTORY, at 118, 120. One famous photograph depicts a crowd of Black men with their hands in the air as they are marched to the Convention Hall, clearly looking to be unwilling captives. *Id.* at 122. It is unclear from this photograph if guardsmen, white civilians, police, or special deputies escorted these captives.

[366] Ellsworth, THE COMMISSION REPORT, at 82.

[367] *Id.* at 83-84 ("Upon their arrival in Tulsa, the State Troops apparently did not proceed immediately to where the fighting was still in progress . . . . The reasons for this seeming hold-up appear to be largely due to the fact that certain steps needed to be fulfilled.").

[368] Tulsa Race Riot Map 9, THE COMMISSION REPORT ("One account of the race riot also claims that the State Troops also broke ranks and ate breakfast.").

[369] HILL, THE 1921 TULSA RACE MASSACRE: A PHOTOGRAPHIC HISTORY, at 64.

[370] *See* PARRISH, THE NATION MUST AWAKE, at 23 ("Just as praise for the state troops was on every tongue so was denunciation of the Home Guard on every lip.").

[371] HALLIBURTON, THE TULSA RACE WAR OF 1921, at 14 ("Guardsmen quickly confiscated a truck load of weapons and arrested and jailed sixty-five looters."); *Guards Return with Governor*, THE DAILY OKLAHOMAN, June 3, 1921, at 1 ("Looters, carrying flour sacks, went from house to house in the devastated district Wednesday, blowing safes and carrying away silver and other valuables until the arrival of the guard units. Sixty-five men were arrested and put in jail by the soldiers charged with looting.").

[372] Ellsworth, THE COMMISSION REPORT, at 84 ("For several hours that morning, John A. Oliphant[,] a white attorney who lived nearby, had been telephoning police headquarters in an effort to save these homes [on North Detroit Avenue], that had been looted but not burned. Oliphant believed that a handful of officers, if sent over immediately, could see to it that the homes were spared.").

[373] Kimberly C. Ellis, *We Look Like Men of War: Africana Male Narratives and the Tulsa Race Riot, War and Massacre of 1921* 49 (2002) (Ph.D. dissertation, Purdue University) (ProQuest).

[374] *See* Interview with Eunice Jackson, *Guide to the 1921 Tulsa Race Massacre Oral History Collection, 2004-2007. National Museum of African American History and Culture, Smithsonian Institution; see also generally* ELLSWORTH, THE GROUND BREAKING, at 35. Some witnesses attributed this action to "armed whites," not National Guardsmen. *See* Ellsworth, THE COMMISSION REPORT, at 76 (quoting an interview with Harold M. Parker, a white bookkeeper, who stated that guards sometimes shot at the heels of their [B]lack prisoners, adding, "[s]ometimes they missed and shot their legs. . . [i]t was sheer cruelty coming out").

[375] KREHBIEL, TULSA 1921: REPORTING A MASSACRE, at 53.

[376] *See, e.g. P.S. Thompson v. T.D. Evans et. al.*, No. 23,375 (Tulsa Cty. Dist. Ct. May 31, 1923); *M. J. and Ellie Lathon v. T.D. Evans, et al.*, No. 23,393 (Tulsa Cty. Dist. Ct. May 31, 1923); *Mary E. Titus v. T. D. Evans et al.*, No. 23,316 (Tulsa Cty. Dist. Ct. May 31, 1923); *Mittie Robinson v. T.D. Evans et. al*, No. 23,399 (Tulsa Cty. Dist. Ct. May 31, 1923); *N. L. Gilliam v. T. D. Evans, et al.*, No. 23,312 (Tulsa Cty. Dist. Ct. May 31, 1923); *J. S. Gish v. T. D. Evans, et al.*, No. 23,315, (Tulsa Cty. Dist. Ct. May 31, 1923).

[377] *See, e.g.*, Petition at 5, *Dora Wells Jones v. City of Tulsa, et al*, No. 23,389 (Tulsa Cty. Dist. Ct. June 1, 1923) ("[T]he acting mayor of said City, as your petitioner is informed and believes, together with the Commissioners thereof, directed its officers and divers and sundry to 'go and kill you a dam [ni**er]' and further stated and asserted that no police protection would be given to them."); Petition at 2, *M. J. and Ellie Lathon v. T.D. Evans, et al.*, No. 23,393 (Tulsa Cty. Dist. Ct. May 31, 1923) (alleging that Mayor and Commissioners handed out weapons to white people while saying in substance to "go out and kill you a dam [ni**er]"); *see also, e.g.*, Petition at 2, *P.S. Thompson v. T.D. Evans et. al.*, No. 23,375 (Tulsa Cty. Dist. Ct. May 31, 1923) (same); Petition at 2, *E.R. Brown v. T.D. Evans* et.al., No. 23,415 (Tulsa Cty. Dist. Ct. May 31, 1923) (same); Petition at 2, *Ruth Calhoun v. City of Tulsa, et al.*, No. 23,311 (Tulsa Cty. Dist. Ct. May 31, 1923) (same); Petition at 2, *Stalie Webb v. City of Tulsa, et al.*, No. 23,313 (Tulsa Cty. Dist. Ct. May 31,1923) (same); Petition at 2, *Mary E. Titus v. T. D. Evans et al.*, No. 23,316 (Tulsa Cty. Dist. Ct. May 31, 1923) (same); Petition at 2, *Emmett Johnson v. The City of Tulsa et al.*, No. 23,317 (Tulsa Cty. Dist. Ct. May 31, 1923) (same); Petition at 2, *Rev. J. R. McClain v. City of Tulsa et al.*, No. 23,319 (Tulsa Cty. Dist. Ct. May 31, 1923) (same); Petition at 2, *E. I. Saddler v, City of Tulsa*, et al., No. 23,321 (Tulsa Cty. Dist. Ct. May 31, 1923) (same).

[378] *See, e.g.*, Petition at 4, *M. J. and Ellie Lathon v. T.D. Evans, et al.*, No. 23,393 (Tulsa Cty. Dist. Ct. May 31, 1923); Petition at 4, *P.S. Thompson v. T.D. Evans et. al.*, No. 23,375 (Tulsa Cty. Dist. Ct. May 31, 1923) (same); Petition at 4, *Mittie Robinson v. T.D. Evans et. al*, No. 23,399 (Tulsa Cty. Dist. Ct. May 31, 1923) (same); Petition at 4, *Ruth Calhoun v. City of Tulsa, et al.*, No. 23,311 (Tulsa Cty. Dist. Ct. May 31, 1923) (same); Petition at 4, *Stalie Webb v. City of Tulsa, et al.*, No. 23,313 (Tulsa Cty. Dist. Ct. May 31, 1923) (same); Petition at 4, *Mary E. Titus v. T. D. Evans et al.*, No. 23,316 (Tulsa Cty. Dist. Ct. May 31, 1923) (same); Petition at 2, *Emmett Johnson v. The City of Tulsa et al.*, No. 23,317 (Tulsa Cty. Dist. Ct. May 31, 1923) (same); Petition at 4, *Rev. J. R. McClain v. City of Tulsa et al.*, No. 23,319 (Tulsa Cty. Dist. Ct. May 31, 1923) (same); Petition at 4, *E. I. Saddler v, City of Tulsa*, et al., No. 23,321 (Tulsa Cty. Dist. Ct. May 31, 1923) (same).

[379] *Public Welfare Board Vacated by Commission: Mayor in Statement on Race Trouble*, TULSA TRIB., June 14, 1921, at 2 (Mayor Evans suggested that if the white community had not destroyed Greenwood, Black residents would have destroyed white Tulsa. He said, in a public address, "I say it was good generalship to let the destruction come to that section where the trouble was hatched up, put in motion and where it had its inception.").

[380] *See, e.g.*, *Air Observers Watched Blacks for Police*, TULSA TRIB., June 2, 1921, at 3 ("Six airplanes from Curtiss flying field took an active part in the campaign carried on yesterday by the National Guard and police to gain control of the city and end the fighting.").

[381] Thomas Van Hare, *The Bombing of Tulsa*, HIST. WINGS (Feb. 27, 2017).

[382] *The JN-4 Jenny: The Plane that Taught America to Fly*, NAT. PARK SERV. (Feb. 2020). The Commission Report indicates that another plane available at Tulsa might have been the Stinson Detroiter, "a single engine plane with an enclosed cabin capable of holding several people." Warner, THE COMMISSION REPORT, at 104. However, some sources suggest that the earliest version of the Stinson Detroiter did not make its first flight until 1926. *See, e.g.*, Roger Guillemette, *Stinton Aircraft Corporation*, U.S. CENTENNIAL OF FLIGHT COMM. The Commission Report credits an interview with airfield employees to support the proposition that a version of the Detroiter existed in 1921, *see* Warner, THE COMMISSION REPORT, at 104 & n.11, and we cannot corroborate or contradict this information.

[383] *Air Observers Watched Blacks for the Police*, TULSA TRIB., June 2, 1921, at 3 ("Piloted by staff aviators from the Curtis Southwestern hangars east of Tulsa, the planes circled round and round over the embattled area."); *see also Transportation (1850-1945)*, TULSA PRES. COMM'N ("In 1917, the first official airfield was opened by Tulsa oilman Harold Breene near

what is now Admiral Place and Hudson Avenue. By 1919, the Curtiss-Southwest Airplane Company, the nation's first commercial interstate air freight shipping business, was formed. The Company opened an airfield near what is now Apache Street and Memorial Drive in 1921."); Warner, THE COMMISSION REPORT, at 104 (discussing Curtiss Southwest Airfield).

[384] Warner, THE COMMISSION REPORT, at 104, 106.

[385] *Air Observers Watched Blacks for the Police*, TULSA TRIB., June 2, 1921, at 3 (reporting that the purpose of the planes was to "note the progress of the fighting and the spread of the fires," to observe the roads to the country filled with "fleeing [N]egroes," and to "periodically" drop messages reporting their observations as the planes "flew low over the police headquarters"); Gill, *The Tulsa Race Riot*, at 40 (citing both the *Tribune* article and an interview with George Henry Blaine to support the same proposition).

[386] *See generally* Ellsworth, THE COMMISSION REPORT, at 73-74 (citing sources); *see also* accounts collected by Eddie Faye Gates, GATES, RIOT ON GREENWOOD, at 53-54 (J.B. Bates said he saw a man shot from a plane), 79 (Vera Ingram reported seeing a woman shot from a plane), 80 (Genevieve Elizabeth Tillman Jackson said that at first she thought she saw "little black birds dropping out of the sky" but later realized it was airplanes dropping "bullets, and devices to set fires, and debris"), 85-86 (Eldoris Mae Ector McCondichie said airplanes flew low overhead and dropping bullets as they were running), 88-89 (Mary Tacoma Maupin said that "[w]hile we were running, airplanes flew over us and began dropping some kind of devices. I don't know exactly what they were dropping, but whatever it was, the devices exploded and set everything they touched on fire. I remember hearing someone yell 'Move on! They're bombing us from the air!'"), 105 (Oscar Washington said that there were "airplanes, dropping something from the air, (we thought they were bombs) that set everything on fire"); FLETCHER, DON'T LET THEM BURY MY STORY, at 9 ("An Airplane flew above us dropping firebombs."); *see also Men Returning to City Tell Story of Riot*, OKLA. CITY TIMES, June 1, 1921, at 33 (report from A.L. Sherburn, a "traveling man" returning to Oklahoma City from Tulsa, stating that he saw "two airplanes in action this morning, and when they got to fighting in the air, there's bound to be a bad situation"); Interview by Cold Case Team with XXXXXX in Tulsa, Okla. (Nov. 15, 2024) (relaying account he heard from an elderly Black man that white men were shooting people from planes as well as dropping cocktail bombs from them from the planes).

[387] *See generally* Warner, THE COMMISSION REPORT, at 105-06 (collecting accounts); Franklin, *The Tulsa Race Riot and Three of Its Victims* at 9-11 (describing planes) and 11 (describing turpentine balls dropped by planes); JOHNSON, BLACK WALL STREET 100, at 233 (account of J.B. Bates); *id.* at 235 (account of Ernestine Gibbs).

[388] Franklin, *The Tulsa Race Riot and Three of Its Victims*, at 7; FRANKLIN, MY LIFE AND AN ERA: THE AUTOBIOGRAPHY OF BUCK COLBERT FRANKLIN, at 197.

[389] *Ex-Police Bares Plot of Tulsans: Officer of Law Tells Who Ordered Aeroplanes to Destroy Homes*, CHI. DEFENDER, Oct. 14, 1921, Ruth Sigler Avery Collection. According to this article, a former white Tulsa policeman named Van B. Hurley signed an affidavit to this effect, but we have been unable to find one. In 2001, the Oklahoma Commission determined that there is no record that a "Van B. Hurley" ever was a policeman or even existed and noted that, if such an affidavit existed, it was never used in any lawsuits. Warner, THE COMMISSION REPORT, at 106.

[390] Petition at 3, *Mrs. J. H. Goodwin [Carlie M. Goodwin] v. City of Tulsa, et al*, No. 23,368, (Tulsa Cty. Dist. Ct. 1923); Petition at 3, *Jackson Undertaking Co. v. City of Tulsa, et al*, No. 23,371 (Tulsa Cty. Dist. Ct. 1923); Petition at 3, *W. S. Holloway v. City of Tulsa, et al.*, No. 23,372 (Tulsa Cty. Dist. Ct. May 31, 1923); Petition at 3, *Daisy Williams v. City of Tulsa, et al.*, No. 23,360 (Tulsa Cty. Dist. Ct. May 31, 1923); Petition at 3, *Edith Patterson v. City of Tulsa, et al.* No. 23,363 (Tulsa Cty. Dist. Ct. May 31, 1923); Petition at 3, *Thomas R. Gentry v. City of Tulsa et al*, No. 23,333 (Tulsa Cty. Dist. Ct. May 31, 1923); Petition at 3, *Julia A. Jackson Ferguson v. City of Tulsa et al*, No. 23,334 (Tulsa Cty. Dist. Ct. May 31, 1923); Petition at 3, *William Walker v. City of Tulsa et al*, No. 23,337 (Tulsa Cty. Dist. Ct. May 31, 1923); Petition at 3, *O. C. Mann v. City of Tulsa et al.*, No. 23,338 (Tulsa Cty. Dist. Ct. May 31, 1923); Petition at 3, *Dr. J. M. Keys v. City of Tulsa et al.*, No. 23,342 (Tulsa Cty. Dist. Ct. May 31, 1923); Petition at 3, *Hosea Vaden v. City of Tulsa et al.*, No. 23,343 (Tulsa Cty. Dist. Ct. May 31, 1923); Petition at 3, *Caroline Lollis v. City of Tulsa, et al.*, No. 23,327 (Tulsa Cty. Dist. Ct. May 31, 1923); Petition at 3, *G. W. Walker v. City of Tulsa et al.*, No. 23,328 (Tulsa Cty. Dist. Ct. May 31, 1923).

---

[391] Warner, THE COMMISSION REPORT, at 107.

[392] *Personal Experiences of Those Who Came Out from the Shambles of Loot, Arson and Murder*, THE BLACK DISPATCH, June 10, 1921, at 8 (reporting the account of massacre survivor Dr. S. P. Thompson that planes would "swoop down on defenseless [B]lack men, women and children and rain a hail of deadly lead into their midst").

[393] PARRISH, THE NATION MUST AWAKE, at 14.

[394] KREHBIEL, TULSA 1921: REPORTING A MASSACRE, at 76 ("[E]xplosives seem unlikely, if only because no explosions were reported . . . Built of flammable materials with the pilot sitting on top of the gas tank, Jennies were more or less flying Molotov cocktails just waiting for a spark.[] Turning one into an impromptu bomber would have required igniting the turpentine balls or kerosene soaked rags in an open cockpit, against the wash of the propeller and the flow of air around the moving aircraft, without setting the airplane on fire, and then hurling the incendiary clear of the biplane's lower wingspan.").

[395] *Id.* ("This [referring to turning Jennies into "impromptu bombers"] seems foolhardy, especially when the whites on the ground were setting all the fires they wanted, and with much greater precision. However, that does not mean that it did not happen, for foolhardiness ruled the day.").

[396] LUCKERSON, BUILT FROM THE FIRE, at 99.

[397] *Id.; see also Air Police Sworn in by Mayor*, TULSA TRIB., May 1, 1920, at 1 (reporting that Tulsa swore in three pilots to keep "an alert lookout for any gathering of radicals" at a May Day celebration, giving Tulsa "[t]he distinction of being the only city in the United States to use airplanes as a combatant to the Red menace" that day); Hopkins, *The Plot to Kill "Diamond Dick" Rowland and the Tulsa Race Riot*, at 27 ("The police department even had its own air force, or 'air police' as the Tribune called it.").

[398] *See Air Police Sworn in by Mayor*, TULSA TRIB., May 1, 1920, at 1 ("[F]lyers . . . divided the city into zones and patrolled it vigilantly.").

[399] *See, e.g., id.*

[400] According to the Smithsonian, "[s]ignal rockets [] resembled ordinary firework rockets and used gunpowder." *Rocket, Signal, World War I*, NAT. AIR & SPACE MUSEUM.

[401] *Id.* ("This specimen is marked 'Green' on its label and therefore had a green signal.").

[402] The Commission Report similarly suggests that pilots communicated by dropping canisters containing messages, which might have been mistaken for bombs. *See* Warner, THE COMMISSION REPORT, at 107.

[403] *See* Petition at 3, *Mrs. J. H. Goodwin [Carlie M. Goodwin] v. City of Tulsa, et al*, No. 23,368, (Tulsa Cty. Dist. Ct. 1923); Petition at 3, *Jackson Undertaking Co. v. City of Tulsa, et al*, No. 23,371 (Tulsa Cty. Dist. Ct. 1923); Petition at 3, *W. S. Holloway v. City of Tulsa, et al.*, No. 23,372 (Tulsa Cty. Dist. Ct. May 31, 1923); Petition at 3, *Daisy Williams v. City of Tulsa, et al.*, No. 23,360 (Tulsa Cty. Dist. Ct. May 31, 1923); Petition at 3, *Edith Patterson v. City of Tulsa, et al.* No. 23,363 (Tulsa Cty. Dist. Ct. May 31, 1923); Petition at 3, *Thomas R. Gentry v. City of Tulsa et al*, No. 23,333 (Tulsa Cty. Dist. Ct. May 31, 1923); Petition at 3, *Julia A. Jackson Ferguson v. City of Tulsa et al*, No. 23,334 (Tulsa Cty. Dist. Ct. May 31, 1923); Petition at 3, *William Walker v. City of Tulsa et al*, No. 23,337 (Tulsa Cty. Dist. Ct. May 31, 1923); Petition at 3, *O. C. Mann v. City of Tulsa et al.*, No. 23,338 (Tulsa Cty. Dist. Ct. May 31, 1923); Petition at 3, *Dr. J. M. Keys v. City of Tulsa et al.*, No. 23,342 (Tulsa Cty. Dist. Ct. May 31, 1923); Petition at 3, *Hosea Vaden v. City of Tulsa et al.*, No. 23,343 (Tulsa Cty. Dist. Ct. May 31, 1923); Petition at 3, *Caroline Lollis v. City of Tulsa, et al.*, No. 23,327 (Tulsa Cty. Dist. Ct. May 31, 1923); Petition at 3, *G. W. Walker v. City of Tulsa et al.*, No. 23,328 (Tulsa Cty. Dist. Ct. May 31, 1923).

[404] *See* discussion, BROPHY, RECONSTRUCTING THE DREAMLAND, at 47 & n.81.

[405] *See generally* Ellsworth, THE COMMISSION REPORT, at 45 (discussing effect of *Birth of a Nation* on Klan in Oklahoma).

[406] KREHBIEL, TULSA 1921: REPORTING A MASSACRE, at 199 ("By the following spring [1922], the Tulsa Klan had grown in size and influence to such an extent that it was poised to seize control of local government. On April 1, just ahead of the city elections, some 1,700 robed and hooded members marched through downtown Tulsa while an airplane with a lighted cross fixed to the underside of its wings and fuselage flew overhead."); ELLSWORTH, DEATH IN A PROMISED LAND, at 20-21 (noting that by "late 1921, the Tulsa 'Klan No. 2' claimed a membership of 3200," and that Tulsa had "the distinction of being one of the few places where the 'Junior' Ku Klux Klan existed").

[407] *KKK Membership Roster, Honorary Members 1928 Dues Issued*, Vols. 1 & 2, The University of Tulsa, McFarlin Library, Department of Special Collections & University Archives (examined by Cold Case Team).

[408] Ellsworth, THE COMMISSION REPORT, at 48 (surveying evidence of pre-massacre Klan activity, but noting that "other evidence suggests that, if anything, the Klan had a very limited presence in Tulsa" before the massacre and surveying evidence that Klan was not as developed in Tulsa as it was elsewhere in Oklahoma).

[409] *See* Norris, *The Oklahoma National Guard*, at 111 (opining that "[t]he riot made the Klan in Tulsa, rather than the Klan making the riot").

[410] O'BRIEN, WHO SPEAKS FOR US? at IV-11 & nn.4-59.

[411] *Id.* at V-11.

[412] Aldrich Blake, *The Ku Klux Kraze: A Lecture* (1924), available in the McFarlin Library Special Collection. In the 1970s, a massacre scholar opined that at the time of the massacre, "[l]awlessness and violence by organized societies such as the Ku Klux Klan, Industrial Workers of the World, Working Class Union and the Knights of Liberty was tolerated." HALLIBURTON, THE TULSA RACE WAR OF 1921, at 2.

[413] Interview with Wilkes and Wilsey, Oklahoma State University – Tulsa Library, Ruth Sigler Avery Collection, Box 7 Folder 3 at 44 ("I had several good friends who became Klansmen at the time it was first organized . . . in 1918 or 1919.").

[414] For example, between September 24 and September 27, 1918, Confederate Veterans held a "Brother Meets Brother" Convention in Tulsa's Convention Hall. *See* Program, TULSA DAILY WORLD, Sept. 25, 1918, at 39.

[415] LUCKERSON, BUILT FROM THE FIRE, at 67 (explaining that the Knights of Liberty were "a vigilante offshoot" of the Great War's council of defense, which had "once tarred and feathered a group of oil industry unionists that they deemed to be meddlesome, forcing their victims to flee Tulsa forever"); *see also id.* at 118 ("Tulsa already had experience developing vigilante networks among the city's business elite through the World War I Council of Defense, the Home Guard, and rogue groups like the Knights of Liberty that often worked closely with police.").

[416] *Id.* at 115-118 ("At a June 2 meeting with city leaders . . . an association of the city's top realty developers called the Tulsa Real Estate Exchange proposed to buy out all the area landowners and build an industrial site there. . . . The face of the gambit was Merritt J. Glass, the Real Estate Exchange's president.").

[417] *Id.* at 118 ("Given the sheer speed and scale of the scheme, there was already speculation across the state that the fiery destruction had been part of the land grab, planned out beforehand by leading city officials.").

[418] *See generally* KREHBIEL, TULSA 1921: REPORTING A MASSACRE, at 30-32 (discussing the inconsistencies and conspiracies surrounding the elevator incident).

[419] *See National Association for the Advancement of Colored People*, 22 CRISIS: A RECORD OF THE DARKER RACES 113, 116 (July 1921).

[420] *See id.* ("The refugees said warnings had been distributed weeks and months before the riot, telling colored people they would have to leave Oklahoma before June 1, or suffer the consequences.").

[421] ELLSWORTH, THE GROUND BREAKING, at 81.

[422] *Survivors' Stories*, Interview with Jackson, The Eddie Faye Gates Tulsa Race Massacre Collection (Gilcrease Museum) (providing no specific time period and suggesting, through context, that it was shortly before the massacre started; "when this riot thing started, the people that my mother worked for sent for her so that she wouldn't be in the riot"). In Eddie Faye Gates' narrative of Jackson's account, Jackson stated that her mother's employer invited them "in the days before the riot," which might suggest a longer time period. *See* GATES, RIOT ON GREENWOOD, at 80-81. But, given the prior recorded statement, this account is insufficient to prove a long-standing plan. One other survivor inferred, because his employer's business was ready for him when he arrived after the start of the massacre, that the employer must have known about the massacre ahead of time. *See* GATES, RIOT ON GREENWOOD, at 90 (account of survivor Ishmael S. Moran that, "[b]efore the riot got out of hand, people from the bank [where my father worked] came and got us. We lived there for a week. It seems like the people there were aware that the riot was going to happen, for the bank was all set up for us—cots, mattresses, bed coverings, food, etc.").

[423] *See, e.g.*, GATES, RIOT ON GREENWOOD, at 90 (account of survivor Ishmael S. Moran that the invitation from employer came "[b]efore the riot got out of hand").

[424] KREHBIEL, TULSA 1921: REPORTING A MASSACRE, at 47 ("Surely, if the objective was to wipe out the [B]lack section of town, a pretext could have been found that did not include running gun battles the length and breadth of the white business district, resulting in white deaths and the looting of white-owned stores."); *see also* LUCKERSON, BUILT FROM THE FIRE, at 118 (noting that while some believed in a pre-massacre plan, the speed at which the post-massacre efforts took place could also be attributed to the fact that men were used to working together for purposes of vigilantism).

[425] KREHBIEL, TULSA 1921: REPORTING A MASSACRE, at 47; *see also* LUCKERSON, BUILT FROM THE FIRE, at 118.

[426] Ellsworth, THE COMMISSION REPORT, at 61 ("The visit of the African American veterans had an electrifying effect, however, on the white mob, now estimated to be more than one thousand strong. . . . The visit of the [B]lack veterans had not at all been foreseen. Shocked, and then outraged, some members of the mob began to go home to fetch their guns.").

[427] LUCKERSON, BUILT FROM THE FIRE, at 118-119 (relying on 1936 thesis by Oklahoma Graduate student Francis Burke, who talked to Tulsa business leaders, and who explained that businessmen had discussed attempting to obtain the land before the massacre and stated that, "[o]n the night of the riot, a number of businessmen participating in this plan actually did much to stimulate the rioters to destroy completely the community").

[428] *Barrett Placed in Full Command, Governor Comes*, TULSA TRIB., June 1, 1921, at 1; Tulsa Race Riot Map 10, THE COMMISSION REPORT (indicating martial law declared on June 1, 1921, at 11:30 a.m.).

[429] *Militia's Reign Brought to End*, TULSA DAILY WORLD, June 3, 1921, at 1 (reporting that martial law was lifted the previous Friday at 5:00 p.m.).

[430] *Id.*

[431] *Id.*

[432] LUCKERSON, BUILT FROM THE FIRE, at 102 ("Greenwood residents were marched into confinement at gunpoint. . . . Blacks who resisted arrest risked immediate execution."). The camps were, at the time, called concentration camps (although that term did not have the same connotation as it would after the Second World War). *See Militia's Reign Brought to End*, TULSA DAILY WORLD, June 3, 1921, at 1 ("A military commission . . . to pass upon the guilty of the 6,000

[N]egroes now held in concentration camp, was formed shortly before noon . . ."); *Black Camp at Fairgrounds Is Nearly Empty*, TULSA TRIB., June 12, 1921, at 13 ("Fewer than a hundred [N]egroes will respond to the breakfast reveille this morning at the Red Cross concentration camp in the Free Fair Grounds . . . scores have found quarters and work somewhere in Tulsa or nearby towns."). The National Guard and other law enforcement arrested and disarmed Black men and led them to the camps. *See* Report of Frank Van Voorhis, 3rd Inf. Okla. Natl Gd. (July 30, 1921) at 90-93 (discussing numerous times the guard arrested and disarmed Black men and sent them to civil authorities).

[433] *Roundup of 64 Indicted Blacks Is On: No Warrants Issued for Whites*, TULSA TRIB., June 17, 1921, at 1 ("Warrants for alleged race rioters to the number of 64 . . . were all against [N]egroes charged with leading the armed invasion of the downtown district by members of their race.").

[434] ELLSWORTH, DEATH IN A PROMISED LAND, at 59.

[435] *Id.* at 71.

[436] PARRISH, THE NATION MUST AWAKE, at 32 (account of Roseatter Moore).

[437] G.A. Gregg, *Tulsa Then and Now*, Oklahoma YMCA at 7 (undated; included in letter to Department of Justice dated June 9, 1921).

[438] *See Fire Razes Black District; All Negroes Interned as Guardmen Patrol City*, TULSA TRIB., June 1, 1921, at 1 ("Mayor Evans estimated at noon today that 6,000 [B]lack men, women and children, race war refugees, are held in the various encampments."). Other estimates put the number at 4,000. *See* HALLIBURTON, THE TULSA RACE WAR OF 1921, at 21 ("By Wednesday evening four thousand people were in detention.").

[439] Victor Luckerson, *Black Wall Street: The African American Haven That Burned and Then Rose From the Ashes*, THE RINGER (June 28, 2018) ("Some residents were imprisoned [at internment camps] for as long as two weeks."); Oklahoma Historical Society, *The Tulsa Race Massacre: The Aftermath* ("The length of stay [at internment camps] varied for most of those imprisoned.").

[440] Interview by Cold Case Team with Michael Eugene Penny, in Tulsa, Okla. (Oct. 16, 2024) (relaying what his grandfather, who lived in a camp for a month, told him about the camp).

[441] An example of such a badge can be found here, courtesy of the Tulsa Historical Society.

[442] Police Commissioner Adkison issued a notice that Black residents of Tulsa would have to have an identification card showing their employment. *See Notice*, TULSA TRIB., June 7, 1921, at 1 ("In order to permit [N]egroes who are peaceful and working in permanent jobs free use of the streets there will be provided a green identification card WHICH MUST BE SIGNED BY THE EMPLOYER AS A MATTER OF IDENTIFICATION."). The notice states that any Black person found without such an identification card would be subject to arrest. *Id.* The same notice appeared in the *Tulsa Daily World*. *See Notice*, TULSA DAILY WORLD, June 7, 1921, at 2. Further orders prohibited any Black person who was not regularly employed by a white person from living in the servants' quarters of that home, even with permission of the white homeowner. *See All Blacks Must Wear Green Tags*, TULSA DAILY WORLD, June 7, 1921, at 9; *see also* PARRISH, THE NATION MUST AWAKE, at 49 (account of J.C. Lattimer).

[443] *See* HILL, THE 1921 TULSA RACE MASSACRE: A PHOTOGRAPHIC HISTORY, at 133 (photograph of green identification card requiring signature of a white employer).

[444] LUCKERSON, BUILT FROM THE FIRE, at 103-04 ("[U]nemployed [B]lacks had to renew their cards every day."); *see also* HILL, THE 1921 TULSA RACE MASSACRE: A PHOTOGRAPHIC HISTORY, at 139 (photograph of red travel card).

[445] LUCKERSON, BUILT FROM THE FIRE, at 104; *see also* Ed Wheeler, *Profile of a Race Riot*, OKLA. IMPACT MAG. (1971) (noting that the Black population was "forced by municipal edict to have identification tags on their person when found on

the street, if employed they were ordered to wear green 'job' tags countersigned by their employer and their movements were highly restricted"); HILL, THE 1921 TULSA RACE MASSACRE: A PHOTOGRAPHIC HISTORY, at 139 (photograph of red identification card needed for "passage").

[446] *Police Order Negro Porters Out of Hotels*, TULSA TRIB., June 14, 1921, at 1.

[447] LUCKERSON, BUILT FROM THE FIRE, at 104.

[448] *Dick Rowland in South Omaha, No Trace of Girl*, THE BLACK DISPATCH, June 17, 1921, at 1 (quoting a Black doctor who left the city as saying, "[i]t is humiliating to the greatest degree to the Negroes of the city to have to go around labeled with green cards as though they are dogs or some other kind of animals").

[449] *Red Cross to Spend Months Aiding Blacks*, TULSA TRIB., June 4, 1921, at 6 ("Out in the black belt today gangs of [N]egroes are at work clearing away the rubbish and debris from residence lots."); Interview by Cold Case Team with XXXXXX in Tulsa, Okla. (on 11/15/2024) (relaying account of how her ancestor was taken out of camp because he was an undertaker who could embalm the dead).

[450] Brig. General Chars F. Barrett, Field Order No. 4, reprinted in HOWER, ANGELS OF MERCY, at 130.

[451] AMERICAN RED CROSS REPORT at 32-33 ("All relief to able-bodied men was in the form of work, at a wage rate of 25 cents per hour.").

[452] *Id.* at 33 ("[F]ood was supplied to the people at the rate of 20 cents per meal.").

[453] *Id.* at 29 ("Mayor Evans early in the day, by written communication designated the Red Cross as the official Relief Agency."); HIRSCH, RIOT AND REMEMBRANCE, at 131 (describing how Tulsa and its mayor "cede[d] basic relief services" to the Red Cross).

[454] AMERICAN RED CROSS REPORT at 32-33 ("All relief to able-bodied men was in the form of work, at a wage rate of 25 cents per hour.").

[455] Kimberly C. Ellis, *We Look Like Men of War: Africana Male Narratives and the Tulsa Race Riot, War and Massacre of 1921* (2002) (Ph.D. dissertation, Purdue University) (ProQuest), at 51 ("Black men who did not have former employment were forced to clean up the district with *no pay*. . . .").

[456] ELLSWORTH, DEATH IN A PROMISED LAND, at 72.

[457] HIRSCH, RIOT AND REMEMBRANCE, at 118 ("Some refugees lived in tents for well over a year."); Ellsworth, THE COMMISSION REPORT, at 88-89 ("Despite the Herculean efforts of the American Red Cross, thousands of [B]lack Tulsans were forced to spend the winter of 1921-22 living in tents.").

[458] LUCKERSON, BUILT FROM THE FIRE, at 130 ("Some [tents] had wooden siding and flooring, but others were little more than a shield from the rain as residents slept in the dirt."). The weeks following the massacre were particularly rainy, adding to the misery of the dispossessed residents. HIRSCH, RIOT AND REMEMBRANCE, at 145 ("It rained like hell. Heavy storms from June 18 to June 28 caused massive floods on the Arkansas River, which sometimes rose two inches an hour. Sewers everywhere were clogged with water and debris. Low crossings were turned into lakes; two feet of water stood in some intersections. . . . The driving rain blew down [the tents of Black survivors] and soaked their bedding, and their stoves and firewood were so drenched that they could not start fires until the following afternoon."). When winter arrived, many Black residents still slept in tents. Ellsworth, THE COMMISSION REPORT, at 88-89 ("[T]thousands of [B]lack Tulsans forced to spend the winter of 1921-22 living in tents.").

[459] Letter from Edward Stuart, Director, Disaster Relief Service to W. Frank Persons, Vice Chairman, American Red Cross (Oct. 15, 1921) ("The worst feature of the whole situation is the bad sanitary condition of the whole district, the [N]egroes defecating all over the ground, the privies being very few and very bad. Flies are very prevalent.").

[460] LUCKERSON, BUILT FROM THE FIRE, at 108, 130.

[461] HIRSCH, RIOT AND REMEMBRANCE, at 118 (noting that the number of fatalities "would have been even higher if they had included those who died from disease or exposure while living in tents after the riot. . . . Some refugees lived in tents for well over a year, combating floods, heat, and cold. Pneumonia, typhoid fever, malnutrition, smallpox, and stress all took their toll.") and 159 (quoting Maurice Willows of the Red Cross as saying at the end of 1921 that "[t]he people of Tulsa can't realize conditions as they exist out here . . . . We are fighting pneumonia from the exposure that is inevitable.").

[462] See HIRSCH, RIOT AND REMEMBRANCE, at 130-32.

[463] AMERICAN RED CROSS REPORT at 89 (Resolution from Committee representing Black community, including B.C. Franklin, referring to Red Cross as "that Angel of Love and Mercy"); see also generally HOWER, ANGELS OF MERCY.

[464] Brooks & Witten, THE COMMISSION REPORT, at 124; Franklin & Ellsworth, THE COMMISSION REPORT, at 23.

[465] Brooks & Witten, THE COMMISSION REPORT, at 124 ("There are reports of victims being placed on flatbed railroad cars and moved by rail from Tulsa. Other accounts have victims being thrown in the Arkansas River or being incinerated. However, the most frequently reported version is of victims being buried in mass graves.").

[466] AMERICAN RED CROSS REPORT at 34.

[467] PARRISH, THE NATION MUST AWAKE, at 22.

[468] Red Cross to Spend Months Aiding Blacks, TULSA TRIB., June 4, 1921, at 6.

[469] O'Dell, THE COMMISSION REPORT, at 144.

[470] Weiss Reports at 12 (Appendix C).

[471] Id.

[472] O'Dell, THE COMMISSION REPORT, at 149.

[473] See CPI Inflation Calculator.

[474] Sub-Station of Postoffice is Razed by Fire, TULSA TRIB., June 4, 1921, at 6.

[475] Id.

[476] Id.

[477] See KREHBIEL, TULSA 1921: REPORTING A MASSACRE, at 148 (citing news stories).

[478] Brophy, THE COMMISSION REPORT, at 166-67. The men indicted included newspaper editor A.J. Smitherman, his brother John Smitherman, and hotel owner J.B. Stradford—all pillars of the Black community. Brent Staples, Unearthing a Riot, N.Y. TIMES (Dec. 19, 1999) ("Stradford and Smitherman were unfairly indicted for the riot and fled the city."); Ellsworth, THE COMMISSION REPORT, at 42, 52-54; Ross, THE COMMISSION REPORT, at vii ("[Smitherman] and Stradford were among the leading [B]lack citizens arrested for causing the riot."). Charges were also filed against "Peg Leg" Taylor, who had fought at Standpipe Hill. See KREHBIEL, TULSA 1921: REPORTING A MASSACRE, at 148; Roundup of 64 Indicted

Blacks Is On: No Warrants Issued for Whites, TULSA TRIB., June 17, 1921, at 1 (naming several Black men indicted). Two white men were arrested for looting at the end of the grand jury investigation, but it is not clear whether they were ever tried or convicted (or whether they were accused of stealing from Black victims or white shops). *See Official Heads Named in Probe*, TULSA TRIB., June 25, 1921, at 1 ("Two white men, C.L. Deaver and E.P. Tutoe, were arrested Thursday on warrants based upon grand jury indictments charging the defendants with grand larceny in connection with looting following the race disturbances here.").

[479] Brophy, THE COMMISSION REPORT, at 167.

[480] ELLSWORTH, DEATH IN A PROMISED LAND, at 97 ("No white Tulsans were ever sent to prison for the killing, burning, and looting of the race riot of 1921.").

[481] *Grand Jury Blames Negroes for Inciting Race Rioting; Whites Clearly Exonerated*, TULSA DAILY WORLD, June 26, 1921, at 1.

[482] *Id.*

[483] *Id.*

[484] The grand jury indicted other police officers for corruption unrelated to the massacre. *Police Head Hit on Five Counts; 11 Others Named*, TULSA TRIB., June 25, 1921, at 1 ("In the same report the grand jury accused four other policemen and indicted seven civilians. The seven are accused in connection with the race riots. The policemen are not.").

[485] *Jury Convicts Gustafson on Both Counts*, TULSA TRIB., July 23, 1921, at 1 ("By a unanimous verdict, a jury... last night, found John A. Gustafson, suspended police chief, guilty of 'failing to make a reasonable effort to disarm various parties assembled during the race trouble in a riotous and tumultuous manner and of permitting the law abiding citizens of Tulsa and their property and houses to be and remain at the mercy of armed men.'").

[486] Letter of Thomas James Sharp to Joseph Anthony Sharp (June 28, 1921) [2021.170.001], Tulsa Historical Society & Museum, Tulsa, OK (noting that the grand jury had "layed [sic] the whole blame on the ni**ers where it rightfully belonged"); Amy Comstock, *"Over There": Another View of the Tulsa Riots*, SURVEY, July 2, 1921, at 460 (account by white survivor using racist language to blame the massacre on Black Greenwood residents).

[487] *Black Agitators Blamed for Riot*, TULSA DAILY WORLD, June 6, 1921, at 1, 5.

[488] *Red Cross to Spend Months Aiding Blacks*, TULSA TRIB., June 4, 1921, at 6. The author further described the "incessant paging of names" at the fairgrounds "from morning till night," as white people were searching for their "[N]egro laundresses, maids and porters" but "[m]ost of them only know these [N]egroes by 'Annie,' or 'Luella,' or 'Aunt Lizzie,'" making it difficult to locate them. *Id.*

[489] *Niles Blames Lawlessness for Race War*, TULSA TRIB., June 2, 1921, at 4.

[490] *Id.*

[491] AMERICAN RED CROSS REPORT at 30.

[492] *Martin Blames Riots to Lax City Hall Rule*, TULSA TRIB., June 2, 1921, at 1 (quoting Judge Loyal J. Martin, the unanimous choice to head the public welfare board, as saying that "[w]e have had a failing police protection here, and now we have got to pay the costs of it. The city and county is legally liable for every dollar of the damage which has been done"); *see also* LUCKERSON, BUILT FROM THE FIRE, at 116-117.

[493] BROPHY, RECONSTRUCTING THE DREAMLAND, at 90; LUCKERSON, BUILT FROM THE FIRE, at 116-17.

[494] BROPHY, RECONSTRUCTING THE DREAMLAND, at 90 ("Yet, the board passed a resolution to refuse contributions from outside Tulsa. A $1000 contribution from the *Chicago Tribune* was returned, as was an offer of aid from the Dallas NAACP."); *see also City to Meet Demands Out of Its Own Purse*, TULSA TRIB., June 3, 1921, at 1 ("Tulsa is going to take care of this problem herself. That was made certain at the reconstruction board meeting this morning.").

[495] *City to Meet Demands Out of Its Own Purse*, TULSA TRIB., June 3, 1921, at 1 ("The $1,000 offered by the Chicago Tribune will be sent back at once with the courteous statement that the city is able to take care of its own problems here.").

[496] *See* KREHBIEL, TULSA 1921: REPORTING A MASSACRE, at 106.

[497] *Public Welfare Board Vacated by Commission: Mayor in Statement on Race Trouble*, TULSA TRIB., June 14, 1921, at 2.

[498] *Id.*

[499] LUCKERSON, BUILT FROM THE FIRE, at 26, 118; *see also* Lee Roy Chapman, *The Nightmare of Dreamland*, THIS LAND PRESS (April 18, 2012).

[500] ELLSWORTH, DEATH IN A PROMISED LAND, at 84-85; BROPHY, RECONSTRUCTING THE DREAMLAND, at 93.

[501] *Id.*

[502] FRANKLIN, MY LIFE AND AN ERA: THE AUTOBIOGRAPHY OF BUCK COLBERT FRANKLIN, at 198.

[503] *Negro Section Abolished by City's Order*, TULSA TRIB., June 7, 1921, at 1.

[504] *Id.*

[505] FRANKLIN, MY LIFE AND AN ERA: THE AUTOBIOGRAPHY OF BUCK COLBERT FRANKLIN, at 198. Franklin's grandson referred to the tent as the "first pop-up law firm." Interview by Cold Case Team with John W. Franklin, in Washington, D.C. (Oct. 24, 2024).

[506] Brophy, THE COMMISSION REPORT, at 168.

[507] *Id.*; *Cannot Enforce Fire Ordinance: Court Holds Unconstitutional Act Against the Burned District*, TULSA DAILY WORLD, Sept. 2, 1921, at 1 (reporting that a three-judge panel held the fire ordinance was illegal and that "[b]y the decision it was declared invalidated without force or effect").

[508] FRANKLIN, MY LIFE AND AN ERA: THE AUTOBIOGRAPHY OF BUCK COLBERT FRANKLIN, at 198.

[509] Robert M. Jarvis, *Remembering Isaiah: Attorney I.H. Spears and the 1921 Tulsa Race Massacre*, 57 TULSA L. REV. 429, 442 (2022) (quoting PARRISH, EVENTS OF THE TULSA DISASTER at 88).

[510] *Redfearn*, 243 P. at 929 ("This suit is to recover on fire insurance policies on a theater building and a hotel building located in the [N]egro section of the city of Tulsa, conceded to have been in force at the time the buildings were totally destroyed by fire. The defense was that the loss was caused directly or indirectly by a riot. Each of the policies contained [a riot clause]."); BROPHY, RECONSTRUCTING THE DREAMLAND, at 95-96 ("On the day after the riot, insurance companies were already telling their customers that they would not pay on the policies containing 'riot exclusion' clauses. Most of the policies had such clauses, which absolved the companies of liability for damage caused by riot.").

[511] *See Redfearn*, 243 P. at 929-931.

[512] *Mrs. J. H. Goodwin [Carlie M. Goodwin] v. City of Tulsa, et al*, No. 23,368, (Tulsa Cty. Dist. Ct. 1923); *Annie Talley v. City of Tulsa, et al.*, No. 23,374 (Tulsa Cty. Dist. Ct.1923), *Jackson Undertaking Co. v. City of Tulsa, et al*, No. 23,371

(Tulsa Cty. Dist. Ct. 1923); *Birdie Lynch Farmer v. City of Tulsa, et al*, No. 23,367 (Tulsa Cty. Dist. Ct. May 31, 1923); *W. S. Holloway v. City of Tulsa, et al.*, No. 23,372 (Tulsa Cty. Dist. Ct. May 31, 1923); *P.S. Thompson v. T.D. Evans et. al.*, No. 23,375 (Tulsa Cty. Dist. Ct. May 31, 1923); *J. S. Gish v. T. D. Evans, et al.*, No. 23,315, (Tulsa Cty. Dist. Ct. May 31, 1923); *Daisy Williams v. City of Tulsa, et al.*, No. 23,360 (Tulsa Cty. Dist. Ct. May 31, 1923); *Jack Wren v. City of Tulsa, et al.*, No. 23,365 (Tulsa Cty. Dist. Ct. May 31, 1923); *J. W. Williams v. City of Tulsa, et al.*, No. 23,370 (Tulsa Cty. Dist. Ct. May 31, 1923); *Belle Harrison v. City of Tulsa, et al.*, No. 23,373 (Tulsa Cty. Dist. Ct. May 31, 1923); *N. L. Gilliam v. T. D. Evans, et al.*, No. 23,312 (Tulsa Cty. Dist. Ct. May 31, 1923); *Edith Patterson v. City of Tulsa, et al.* No. 23,363 (Tulsa Cty. Dist. Ct. May 31, 1923). These pleadings are available from the Tulsa Historical Society,

[513] Brophy, THE COMMISSION REPORT, at 166-67.

[514] *Alexander v. Oklahoma*, 382 F.3d 1206, 1212 (10th Cir. 2004) ("Plaintiffs filed their initial complaint on February 24, 2003. In it, they alleged civil rights claims under 28 U.S.C. §§ 1981, 1983, and 1985. They also brought claims under the Fourteenth Amendment to the Federal Constitution and the Equal Protection Clause. Finally, they submitted state law claims based on negligence and promissory estoppel.").

[515] *Alexander*, 382 F.3d at 1212.

[516] The district court dismissed the complaint, but the Tenth Circuit treated the dismissal as a grant of a motion for summary judgment and held that the complaint should be dismissed on that basis. *Alexander*, 382 F.3d at 1214.

[517] *Alexander*, 382 F.3d at 1217-1218.

[518] *Randle v. City of Tulsa*, 556 P.3d 612, 615, *reh'g denied* (Sept. 9, 2024). The Oklahoma Supreme Court explained that, to prove a violation of Oklahoma nuisance law, 50 O.S. § 1, there must be a showing that an offending party, unlawfully does an act, or omits to perform a duty, which act or omission either:

> First. Annoys, injures or endangers the comfort, repose, health, or safety of others; or
> Second. Offends decency; or
> Third. Unlawfully interferes with, obstructs or tends to obstruct, or renders dangerous for passage, any lake or navigable river, stream, canal or basin, or any public park, square, street or highway; or
> Fourth. In any way renders other persons insecure in life, or in the use of property, provided, this section shall not apply to preexisting agricultural activities.

The court further explained that "[a] nuisance is public when it 'affects at the same time an entire community or neighborhood, or any considerable number of persons, although the extent of the annoyance or damage inflicted upon the individuals may be unequal.'" *Id. at* 617 (quoting 50 O.S. § 2).

[519] *Randle*, 556 P.3d at 615.

[520] *Id.* at 618.

[521] *Id.* at 619.

[522] *Id.* at 621.

[523] *Probe of Tulsa Riot Ordered by Daugherty*, THE SUN, June 4, 1921, at 3.

[524] *Sub-Station of Postoffice is Razed by Fire*, TULSA TRIB., June 4, 1921, at 6.

[525] Weiss Reports at 2-3 (Appendix C) (report of Agent Findlay dated June 3, 1921, including a telegram from Agent Weiss dated June 2).

[526] *Id.* at 3; *see also Attorney General's Office Wires to Federal Officers Here to Conduct Thorough Probe to Fix Blame; Governor Gives Directions to Freeling,* OKLA. CITY TIMES, June 3, 1921 at 33 ("Just what Washington officials intend to do in regard to the situation is not known, [Agent] Findlay said, as, technically speaking, no federal law has been violated.").

[527] Weiss Reports at 13 (Appendix C).

[528] *Id.*

[529] *Id.* at 3.

[530] *Id.* at 13.

[531] *Id.* at 6-11.

[532] *Id.* at 12.

[533] *Id.*

[534] *Id.*

[535] *Id.*

[536] *Id.*

[537] *Id.* at 7 ("WILLIAM ELLIS, Deputy United States Marshal, Tulsa, stated to Agent that May 31st he heard rumors that ROWLAND was to be lynched that night, and took his wife with him in his car to the jail about 6 P.M. to see the lynching, but to take no part."). Ellis did tell Agent Weiss that he counseled the sheriff to disarm everyone and offered to help him, "before the tension became dangerous." *Id.*

[538] *Id.* at 11.

[539] *Id.*

[540] *Id.*

[541] *Id.*

[542] *Id.* (noting that Dyer stated that, during the burning and looting, "there was absolutely no effort" made by city officers "to preserve order or enforce the law").

[543] *See* Miscellaneous Notes at 2, *Oklahoma v. Gustafson.*

[544] A news article about the post-massacre grand jury investigation identifies "Jack Rigden" as one of the "[p]rominent Tulsans" to testify in the grand jury. *See Grand Jury Gives Report to Court,* TULSA DAILY WORLD, June 16, 1921, at 1.

[545] Several contemporaneous news articles identify Jack Rigdon as a Red Fork Motorcycle officer. One article indicates that Rigdon had held the same role as part of the Tulsa Police Department. *See Romance of War Told in Court Trial,* TULSA TRIB., Oct. 1, 1921, at 6 ("Rigdon was formerly a motorcycle cop on the police force. He is serving at Red Fork in the same capacity now."). In October 1921, newspapers reported allegations that Officer Jack Rigdon of Red Fork was accused of making arrests on "trumped up" charges. *See Await Action of County Board: Red Fork Officials Still Have Several Days of Grace,* TULSA DAILY WORLD, Oct. 22, 1921, at 18. Rigdon and two other Red Fork officials were charged with extortion, but the charges were ultimately dismissed. *See You Tell the World,* TULSA DAILY WORLD, Feb. 12, 1922, at 3.

[546] In contrast to the attitude Weiss displayed in his report toward those responsible for destroying Greenwood, it is worth noting that, a month later, he arranged to be kept informed of any "radical organization . . . among the [N]egroes," including the African Blood Brotherhood, that were rumored to be planning an attack in revenge for the massacre, even though his report indicated that he had received no credible information that this group posed a danger. Weiss Reports at 4-5 (Appendix C) (report from Agent Weiss on the African Blood Brotherhood as a "Possible Radical Matter"). He documented this information in a report, dated July 5, 1921, which ends with the word "open," indicating an ongoing investigation. *Id.* at 5.

[547] *History, Northern District of Oklahoma*, DEP'T OF JUSTICE (June 26, 2024).

[548] *Lee Not Yet Advised*, MUSKOGEE DAILY PHOENIX & TIMES-DEMOCRAT, June 4, 1921, at 1.

[549] *Id.*

[550] It is of course possible that someone in the United States Attorney's Office or at Main Justice conducted an analysis and that the relevant files have been misfiled, lost, or stored in an unindexed box. Future researchers may wish to examine Daugherty's files, which are on microfiche in the H.M. Daugherty Collection in the Ohio History Collection, as well as boxes from 1921 in the National Archives repository in Texas, which holds records for the Eastern District of Oklahoma.

[551] *President Harding at Lincoln University*, LINCOLN UNIV. HERALD, Aug. 1921, at 11 ("[C]ontrasting the commencement scene before him with the recent riots in Tulsa, [President Harding] said: 'God grant that in the soberness, the fairness and the justice of the country, we shall never again have a spectacle like it.'").

[552] *Assistant Attorney General Kristen Clarke Delivers Remarks at the Civil Rights Division's Cold Case Convening*, DEP'T OF JUST., Office of Public Affairs (Sept. 30, 2024) ("When we have finished our federal review, we will issue a report analyzing the massacre in light of both modern and then-existing civil rights law."). This Report does not purport to opine on whether any person or entity can be held civilly responsible for any harm inflicted during the massacre.

[553] *See, e.g.*, Plaintiff's Brief, *Redfearn*, at 25-91.

[554] Ellsworth, THE COMMISSION REPORT, at 80 (recounting experience of a young white man whose boss told him that there would be no work that day because it was "ni**er day" and that he was "going hunting ni**ers,").

[555] Witness Testimony of Laurel Buck at 2, *Oklahoma v. Gustafson*.

[556] The government might not be able to prove bias motivation in those cases in which a Black person was killed or injured while they were firing at white men, as the white men responsible would be able to claim self-defense or defense of others.

[557] Subsection (a)(1) of the HCPA prohibits willfully causing bodily injury because of the actual or perceived race or color of any person and likewise punishes attempting to cause such injury with a dangerous weapon (like a gun).

[558] The criminal provisions of the Fair Housing Act prohibit anyone (whether or not they act under color of law) from using force or threat of force to willfully injure, intimidate, or interfere with a victim because of that victim's race or color (among other characteristics) and because the victim was enjoying a housing right, such as the right to peacefully occupy a dwelling that victim owned, rented, or occupied. 42 U.S.C. § 3631; *United States v. Porter*, 928 F.3d 947, 956 (10th Cir. 2019) (citing elements).

[559] HILL, TULSA RACE MASSACRE: A PHOTOGRAPHIC HISTORY, at 59.

[560] The government could use either the civil rights conspiracy law, 18 U.S.C. § 241, or the general conspiracy law, 18 U.S.C. § 371.

---

[561] Section 247(c) of the Church Arson Prevention Act prohibits intentionally defacing, damaging, or destroying religious real property because of the race, color, or ethnic characteristics of any individual associated with that religious property.

[562] For a history of 18 U.S.C. § 242, see *United States v. Williams*, 341 U.S. 70, 83 (1951) (Appendix to Opinion of J. Frankfurter, tracing the history of 18 U.S.C. § 242).

[563] *United States v. Lanier*, 520 U.S. 259, 264 (1997) ("Section 242 is a Reconstruction Era civil rights statute making it criminal to act (1) willfully and (2) under color of law (3) to deprive a person of rights protected by the Constitution or laws of the United States.") (internal quotations omitted); *United States v. Rodella*, 804 F.3d 1317, 1323 (10th Cir. 2015) ("Section 242 of Title 18 prohibits, in pertinent part, a person acting under color of any law from willfully subject[ing] any person in any State, Territory, Commonwealth, Possession, or District to the deprivation of any rights, privileges, or immunities secured or protected by the Constitution or laws of the United States.") (internal quotations omitted). The key difference between the current version of § 242 and its 1921 version is that, in 1921, the statute protected only the rights of "citizens" not all "persons." *See United States v. Otherson*, 637 F.2d 1276, 1280-84 (9th Cir. 1980).

[564] Current Fourth Amendment jurisprudence would allow prosecution of any law enforcement officer who intentionally used more force than reasonably necessary to take a Black person into custody or who seized a Black person by killing him when that person was not posing an imminent threat of death or serious bodily injury. *Graham v. Connor*, 490 U.S. 386, 394, 396 (1989) (holding that the Fourth Amendment governs an arrestee's excessive force claims and stating that the "test of reasonableness under the Fourth Amendment is not capable of precise definition or mechanical application, however, its proper application requires careful attention to the facts and circumstances of each particular case, including the severity of the crime at issue, whether the officers or others, and whether he is actively resisting arrest or attempting to evade arrest by flight") (internal quotations and citation omitted); *Packard v. Budaj*, 86 F.4th 859, 865-66 (10th Cir. 2023) ("When an excessive force claim arises in the context of an arrest or investigatory stop of a free citizen, it is most properly characterized as one invoking the protections of the Fourth Amendment. . . . The Supreme Court outlined three factors that guide the reasonableness analysis: (1) the severity of the crime at issue, (2) whether the suspect poses an immediate threat to the safety of the officers or others, and (3) whether the suspect is actively resisting arrest or attempting to evade arrest by flight.") (internal quotations and citations omitted).

[565] *Cronick v. Pryor*, 99 F.4th 1262, 1268 (10th Cir. 2024) ("An officer has probable cause to arrest a person when the facts and circumstances surrounding the situation would lead a reasonably prudent officer to believe that the arrestee has committed a crime . . . . Whether probable cause exists is determined by looking at the totality of the circumstances, based on what an objective officer would have known in the situation.") (internal citation omitted).

[566] *United States v. Hill*, 805 F.3d 935, 937 (10th Cir. 2015) ("A seizure within the contemplation of the Fourth Amendment occurs when there is some meaningful interference with an individual's possessory interest in his property.").

[567] *Ramirez v. Department of Corrections*, 222 F.3d 1238, 1243 (10th Cir. 2000) ("The Equal Protection Clause of the Fourteenth Amendment mandates that no state deny any person within its jurisdiction the equal protection of the laws. [] Racial and national origin discrimination can violate the Fourteenth Amendment right to equal protection of the law.") (internal quotations and citation omitted).

[568] The Tenth Circuit had held that, to show a constitutional violation under the danger-creation theory, a plaintiff must show that a state actor "affirmatively acted to create or increases a plaintiff's vulnerability to, danger from private violence." *T.D. v. Patton*, 868 F.3d 1209, 1222 (10th Cir. 2017) (internal quotations, citations, and alterations omitted). Once this threshold is met, a plaintiff may recover if he or she demonstrates that "(1) the charged state entity and the charged individual actors created the danger or increased plaintiff's vulnerability to the danger in some way; (2) plaintiff was a member of a limited and specifically definable group; (3) defendants' conduct put plaintiff at substantial risk of serious, immediate, and proximate harm; (4) the risk was obvious or known; (5) defendants acted recklessly in conscious disregard of that risk; and (6) such conduct, when viewed in total, is conscience shocking." *Id.* The government would have to prove these facts beyond a reasonable doubt to prosecute someone under this theory and would also have to show that any defendant it prosecuted under this theory acted willfully, understanding the wrongfulness of their conduct. *See* 18 U.S.C. § 242.

[569] Courts first began to interpret § 242 in the 1940s. Early prosecutions of law enforcement officers who engaged in assault and murder generally charged a violation of the right to be free from the deprivation of life, without due process or the right to be free from summary punishment. *See Screws v. United States*, 325 U.S. 91, 93-94 (1945) (discussing indictment); *Culp v. United States*, 131 F.2d 93, 96-97 (8th Cir. 1942) (discussing conspiracy indictment). They did not charge unreasonable seizure theories.

[570] *Uhlrig v. Harder*, 64 F.3d 567, 572-73 (10th Cir. 1995) (discussing doctrine).

[571] *Graham v. Connor*, 490 U.S. 386 (1989).

[572] Moreover, any prosecutor who wished to bring charge now (assuming someone was alive to prosecute and that the statute of limitations had not run) would have to apply constitutional interpretations from the time of the offense. The Supreme Court has recognized that a defendant cannot be prosecuted for violating § 242 unless he has fair warning that his conduct is unconstitutional. *Lanier*, 520 U.S. at 270-71. Referring just to the general language of the constitution is insufficient; there must be case law making clear that the act in question is unconstitutional. *Sanchez v. Guzman*, 105 F.4th 1285, 1293 (10th Cir. 2024) (explaining that clearly established law should not be defined at a high level of generality; rather, noting that "general statements of the law are not inherently *incapable* of giving fair and clear warning' to officers, . . . but in the light of pre-existing law the unlawfulness must be apparent") (cleaned up).

[573] *Ex parte Commonwealth of Virginia*, 100 U.S. 339, 347 (1879); *see also Buchanan v. Warley*, 245 U.S. 60, 82 (1917) (holding that municipally mandated zoning ordinance prohibiting transfer of property to people of color was in "direct violation of the fundamental law enacted in the Fourteenth Amendment of the Constitution preventing state interference with property rights except by due process of law").

[574] The Supreme Court has recognized that while fair warning is usually needed, there are extreme cases when there need not be a case exactly on point to establish fair warning. *Lanier*, 520 U.S. at 271 ("The easiest cases don't even arise. There has never been . . . a section 1983 case accusing welfare officials of selling foster children into slavery; it does not follow that if such a case arose, the officials would be immune from damages [or criminal] liability.") (internal quotations and citation omitted).

[575] After *Graham*, such an offense would be prosecuted as an unreasonable seizure through the use of excessive force. *Graham v. Connor*, 490 U.S. 386, 396-97 (1989).

[576] Such actions would, under current law, be prosecuted as an arrest without probable cause.

[577] *Moyer v. Peabody*, 212 U.S. 78, 84-85 (1909).

[578] *Id.*

[579] *Id.* at 85.

[580] The Supreme Court subsequently held that, notwithstanding the holding of *Moyer*, "it does not follow . . . that every sort of action the Governor may take, no matter how unjustified by the exigency or subversive of private right and the jurisdiction of the courts, otherwise available, is conclusively supported by mere executive fiat." *Sterling v. Constantin*, 287 U.S. 378, 400 (1932). The Tenth Circuit has approved the *Moyer* language in jury instructions in civil rights cases involving the National Guard. *See, e.g., Valdez v. Black*, 446 F.2d 1071, 1076 (10th Cir. 1971) (upholding instruction: "If you find from the evidence that the Governor had called out the National Guard and declared a state of extreme emergency in Rio Arriba County, and that the detention of plaintiffs was accomplished by the National Guard pursuant to such proclamation, and that such detention was made in good faith and in the honest belief that it was necessary under the circumstances to preserve peace, then you should find for the defendant [] and against the plaintiffs.").

[581] Section 241 prohibits conspiring to "injure, oppress, threaten, or intimidate any person . . . in the free exercise or enjoyment of any right or privilege secured to him by the Constitution or laws of the United States." 18 U.S.C. § 241.

[582] For a history of 18 U.S.C. § 241, see *Williams*, 341 U.S. at 83 (Appendix to Opinion of J. Frankfurter, tracing the history of 18 U.S.C. § 241).

[583] 18 U.S.C. § 241; *United States v. Magleby*, 241 F.3d 1306, 1314 (10th Cir. 2001) (describing elements of § 241 in a case involving a conspiracy to violate housing rights).

[584] There are allegations that in the years after the massacre, city officials destroyed records or otherwise acted to prevent the community and the world from learning the truth of what happened. Some have suggested that these acts of concealment or obstruction, if they occurred, make violation of § 19 a continuing offense. But acts of concealment, undertaken after the objects of a conspiracy have been achieved, do not extend the statute of limitations. *United States v. Silverstein*, 737 F.2d 864, 867 (10th Cir. 1984) ("The duration of a conspiracy does not extend to attempts to conceal the crime.") (citing *Grunewald v. United States*, 353 U.S. 391, 399-406 (1957) and *Krulewitch v. United States*, 336 U.S. 440, 443 (1949)).

[585] *Lee Not Yet Advised*, MUSKOGEE DAILY PHOENIX & TIMES-DEMOCRAT, June 4, 1921, at 1.

[586] *United States v. Price*, 383 U.S. 787, 794 (1966) ("Private persons, jointly engaged with state officials in the prohibited action, are acting 'under color' of law for purposes of the statute. To act 'under color' of law does not require that the accused be an officer of the State. It is enough that he is a willful participant in joint activity with the State or its agents.").

[587] *See, e.g., Hodges v. United States*, 203 U.S. 1, 14-15 (1906) (holding that Section 5508 (a previous codification of 18 U.S.C. § 241) did not preclude private acts of racial violence that did not impose a condition of slavery or servitude), *overruled in part by Jones v. Alfred H. Mayer Co.*, 392 U.S. 409 (1968); *United States v. Cruikshank*, 92 U.S. 542, 543 (1875) (holding that most rights secured and protected by the Constitution are limitations on governmental power and that private persons who interfere with such rights through force and violence may not be prosecuted for their actions). The Constitutional rights described above, protected by the Fourth and Fourteenth Amendment, are limitations on the power of the government (and government actors). Section 241 does not, by its plain language, require proof that a defendant acted under color of law. However, courts have held that if the constitutional right allegedly violated was one that serves as a limitation on the power of the federal government, then that right cannot be violated by private persons.

[588] It is also possible, perhaps likely, that there was not one big master plan but, instead, multiple groups who understood the plan differently or who had different plans. Some may have believed the objective was limited to keeping Black people confined to Greenwood (and excluded from the white section of Tulsa). Others may have had the objective of rounding up Black men, on the (mistaken) assumption that such men posed a threat, without intending to take any further action against the residents of Greenwood. But the evidence shows that at least some of the white Tulsans were, from fairly early in the evening, bent on causing as much destruction as possible. Evidence indicates that at least some of these were law enforcement officers. *See generally* Sections E(1)-(3).

[589] *Sub-Station of Postoffice is Razed by Fire*, TULSA TRIB., June 4, 1921, at 6.

[590] 18 U.S.C. § 1701.

[591] *United States v. Kirby*, 74 U.S. 482, 485–86 (1868) (discussing statute and explaining it applies to those who knowingly and willfully obstruct or retard the passage of the mail or its carrier); *Taylor v. United States*, 2 F.2d 444, 446 (7th Cir. 1924) (discussing statute as codified under Section 201 of the Penal Code).

[592] 18 U.S.C. § 7; *Bowen v. Johnston*, 306 U.S. 19, 23 (1939); *Hayes v. United States*, 367 F.2d 216, 218-220 (10th Cir. 1966); *United States v. Davis*, 726 F.3d 357, 366–67 (2d Cir. 2013) ("One cannot simply assume that a federal installation on federal land 'automatically comes within Federal jurisdiction.'") (quoting *United States v. Williams*, 17 M.J. 207, 211 (C.M.A. 1984)); *Scaggs v. United States*, No. 06-CR-00206-JAH-4, 2024 WL 3094622, at *1 (S.D. Cal. June 20, 2024)

(generally discussing federal enclave jurisdiction); *cf. Wackerly v. State*, 237 P.3d 795, 798 (2010) (not mentioning post office in list of property purchases where the Oklahoma legislature consented to cede jurisdiction: "for the United States to exercise exclusive jurisdiction over the [property it] must have been purchased for use as a fort, magazine, arsenal, dock-yard, or irrigation or drainage project").

[593] Nor could the federal government prosecute anyone for killing a postal employee inside the substation (or anywhere else, for that matter) if a Black victim worked at the post office and was killed during the massacre. The law prohibiting the murder of federal employees was not enacted until 1934 and, at that time, covered only a limited class of employees (including a "post-office inspector" but not postal employees). *See* 18 U.S.C. § 253, *as amended*, 18 U.S.C. § 1114; *see also United States v. Feola*, 420 U.S. 671, 700 n.8 (1975) (Stewart, J., dissenting) (explaining history of statute prohibiting the killing of federal officers). More importantly, our review has uncovered no information indicating anyone was killed in the post office or that any postal worker was killed during the massacre. And as explained above, even if such a crime did take place, any perpetrator is now deceased.

[594] *McGirt v. Oklahoma*, 591 U.S. 894, 897-99, 937-38 (2020) (holding that land in present-day Oklahoma that was subject to the 1832 treaty with the Creek Indians, "including a portion of Northeastern Oklahoma that includes most of the city of Tulsa," is considered an Indian reservation for purposes of federal criminal law).

[595] Initially enacted in 1817, the General Crimes Act extended federal criminal jurisdiction over crimes committed in Indian country where the offender is non-Indian and the victim is Indian. *See* 18 U.S.C. § 1152; *see also United States v. Prentiss*, 256 F.3d 971, 974 (10th Cir. 2001) (*en banc*), *overruled in part on other grounds by United States v. Cotton*, 535 U.S. 625 (2002) ("Read in conjunction with the Supreme Court's decision in *McBratney*, § 1152 establishes federal jurisdiction over interracial crimes only (i.e., when the defendant is an Indian and the victim is a non-Indian, or vice versa).").

[596] Initially enacted in 1885, the Major Crimes Act extended federal jurisdiction over certain enumerated crimes, such as murder, committed in Indian country where the offender is Indian, regardless of the status of the victim. *See* 18 U.S.C. § 1153; *see also Keeble v. United States*, 412 U.S. 205, 205-06 (1973) (noting that § 1153 "authorizes the prosecution in federal court of an Indian charged with the commission on an Indian reservation of certain specifically enumerated offenses").

[597] *See, e.g., United States v. Antelope*, 430 U.S. 641, 643-44 (1977) (law providing for prosecution in federal court of Indians charged with murdering non-Indians is constitutional); *United States v. Pierce*, No. 23-7062, 2024 WL 2930939, *1 (10th Cir. June 11, 2024) (discussing prosecution of non-Indian for murder of Indian victim in Indian country).

[598] *See, e.g., United States v. Wood*, 109 F.4th 1253, 1257 (10th Cir. 2024) (citing *Prentiss*, 256 F.3d at 974).

[599] *See* 18 U.S.C. § 3281.

[600] *Prentiss*, 256 F.3d at 974.

[601] *See, e.g., United States v. Walker*, 85 F.4th 973, 979 (10th Cir. 2023) ("'[T]he Indian/non-Indian statuses of the victim and the defendant are essential elements of [a] crime' under [the General Crimes Act] that the government must prove beyond a reasonable doubt.") (quoting *Prentiss*, 256 F.3d at 974); *see also United States v. Brown*, 705 F. Supp. 3d 1289, 1291 (N.D. Okla. 2023) ("In order to prosecute under [the Major Crimes Act], the Government must prove, as a jurisdictional requisite, that an Indian committed one of the fourteen enumerated crimes against another Indian, or any person, within Indian country.") (quoting *United States v. Torres*, 733 F.2d 449, 453-54 (7th Cir. 1984) and collecting cases).

[602] 18 U.S.C. § 3282(a).

[603] 18 U.S.C. § 3231.

[604] Pub. L. No. 103-322, 108 Stat. 1796 (1994).

[605] Once the statute of limitations has expired, it may not be extended. *Stogner v. California*, 539 U.S. 607, 610 (2003).

[606] *Monell v. Dep't of Soc. Servs. of City of New York*, 436 U.S. 658, 694 (1978). "To state a claim against a municipal entity [under *Monell*], a plaintiff must allege facts showing (1) an official policy or custom, (2) causation, and (3) deliberate indifference." *Lucas v. Turn Key Health Clinics, LLC*, 58 F.4th 1127, 1145 (10th Cir. 2023). An official custom or policy may include "(1) a formal regulation or policy statement; (2) an informal custom amounting to a widespread practice that, although not authorized by written law or express municipal policy, is so permanent and well settled as to constitute a custom or usage with the force of law; (3) the decisions of employees with final policymaking authority; (4) the ratification by such final policymakers of the decisions—and the basis for them—of subordinates to whom authority was delegated subject to these policymakers' review and approval; or (5) the failure to adequately train or supervise employees, so long as that failure results from deliberate indifference to the injuries that may be caused." *Lucas*, 58 F.4th at 1145 (quoting *Crowson v. Washington Cnty. Utah*, 983 F.3d 1166, 1184 (10th Cir. 2020)). The exact standard for analyzing *Monell* liability in any civil case will, of course, be subject to the controlling law in the relevant circuit.

[607] This issue would likely be litigated, as the government has never used the civil rights laws to prosecute a city or other municipality. Such entities have been criminally prosecuted by the government for violating other criminal laws, particularly for violation of criminal environmental statutes. *See, e.g., United States v. City of Lake Ozark*, No. 2:08-cr-4036 (W.D. Mo. 2008) (33 U.S.C. § 1311(a) (Clean Water Act)); *United States v. City of Venice*, No. 8:05-cr-190 (M.D. Fla. 2005) (§§ 1311, 1318 (Clean Water Act)); *United States v. County of Kauai*, No. 1:10-cr-614 (D. Haw. 2010) (16 U.S.C. §§ 703, 707(a) (Migratory Bird Treaty Act)). The laws used to prosecute cities often expressly include definitions authorizing such prosecution. *See e.g.,* 33 U.S.C.A. § 1362 (5) (defining the word person, for purposes of the Clean Water Act to include, among other things, a "[s]tate, municipality, commission, or political subdivision of a State, or any interstate body").

Section 241 applies to "persons." 18 U.S.C. § 241 ("If two or more persons conspire to injure, oppress, threaten, or intimidate . . ."). Section § 242 applies to "whoever" violates its precepts. 18 U.S.C. § 242 ("Whoever, under color of any law, statute, ordinance, regulation, or custom . . . ."). Neither civil rights statute expressly states that the term "person" includes a city or other municipality. Under the current version of the Dictionary Act, these terms ("person" and "whoever") include "corporations, companies, associations, firms, partnerships, societies, and joint stock companies, as well as individuals," but the Act does not expressly state that the term "person" incudes "municipalities" or other government entities. *See* 1 U.S.C. § 1. The version of the Dictionary Act in effect shortly after the time these civil rights laws were enacted provided that the word "person" extended to "bodies politic . . . unless the context shows that such words were intended to be used in a more limited sense." Act of Feb. 25, 1871, § 2, 16 Stat. 431. However, at the time of the massacre, in 1921, the Dictionary Act had been amended to remove this provision. *See Ngiraingas v. Sanchez*, 495 U.S. 182, 189-92 (1990) (discussing history of amendments to the Dictionary Act).

The Supreme Court has held that 42 U.S.C. § 1983, the civil analogue of § 242, can be used to sue municipalities and that they are persons under the act. *Monell v. Dep't of Soc. Servs. of City of New York*, 436 U.S. 658, 688–89 (1978) ("Municipal corporations in 1871 were included within the phrase 'bodies politic and corporate' and, accordingly, the 'plain meaning' of § 1 is that local government bodies were to be included within the ambit of the persons who could be sued under § 1 of the Civil Rights Act."); *see also United States v. Bly*, 510 F.3d 453, 463 (4th Cir. 2007) (rejecting the proposition that "the term 'person,' should exclude all sovereign entities and their subparts" and noting it had "little appeal in the criminal law context"). As these statutes are generally given similar interpretations, the government would likely be able to argue that prosecution is possible under the criminal civil rights statutes, however, no court has yet to opine on this issue.

[608] *See Cedric Kushner Promotions, Ltd. v. King*, 533 U.S. 158, 166 (2001); *Imperial Meat Co. v. United States*, 316 F.2d 435, 440 (10th Cir. 1963) (approving jury instructions explaining that to find corporation guilty, it was necessary to find a corporate actor guilty and that the corporate actor's criminal acts were committed while acting as an officer, agent, or employee, within the scope of their employment); *see also United States v. Oceanic Illsabe Ltd.*, 889 F.3d 178, 195 (4th Cir. 2018) (recognizing that a corporation is liable for the criminal acts of its employees and agents that are committed within the scope of their employment and with the intent to benefit the corporation).

[609] *See* U.S. Const. amend. VI; *Smith v. Arizona*, 602 U.S. 779, 783 (2024).

[610] *See* Fed. R. Evid. 801, 802, 803, and 804.

APPENDIX A

Tulsa Race Massacre Sources

BUREAU OF INVESTIGATION & DEPARTMENT OF JUSTICE FILES

Reports of Agents T.F. Weiss & James G. Findlay, Bureau of Investigation (June–July 1921), Department of Justice General Records, Entry 112-B, Straight Numerical Files, #158260. available at https://www.proquest.com/archival-materials/riots-tulsa-oklahoma/docview/2627199297/se-2?accountid=14740

Case File BS 202600-2253: The Tulsa Massacre, Federal Bureau of Investigation, Bureau Section Files (1921), available at https://www.proquest.com/docview/2587282298?sourcetype=Archival%20Materials

Department of Justice Correspondence File (June 1, 1921–July 31, 1921), Department of Justice Classified Subject Files on Civil Rights (1914–1949), Department of Justice General Records, Entry 112-B, Straight Numerical Files No. 158260, available at https://www.proquest.com/docview/2627198766?sourcetype=Archival%20Materials

Letter of Redmond S. Cole to U.S. Department of Justice Official J.G. Findlay (June 6, 1921), M290, Folder 1, Box 12, Redmond S. Cole Collection, Western History Collections, University of Oklahoma [1]

COMMISSION REPORT

DANNEY GOBLE ET AL., TULSA RACE RIOT: A REPORT BY THE OKLAHOMA COMMISSION TO STUDY THE TULSA RACE RIOT OF 1921 (Feb. 2001), https://www.okhistory.org/research/forms/freport.pdf, including the following scholarly essays in the report:

- *Final Report of the Oklahoma Commission to Study the Tulsa Race Riot of 1921*
- Don Ross, *Prologue*
- John Hope Franklin and Scott Ellsworth, *History Knows No Fences: An Overview*
- Scott Ellsworth, *The Tulsa Race Riot*
- Richard Warner, *Airplanes and the Riot*
- Clyde Snow, *Confirmed Deaths: A Preliminary Report*
- Robert Brooks and Alan H. Witten, *The Investigation of Potential Mass Grave Locations for the Tulsa Race Riot*
- Lesley Rankin-Hill and Phoebe Stubblefield, *History Uncovered: Skeletal Remains as a Vehicle to the Past*

---

[1] Thanks to Randall Hopkins for providing this letter.

- Larry O'Dell, *Riot Property Loss*
- Alfred Brophy, *Assessing State and City Culpability: The Riot and the Law*
- *Chronological Maps of the Tulsa Race Riot*

PRIMARY SOURCE MATERIALS

A. Report from American Red Cross

AMERICAN RED CROSS, REPORT: TULSA RACE RIOT DISASTER RELIEF (Loula Watkins, comp.), Tulsa Historical Society & Museum, Accession No. 1984.002.060, https://ppolinks.com/tulsahistory/1984_002_060_pdf.pdf

B. National Guard Reports[2]

Report of Major Jas. A. Bell (July 2, 1921)

Report of Major M.C. Paul R. Brown (July 1, 1921)

Report of Major C. W. Daley (July 6, 1921)

Report of Lieut. Roy R. Dunlap (July 1, 1921)

Report of Major Byron Kirkpatrick (July 1, 1921)

Report of Capt. John W. McCurn B Co 3d Inf. (undated)

Report of L.J.F. Rooney, Lieut. Col. 3rd Infantry and Chas. W. Daley, Inspector General's Dept. (June 3, 1921)

Report of Lt. Col. L.J.F. Rooney (July 29, 1921)

Report of Frank Van Voorhis, Capt. Com. Service (July 30, 1921)

C. Grand Jury Investigation of John A. Gustafson, Tulsa Police Chief

Oklahoma v. Gustafson, No. 10537 (Okl. Dist. 1921), collected by Okla. Dept. of Libraries, Okla. State Archives Division, RG 1-2, Case No. 1062, https://digitalprairie.ok.gov/digital/collection/race-riot/search/searchterm/1062%20Gustafson

D. Ku Klux Klan Materials[3]

Including:

- Form K-115, Application for Citizenship in the Invisible Empire, Knights of the Ku Klux Klan (1920s)
- Constitution of the Women of the Ku Klux Klan (June 2, 1923)
- Form K-114, List of Klan Supplies

---

[2] Thanks to Eric Miller, Greta Smith-Wisnewski, and Damario Soloman Simmons for providing this information, some of which was also found in the McFarlin Library Special Collection.

[3] Available from the McFarlin Library Special Collections at the University of Tulsa.

- Kloran: Knights Kamellia [Primary Order of Knighthood] (1925) (pamphlet)
- Klankraft Card of L.J. Boll (1926)
- Letter to Klansmen from Imperial Wizard (Jan. 18, 1928)
- *KKK Membership Roster, Honorary Members 1928 Dues Issued*, Vols. 1 & 2
- Alvia O. DeRee, *The Bright Fiery Cross: Our Song*
- Why You Should Become a Klansman (pamphlet)

E.   Other Primary Sources[4]

Including:

- Tulsa, Okla., Ordinance No. 1547 (Aug. 4, 1915)
- Anti-Segregation Petition (Tulsa, 1916)
- W.E.B. Du Bois, *Returning Soldiers*, 18 CRISIS: A RECORD OF THE DARKER RACES 7, 13-14 (May 1919)
- Tulsa Board of Commissioners Meeting Minutes (June 7, 1921)
- Tulsa Chamber of Commerce Meeting Minutes (June-July 1921)*
- Letter to the Governor of Oklahoma from T.W. Bell, et al. (June 20, 1921)*
- Letter to Governor J.B.A. Robertson from Chas. F. Barrett (July 2, 1921)*
- *National Association for the Advancement of Colored People*, 22 CRISIS: A RECORD OF THE DARKER RACES 113 (July 1921)
- G.A. Gregg, *Tulsa Then and Now*, Oklahoma YMCA (undated; included in letter to Department of Justice dated June 9, 1921)
- Tulsa Chamber of Commerce, *The Riot—Cause and Effect*, 6 TULSA SPIRIT 4 (July 1921), https://lib.utulsa.edu/speccoll/collections/1990.002_KennedyScrapbook/1900-002-1p18.pdf
- Brig. General Chars F. Barrett, Field Order No. 4 (June 1921), *in* ROBERT N. HOWER, 1921 RACE RIOT AND THE AMERICAN RED CROSS: ANGELS OF MERCY 130 (Homestead Press 1993)
- Maurice Williams, *Personal Account of the 1921 Tulsa Race Riot*, reprinted in ROBERT N. HOWER, 1921 RACE RIOT AND THE AMERICAN RED CROSS: ANGELS OF MERCY 115 (Homestead Press 1993)
- Account of J.W. Hughes, collected by the Red Cross and reprinted in ROBERT N. HOWER, 1921 RACE RIOT AND THE AMERICAN RED CROSS: ANGELS OF MERCY 115 (Homestead Press 1993)
- Letter from Edward Stuart, Director, Disaster Relief Service to W. Frank Persons, Vice Chairman, American Red Cross (October 15, 1921)
- Image of Identification Card, Tulsa Historical Society & Museum, https://tulsahistory.pastperfectonline.com/media/AD47603E-142D-439B-BCA0-115209300740

---

[4] Documents denoted with an asterisk are available from the McFarlin Library Special Collections at the University of Tulsa.

- TWELFTH ANNUAL REPORT OF THE NATIONAL ASSOCIATION FOR THE ADVANCEMENT OF COLORED PEOPLE FOR THE YEAR 1921 (Jan. 1922)
- Stanley Frost, *The Night-Riding Reformers: The Regeneration of Oklahoma*, OUTLOOK (Nov. 14, 1923), https://www.unz.com/PDF/PERIODICAL/Outlook-1923nov14/10-13/
- Walter White, *I Investigate Lynchings*, 16 AM. MERCURY 77 (Jan. 1929), https://nationalhumanitiescenter.org/pds/maai3/segregation/text2/investigatelynchings.pdf
- Tulsa, Okla., Ordinance No. 9708 (July 16, 1963)
- Tate Brady Scrapbook (collection of news articles provided to DOJ by citizen)

LEGAL PROCEEDINGS

A.   Recent Legal Proceedings

Randle v. City of Tulsa, 556 P.3d 612, *reh'g denied* (Sept. 9, 2024)

Randle v. City of Tulsa, No. CV-2020-1179, 2022 WL 17819260, at *1 (Okl. Dist. Aug. 3, 2022)

Randle v. City of Tulsa, No. CV-2020-1179, 2022 WL 22861061 (Okl. Dist. Sept. 2, 2022) (Second Amended Petition), https://www.justiceforgreenwood.org/wp-content/uploads/2022/10/2022-09-02._Second_Amended_Petition.pdf

Alexander v. Oklahoma, 382 F.3d 1206 (10th Cir. 2004)

B.   Historic Legal Proceedings

1.   Published Opinions and Related Documents

Redfearn v. Am. Cent. Ins. Co., 243 P. 929 (Okla. 1926)

Deposition of Green E. Smith, *Redfearn vs. Am. Cent. Ins. Co.*, No. 15,851 (Okl. Sup. Ct. Jan 9, 1925), as appended to Plaintiff's Brief, *Stradford v. Am. Cent. Ins. Co.*, No. 370274 (Sup. Ct. Cook County, Ill.)

Brief of Plaintiff in Error, *Redfearn vs. Am. Cent. Ins. Co.*, No. 15,851, 243 P. 929 (Okla. 1926)

2. Case Documents Available from Tulsa University Law School[5] and the Tulsa Historical Society[6]

- *Mabel Allen v. Cont'l Ins. Co.*
- *Amanda Durham v. Aetna Ins. Co. of Hartford*
- *Sarah E. Mann v. Cont'l Ins. Co.*
- *J. D. Mann v. Cont'l Ins. Co.*
- *J. D. Mann ex rel. P. P. Mann v. Cont'l Ins. Co.*
- *J. L. Northington v. Westchester Fire Ins. Co. of New York*

---

[5] Thanks to Tulsa University Law School and its Dean Oren Griffin, as well as to author Victor Luckerson, who originally compiled this list.
[6] Documents collected by the Tulsa Historical Society are denoted with an asterisk and available at https://tulsahistory.pastperfectonline.com/archive/09CDE527-F1C6-4BAC-B895-055162216370.

- *Mary E. Titus v. Westchester Fire Ins. Co. of New York*
- *(Mrs.) Susie C. Spears v. Cont'l Ins. Co.*
- *Dr. B.A. Waynes & M.C. Waynes v. Nat'l Fire Ins. Co. of Hartford*
- *A. Vernon v. Cont'l Ins. Co.*
- *T. L. Jasper v. Nat'l Union Fire Ins. Co. of Pittsburg*
- *Hope Watson v. Great Am. Ins. Co.*
- *Emma Gurley, Farm & Home Savings & Loan Ass'n v. Hartford Fire Ins. Co.*
- *Emma Gurley v. Commonwealth Ins. Co. of New York*
- *Emma Gurley, Farm & Home Savings & Loan Ass'n v. Orient Ins. Co.*
- *Lillie Shobe v. Westchester Fire Ins. Co.*
- *W. F. Carter v. Nat'l Fire Ins. Co. Columbia Fire Underwriters*
- *W. B. McLeod v. Nat'l Union Fire Ins. Co., of Pittsburg*
- *Osborn Monroe v. The Mercantile Ins. Co. of Am.*
- *Osborn Monroe v. North Am. Assurance Co.*
- *Osborn Monroe v. Mechanics & Traders Ins. Co. of New Orleans*
- *Mary V. Howard v. Glens Falls Ins. Co.*
- *Mary V. Howard v. Columbia Underwriters of the Nat'l Fire Ins. Co. of Hartford*
- *T. J. Elliott & S.D. Hooker v. Fire Ass'n. of Philadelphia*
- *T. J. Elliott & S.D. Hooker v. Union Ins. Co.*
- *T. J. Elliott & S.D. Hooker v. Liverpool & London & Globe Ins. Co.*
- *J. Tyler Smith v. Cont'l Ins. Co.*
- *J. Tyler Smith v. Am. Cent. Ins. Co.*
- *J.J. McKeever & & Myrtle McKeever v. Star Ins. Co. of America*
- *Anderson Williams v. Fire Ass'n of Philadelphia*
- *Mrs. M. L. Lynch v. Columbia Underwriters of the Nat'l Fire Ins. Co. of Hartford*
- *Felix Irvin v. Mechanics & Traders Ins. Co. of New Orleans*
- *C. W. Drummond v. Columbia Underwriters of the Nat'l Fire Ins. Co., of Hartford*
- *H. D. Earl v. North River Ins. Co. of New York*
- *Trustees of Brown C. M. E. Church v. Nat'l Fire Ins. Co. of Hartford*
- *W. M. Curry v. Ins. Co. of North America*
- *H. J. Caver v. Columbia Underwriters of the Nat'l Fire Ins. Co., of Hartford*
- *R. D. Holloway v. Westchester Fire Ins. Co. of New York*
- *A. L. Young v. Glens Falls Ins. Co.*
- *Mary & Elmore Hill v. Aetna Ins. Co. of Hartford*
- *E. I. Saddler v. Nat'l Fire Ins. Co. of Hartford*
- *E. I. Saddler v. Glens Falls Ins. Co.*
- *E. A. Loupe v. Nat'l Fire Ins. Co. of Hartford*
- *A. L. Phillips v. Reliance Fire Ins. Co., of Pema*

- *A. L. Phillips v. Security Fire Ins. Co. of New Haven*
- *W. A. Baker & Sarah Baker v. Fire Ass'n of Philadelphia*
- *W. A. Baker v. Fire Ass'n of Philadelphia*
- *J. L. Donohoe v. London Assurance Co.*
- *J. L. Donohoe v. Patriotic Assurance Co.*
- *Augustus Hicks v. Nat'l Fire Ins. Co. of Hartford*
- *Mrs. J. H. Wells v. Nat'l Fire Ins. Co., Columbia Fire Underwriters*
- *Mazie Singleton v. Palatine Ins. Co. of London*
- *Emma Washington v. Nat'l Fire Ins. Co. of Hartford*
- *J. H. White v. Nat'l Fire Ins. Co. of Hartford & Columbia Underwriter Agcy. of Omaha*
- *Polly Curtis & Elmira Woods v. Mechanics & Traders Ins. Co. of New Orleans*
- *A. C. Brooks v. Nat'l Fire Ins. Co. of Hartford*
- *Lillie Shobe v. Continental Ins. Co.*
- *Virgil Rowe v. Westchester Fire Ins. Co. of New York*
- *Virgil Rowe v. American Eagle Ins. Co.*
- *Virgil Rowe v. New York Underwriters*
- *William Redfearn v. American Cent. Ins Co.*
- *W. T. Brady v. Nat'l Fire Ins Co.*
- *A. W. Brown v. Ins. Co. of North America, Fire Ass'n of Philadelphia, Oklahoma Savings & Loan Co.*
- *I. J. Buck v. Ins. Co. of Pennsylvania*
- *I. J. Buck v. Scottish Union and Nat'l Ins. Co. of Edinburg*
- *I. J. Buck v. Phoenix Assurance Co.*
- *T. J. Elliott & S. D. Hooker v. Star Ins. Co. of America*
- *Willliam Kyle v. Palatine Ins. Co. of London*
- *Dr. P. S. Thompson v. Imperial Assurance Co.*
- *Dr. P. S. Thompson v. Palatine Ins. Co. of London*
- *W. M. Garrison & Sophia Garrison v. Nat'l Fire Ins. Co. of Hartford*
- *D. L. Whitlow v. Nat'l Fire Ins. Co. & Columbia Fire Underwriters*
- *S. M. Jackson v. Camden Fire Ins. Ass'n*
- *Ransom Burk v. Nat'l Fire Ins. Co. of Hartford*
- *J. H. Goodwin & C. M. Goodwin v. Camden Fire Ins. Ass'n*
- *C. M. Goodwin v. Camden Fire Ins. Ass'n*
- *J. H. Goodwin v. Ins. Co. of North America Fire Ass'n of Philadelphia*
- *Link Hollingsworth v. Nat'l Fire Ins. Co.*
- *J. S. Gist & Mary A. Gist v. California Ins. Co.*
- *Caroline Lollis v. Westchester Fire Ins. Co. of New York*
- *J. M. Keys v. Star Ins. Co.*

- *J. H. Rollerson v. Nat'l Union Fire Ins. Co.*
- *Frank Payne v. Nat'l Fire Ins. Co.*
- *S. F. Smart v. Glens Falls Ins. Co.*
- *A. F. Bryant v. Columbia Ins. Co.*
- *A. F. Bryant v. Fire Ass'n of Pennsylvania*
- *C. L. Netherland v. Hartford Fire Ins. Co.*
- *Loula T. Williams v. Central States Fire Ins. Co.*
- *Loula T. Williams v. London, Liverpool & Globe Ins. Co.*
- *Loula T. Williams v. Fire Ass'n of Philadelphia*
- *Jennie M. Wilson v. Aetna Ins. Co. of Hartford*
- *Jennie M. Wilson v. Star Ins. Co. of America*
- *Jennie M. Wilson v. Fire Ass'n of Philadelphia*
- *C. R. Earl v. North River Ins. Co. of New York*
- *Sam Mackley v. Mechanics & Traders Ins. Co. of New Orleans*
- *C. D. Brown v. City of Tulsa*
- *C. L. Netherland v. City of Tulsa*
- *S. F. Smart v. City of Tulsa*
- *J. E. Hardy v. City of Tulsa*
- *Will Robertson v. City of Tulsa*
- *John R. Bell v. City of Tulsa*
- *Virgil Rowe v. City of Tulsa, Oklahoma*
- *William Redfearn v. City of Tulsa*
- *E. J. H. Bryant v. City of Tulsa, et al.*
- *A. L. Stovall v. City of Tulsa*
- *T. E. Hughes v. City of Tulsa*
- *King Ingram v. City of Tulsa*
- *George Hardy v. City of Tulsa*
- *J. Tyler Smith v. City of Tulsa*
- *Elliott and Hooker v. City of Tulsa*
- *Ruth Calhoun v. City of Tulsa*
- *Stalie Webb v. City of Tulsa*
- *Mary E. Titus v. T. D. Evans*
- *Emmett Johnson v. City of Tulsa*
- *Rev. J.R. McClain v. City of Tulsa*
- *E. I. Saddler v. City of Tulsa.*
- *B. A. Waynes v. City of Tulsa*
- *Jack Scott v. City of Tulsa*
- *Caroline Lollis v. City of Tulsa*

7

- *G. W. Walker v. City of Tulsa*
- *Emma Ramsey v. City of Tulsa*
- *Harrison Magill v. City of Tulsa*
- *Barney Cleaver v. City of Tulsa*
- *Cora M. Leamus v. City of Tulsa*
- *S. P. McCormick v. Margaret E. Sykes, Penn Mutual Life Ins. Co., Gum Brothers Co. & City of Tulsa*
- *Thomas R. Gentry v. City of Tulsa*
- *Julia A. Jackson Ferguson v. City of Tulsa*
- *Lula T. Williams & J. W. Williams v. City of Tulsa*
- *W. P. Carter v. City of Tulsa*
- *William Walker v. City of Tulsa*
- *O. C. Mann v. City of Tulsa*
- *James A. & Fannie Johnson v. City of Tulsa*
- *A. L. Ferguson v. City of Tulsa*
- *Dr. J. M. Keys v. City of Tulsa*
- *Hosea Vaden v. City of Tulsa*
- *Ploto Travis v. City of Tulsa*
- *F. C. Smith v. City of Tulsa*
- *R. B. Holloway v. City of Tulsa*
- *Lucy Williams v. City of Tulsa*
- *Albert Vernon v. City of Tulsa*
- *Lula T. Williams v. City of Tulsa*
- *Lacy Little, ex rel. C. S. Little v. Nowata Oil & Refining Co., Seidenback's Inc., H. J. Lichtenstein*
- *Mrs. B. J. Sandredge v. City of Tulsa*
- *Sarah Andrews v. City of Tulsa*
- *Dave Wren v. City of Tulsa.*
- *D. L. Whitlow v. City of Tulsa*
- *Sam Mackey & Lucy Mackey v. City of Tulsa*
- *Henry T. Wilson v. City of Tulsa*
- *J. D. Mann v. City of Tulsa*
- *Robt. A. Bobo v. City of Tulsa*
- *Dr. A. F. Bryant v. City of Tulsa*
- *Ed White v. City of Tulsa*
- *Louis Newman v. City of Tulsa*
- *William Kyle v. City of Tulsa*
- *Dora Wells Jones v. City of Tulsa*

- *B. R. Swinger v. City of Tulsa*
- *M. J. Lathon & Ellie Lathon v. T. D. Evans*
- *Horace Green v. City of Tulsa*
- *Shakespeare Johnson v. City of Tulsa*
- *P. J. Eldridge v. City of Tulsa*
- *Osborn Monroe v. City of Tulsa*
- *Mittie Robinson v. T. D. Evans*
- *Della Smith v. City of Tulsa*
- *E. W. Woods v. City of Tulsa*
- *J. L. Mosley v. City of Tulsa*
- *J. C. Stovall v. City of Tulsa*
- *R. W. Motley v. City of Tulsa*
- *Josh McDonald v. City of Tulsa*
- *Georgia Brown v. City of Tulsa*
- *Garfield Miles v. City of Tulsa*
- *Joan Watson v. City of Tulsa*
- *H. J. Caver v. City of Tulsa*
- *A. Williams v. City of Tulsa*
- *E. R. Brown v. T. D. Evans.*
- *E. W. Williams v. City of Tulsa*
- *Mrs. J. H. Goodwin [Carlie M. Goodwin] v. City of Tulsa,* * https://www.tulsahistory.org/wp-content/uploads/2018/11/Goodwin-Mrs.-J.H.-23368-Reduced-size.pdf
- *Annie Talley v. City of Tulsa,* * https://www.tulsahistory.org/wp-content/uploads/2018/11/Tally-Annie-23374-Reduced-size-1.pdf
- *Jackson Undertaking Co. v. City of Tulsa,* * https://www.tulsahistory.org/wp-content/uploads/2018/11/Jackson-Undertaking-Co-23371-Reduced-size.pdf
- *Birdie Lynch Farmer v. City of Tulsa,* * https://www.tulsahistory.org/wp-content/uploads/2018/11/Farmer-Birdie-Lynch-23367-Reduced-size.pdf
- *W. S. Holloway v. City of Tulsa,* * https://www.tulsahistory.org/wp-content/uploads/2018/11/Halloway-W.S.-23372-Reduced-size.pdf
- *P. S. Thompson v. T.D. Evans,* * https://www.tulsahistory.org/wp-content/uploads/2018/11/Thompson-P.S.-23375-Reduced-size.pdf
- *J. S. Gish v. T.D. Evans,* * https://www.tulsahistory.org/wp-content/uploads/2018/11/Gish-J.S.-23315-Reduced-size.pdf
- *Daisy Williams v. City of Tulsa,* * https://www.tulsahistory.org/wp-content/uploads/2018/11/Williams-Daisy-23360-Reduced-size.pdf
- *Jack Wren v. City of Tulsa,* * https://www.tulsahistory.org/wp-content/uploads/2018/11/Wren-Jack-23365-Reduced-size.pdf

- *J. W. Williams v. City of Tulsa,** https://www.tulsahistory.org/wp-content/uploads/2018/11/Williams-J.W.-23370-Reduced-size.pdf
- *Belle Harrison v. City of Tulsa,** https://www.tulsahistory.org/wp-content/uploads/2018/11/Harrison-Belle-23373-Reduced-size.pdf
- *N. L. Gilliam v. T.D. Evans,** https://www.tulsahistory.org/wp-content/uploads/2018/11/Gilliam-N.L.-23312-Reduced-size.pdf
- *Edith Patterson v. City of Tulsa,** https://www.tulsahistory.org/wp-content/uploads/2018/11/Patterson-Edith-23363-Reduced-size.pdf
- *P.W. Ross v. City of Tulsa,** https://www.tulsahistory.org/wp-content/uploads/2018/11/Ross-P.W.-23362-Reduced-size.pdf
- *Esther Henry v. City of Tulsa,** https://www.tulsahistory.org/wp-content/uploads/2018/11/Henry-Esther-23366-Reduced-size.pdf
- *Joe Lockard v. T.D. Evans,** https://www.tulsahistory.org/wp-content/uploads/2018/11/Lockard-Joe-15730-Reduced-size.pdf
- *Jennie M. Wilson v. City of Tulsa,** https://www.tulsahistory.org/wp-content/uploads/2018/11/Wilson-Jennie-M.-23364-Reduced-size.pdf
- *H. Watson v. City of Tulsa,** https://www.tulsahistory.org/wp-content/uploads/2018/11/Watson-H.-23361-Reduced-size.pdf

SECONDARY SOURCES

A.   Books

CHIEF EGUNWALE AMUSAN, AMERICA'S BLACK WALL STREET (The Real Black Wall Street Tour, 2023)

ALFRED L. BROPHY, RECONSTRUCTING THE DREAMLAND: THE TULSA RIOT OF 1921—RACE, REPARATIONS, AND RECONCILIATION (Oxford University Press, 2002)

SCOTT ELLSWORTH, DEATH IN A PROMISED LAND: THE TULSA RACE RIOT OF 1921 (LSU Press, 1982)

SCOTT ELLSWORTH, THE GROUND BREAKING: THE TULSA RACE MASSACRE AND AN AMERICAN CITY'S SEARCH FOR JUSTICE (Dutton, 2022)

BUCK COLBERT FRANKLIN, MY LIFE AND AN ERA: THE AUTOBIOGRAPHY OF BUCK COLBERT FRANKLIN (John Hope Franklin & John Whittington Franklin, eds., LSU Press, 1997)

EDDIE FAYE GATES, RIOT ON GREENWOOD: THE TOTAL DESTRUCTION OF BLACK WALL STREET (Eakin Press, 2003)

RUDIA M. HALLIBURTON, JR., THE TULSA RACE WAR OF 1921 (R & E Research Associates, 1975)

KARLOS K. HILL, THE 1921 TULSA RACE MASSACRE: A PHOTOGRAPHIC HISTORY (University of

Oklahoma Press, 2021)

JAMES S. HIRSCH, RIOT AND REMEMBRANCE: THE TULSA RACE MASSACRE AND ITS LEGACY (Second Mariner Books, 2021)

ROBERT N. HOWER, 1921 RACE RIOT AND THE AMERICAN RED CROSS: ANGELS OF MERCY (Homestead Press 1993)

HANNIBAL B. JOHNSON, TULSA'S HISTORIC GREENWOOD DISTRICT (Arcadia, 2014)

HANNIBAL B. JOHNSON, BLACK WALL STREET 100 (Eakin, 2020)

RANDY KREHBIEL, TULSA 1921: REPORTING A MASSACRE (U. Okla. Press, 2021)

VICTOR LUCKERSON, BUILT FROM THE FIRE (Random House, 2023)

TIM MADIGAN, THE BURNING (St. Martin's Griffin, 100th Anniversary Ed., 2021)

WILLIAM M. O'BRIEN, WHO SPEAKS FOR US? (2002)

WILLIAM "CHOC" PHILLIPS, MURDER IN THE STREETS: A WHITE CHOCTAW WITNESS TO THE 1921 TULSA RACE MASSACRE (Eakin Press, 2021)

THOMAS E. WRIGHT, ET AL., REPORT OF THE 1898 WILMINGTON RACE RIOT COMMISSION (May 31, 2006)

DAVID ZUCCHINO, WILMINGTON'S LIE: THE MURDEROUS COUP OF 1898 AND THE RISE OF WHITE SUPREMACY (Atlantic Monthly Press, 2020)

B.   Articles

Alex Albright et al., *After the Burning: The Economic Effects of the 1921 Tulsa Race Massacre*, NAT'L BUREAU OF ECON. RSCH. (July 2021), https://www.nber.org/papers/w28985

Alina Ball, *Lost in the Fire: Reflections on the Tulsa Race Massacre Centennial*, 49 HASTINGS CONST. L.Q. 216, 231 (2022)

Biography of Redmond S. Cole - Redmond Selecman Cole Collection, University Libraries of the University of Oklahoma, https://archives.libraries.ou.edu/repositories/2/resources/7969 (last visited Dec. 20, 2024)

Aldrich Blake, *The Ku Klux Kraze: A Lecture* (1924), https://archive.org/details/1924BlakeKKK/mode/2up

Alfred L. Brophy, *The Tulsa Race Riot of 1921 in the Oklahoma Supreme Court*, 54 OKLA. L. REV. 67 (2001)

Archiebald Browne, *Oklahoma's historic all-black towns: Built on hope, survived by pride*, NONDOC.COM (July 25, 2019), https://nondoc.com/2019/07/25/oklahoma-historic-all-black-towns/

Elizabeth M. Burton, *Tulsa Wealth Disparity: The Political Legacy of the 1921 Race Massacre* (2021) (Political Science Honors Projects, Macalester College), https://digitalcommons.macalester.edu/poli_honors/91

DeNeen L. Brown, *Red Summer: When Racist Mobs Ruled*, PBS: AM. EXPERIENCE (Feb. 4, 2021), https://www.pbs.org/wgbh/americanexperience/features/t-town-red-summer-racist-mobs/

DeNeen L. Brown, *They Was Killing Black People*, WASH. POST (Sept. 28, 2018), https://www.washingtonpost.com/news/local/wp/2018/09/28/feature/they-was-killing-black-people/

Jami L. Bryan, *Fighting For Respect: African-American Soldiers in WWI*, ARMY HIST. FOUND., https://armyhistory.org/fighting-for-respect-african-american-soldiers-in-wwi/

Kweku Larry Crowe & Thabiti Lewis, *The 1921 Tulsa Massacre: What Happened to Black Wall Street*, MAG. OF THE NAT. ENDOWMENT FOR THE HUMANITIES (Winter 2021), https://www.neh.gov/article/1921-tulsa-massacre

Natalie Chang, *The Massacre of Black Wall Street*, ATLANTIC.COM (Nov. 23, 2019), https://www.theatlantic.com/sponsored/hbo-2019/the-massacre-of-black-wall-street/3217/

Lee Roy Chapman, *The Nightmare of Dreamland*, THIS LAND PRESS (April 18, 2012), https://thislandpress.com/2012/04/18/tate-brady-battle-greenwood/

Nicole Chavez, *Rosewood, Florida, marks 100 years since race massacre. Here's what happened*, CNN (Jan. 8, 2023), https://www.cnn.com/2023/01/08/us/rosewood-massacre-florida-what-happened-reaj/index.html

Russell Cobb, *'No apology': Richard Lloyd Jones and the 1921 Race Massacre*, TULSAPEOPLE (Feb. 20, 2019), https://www.tulsapeople.com/no-apology/article_d76c97dd-6154-56bc-8d92-4c8a9139a7a4.html

Russell Cobb, *Shifting Collective Memory in Tulsa*, N.Y. TIMES (Feb. 11, 2020), https://www.nytimes.com/2020/02/11/opinion/tulsa-race-massacre.html

Connie Crowley, *That Ugly Day in May*, OKLA. MONTHLY, Aug. 1976, at 30

William A. Darity, Jr. et al., *Racial Disparities in Family Income, Assets, and Liabilities: A Century After the 1921 Tulsa Massacre*, J. FAM. & ECON. ISSUES 45:256–275 (2024)

William A. Darity, Jr. et al., *The Cumulative Costs of Racism and the Bill for Black Reparations*, 36:2 J. ECON. PERSP. 99 (Spring 2022)

Sarah Dewberry, *Victim of 1921 Tulsa Race Massacre identified through DNA genealogy as WWI veteran*, CNN (July 12, 2024), https://edition.cnn.com/2024/07/12/us/tusla-race-massacre-victim-identified-reaj/index.html

Pete Earley, *The Untold Story of One of America's Worst Race Riots*, WASH. POST (Sept. 12, 1982), https://www.washingtonpost.com/archive/opinions/1982/09/12/the-untold-story-of-one-of-americas-worst-race-riots/e37fc963-71dd-45cc-8cb0-04ab8032bcd2/

The East St. Louis Riot, PBS: AM. EXPERIENCE, https://www.pbs.org/wgbh/americanexperience/features/garvey-riot/ (last visited Dec. 4, 2024)

Kimberly C. Ellis, *We Look Like Men of War: Africana Male Narratives and the Tulsa Race Riot, War and Massacre of 1921* (2002) (Ph.D. dissertation, Purdue University) (ProQuest)

Nicquel Terry Ellis, *A Tulsa Race Massacre victim was recently ID'd as a World War I veteran*, CNN (Nov. 17, 2024), https://edition.cnn.com/2024/11/17/us/cl-daniel-tulsa-memorial/index.html

Scott Ellsworth, et. al., *The Long Shadow: The Tulsa Race Massacre a Century Later (An Interview with Scott Ellsworth)*, 54 CONN. L. REV. 907 (2022)

Julia Forrester-Sellers, *The 1921 Tulsa Race Riot and the Politics of Memory* (2000) (Master's Thesis, Oklahoma University of Tulsa) (ProQuest)

Trevion Freeman, *For Freedmens Sake: The Story of the Native Blacks of the Muscogee Nation and Their Fight for Citizenship Post-McGirt*, 57 TULSA L. REV. 513, 525–26 (2022)

Megan Gannon, *Unearthing the True Toll of the Tulsa Race Massacre*, SAPIENS (May 22, 2020), https://www.sapiens.org/archaeology/tulsa-race-massacre/

Loren Gill, *The Tulsa Race Riot* (Master's Thesis, University of Tulsa) (1946) (ProQuest)

Nellie Gilles & Mycah Hazel, *Radio Diaries: Harry Pace and the Rise and Fall of Black Swan Records*, NPR: ALL THINGS CONSIDERED (July 1, 2021), https://www.npr.org/2021/06/30/1011901555/radio-diaries-harry-pace-and-the-rise-and-fall-of-black-swan-records

Roger Guillemette, *Stinton Aircraft Corporation*, U.S. CENTENNIAL OF FLIGHT COMM., https://www.centennialofflight.net/essay/GENERAL_AVIATION/stinson/GA2.htm (last visited Dec. 9. 2020)

David Hedrick, *Early American Fire Alarm Systems*, FFAM (Sept. 17, 2022), https://www.ffam.org/early-american-fire-alarm-systems/?hilite=early+american+fire+alarm+systems

Karlos K. Hill, *Where Did Images of the Tulsa Race Massacre Come From?*, PBS: AM. EXPERIENCE (May 27, 2021), https://www.pbs.org/wgbh/americanexperience/features/t-town-tulsa-race-massacre-photographs/

A History of Racial Injustice Calendar, EQUAL JUST. INITIATIVE, https://calendar.eji.org/racial-injustice/may/24 (entry for May 24, 1911) (last visited Dec. 8, 2024)

Jesse J. Holland, *Hundreds of black deaths during 1919's Red Summer are being remembered*, PBS NEWS (July 23, 2019), https://www.pbs.org/newshour/nation/hundreds-of-black-deaths-during-1919s-red-summer-are-being-remembered

Randy Hopkins, *The Plot to Kill "Diamond Dick" Rowland and the Tulsa Race Riot*, 99 CHRON. OF OKLA. 4, 4-49 (Spring 2021)

Joseph E. Howell, *Noted, Notorious—Tulsan Recalls Sooners*, TULSA TRIB., Nov. 26, 1960, at 11

Robert M. Jarvis, *Remembering Isaiah: Attorney I.H. Spears and the 1921 Tulsa Race Massacre*, 57 TULSA L. REV. 429, 442 (2022)

The JN-4 Jenny: The Plane that Taught America to Fly, NAT. PARK SERV. (Feb. 2020), https://www.nps.gov/articles/jn-4.htm

Hannibal B. Johnson, *As 1921's Centennial Nears, There Is a Reason for Hope in Tulsa's Effort to Face its Painful History Positively*, TULSA DAILY WORLD (July 14, 2019), https://tulsaworld.com/opinion/columnists/hannibal-b-johnson-as-1921s-centennial-nears-there-is-a-reason-for-hope-in-tulsas/article_cd12f4bb-a14a-588d-a971-0a3844dda530.html

Allison Keyes, *A Long-Lost Manuscript Contains a Searing Eyewitness Account of the Tulsa Race Massacre of 1921*, SMITHSONIAN MAG. (May 2016), https://www.smithsonianmag.com/smithsonian-institution/long-lost-manuscript-contains-searing-eyewitness-account-tulsa-race-massacre-1921-180959251/

Allison Keyes, *The East St. Louis Race Riot Left Dozens Dead, Devastating a Community on the Rise*, SMITHSONIAN MAG. (June 30, 2017), https://www.smithsonianmag.com/smithsonian-institution/east-st-louis-race-riot-left-dozens-dead-devastating-community-on-the-rise-180963885/

Randy Krehbiel, *1921 Race Riot: Tribune Mystery Unsolved*, TULSA DAILY WORLD (May 31, 2002), https://tulsaworld.com/archives/race-riot-tribune-mystery-unsolved/article_81f8ac0b-01bd-56a8-97ba-851961c400be.html

Victor Luckerson, *The Promise of Oklahoma*, SMITHSONIAN MAG. (April 2021), https://www.smithsonianmag.com/history/unrealized-promise-oklahoma-180977174/

Lynchings: By State and Race, 1882-1968, ARCHIVES AT TUSKEGEE INSTITUTE (Nov. 2020), https://archive.tuskegee.edu/repository/wp-content/uploads/2020/11/Lynchings-Stats-Year-Dates-Causes.pdf

Lynching in America: Racial Terror Lynchings (Map), EQUAL JUST. INITIATIVE, https://lynchinginamerica.eji.org/explore (last visited Dec. 4, 2024)

Joshua D. Mackey, *Breaking a Century of Silence: A Historiography of the Tulsa Race Riot*, 19 FAIRMOUNT FOLIO: J. OF HIST. 49, 49-61 (May 13, 2019), https://journals.wichita.edu/index.php/ff/article/view/228/220

Suzette M. Malveaux, *A Taxonomy of Silencing: The Law's 100-Year Suppression of the Tulsa Race Massacre*, 102 B.U. L. REV. 2173 (2022), https://www.bu.edu/bulawreview/files/2023/02/MALVEAUX.pdf

Brandy McDonnell, *Tulsa Race Massacre to be examined on Sunday's '60 Minutes,'* THE OKLAHOMAN (June 13, 2020), https://www.oklahoman.com/story/entertainment/columns/brandy-mcdonnell/2020/06/13/tulsa-race-massacre-to-be-examined-on-sundays-60-minutes/60396299007/'

Christopher M. Messer, *The Tulsa Race Riot of 1921: Determining its Causes and Framing* (2003) (Ph.D. dissertation, Oklahoma State University) (ProQuest)

Charles Oquin Meyers, Jr., *The Ku Klux Klan in Tulsa County, Oklahoma During the Early 1920s* (1974) (Honor's Paper, Department of History, University of Tulsa)

Lindsay Myers, *The Continual Erasure of Greenwood*, NEW TULSA STAR (March 22, 2020), https://sarweb.org/wp-content/uploads/2021/01/The-Continual-Erasure-of-Greenwood-%E2%80%93-Tulsa-Star.pdf

1921 Tulsa Race Riot - Reconnaissance Survey, NAT. PARK SER. (Nov. 2005), https://www.nps.gov/parkhistory/online_books/nnps/tulsa_riot.pdf

Robert D. Norris, Jr., *The Oklahoma National Guard and the Tulsa Race Riot of 1921: A Historical, Tactical and Legal Analysis* (2001), available at the University of Tulsa, McFarlin Library, Department of Special Collections & University Archives

Alicia Odewale, *New Efforts in Restorative Justice Archaeology: Tulsa, Oklahoma*, SOC'Y BLACK ARCHAEOLOGISTS NEWSLETTER (Jan. 13, 2020), https://sarweb.org/wp-content/uploads/2021/01/New-Efforts-in-Restorative-Justice-Archaeology-Tulsa-OK.pdf

Guy Harold Parkhurst, *Uses and Legal Questions of Martial Law in Oklahoma* (1955) (Ph.D. Dissertation, University of Oklahoma)

Ottawa W. Gurley: Visionary of Black Wall Street, CENTENNIAL TULSA PILGRIMAGE (2021), https://blackwallstreet.org/owgurley

Deborah Savage, *African American Soldiers in World War One*, LA. PUB. LIBR.: LAPL BLOG (Feb. 27, 2024), https://www.lapl.org/collections-resources/blogs/lapl/african-american-soldiers-world-war-one

Red Summer: The Race Riots of 1919, NAT. WWI MUSEUM & MEM'L., https://www.theworldwar.org/learn/about-wwi/red-summer

Rocket, Signal, World War I, NAT. AIR & SPACE MUSEUM, https://airandspace.si.edu/collection-objects/rocket-signal-world-war-i/nasm_A19960020000 (last visited Dec. 3, 2024)

Greta Katherine Smith, *"The Battling Ground": Memory, Violence, and Resistance in Greenwood, North Tulsa, Oklahoma, 1907-1980* (2018) (Master's Thesis, Portland State University)

Ryan P. Smith, *How Native American Slaveholders Complicate the Trail of Tears Narrative*, SMITHSONIAN MAG. (March 6, 2018), https://www.smithsonianmag.com/smithsonian-institution/how-native-american-slaveholders-complicate-trail-tears-narrative-180968339/

Brent Staples, *Unearthing a Riot*, N.Y. TIMES (Dec. 19, 1999), https://www.nytimes.com/1999/12/19/magazine/unearthing-a-riot.html

Kara W. Swanson, *The Tulsa Race Massacre of 1921: A Lesson in the Law of Trespass*, 54 CONN. L. REV. 1005 (2022)

Marjorie A. Tracy, *The Tulsa Race Riot of 1921: The Politics of Lawlessness* (1996) (Master's Thesis, University of Tulsa) (ProQuest)

Transportation (1850-1945), TULSA PRES. COMM'N, https://tulsapreservationcommission.org/resources/tulsa-history/transportation/ (last visited Dec. 4, 2024)

Tulsa City-County Library, *Tulsa-Area FAQs*, https://www.tulsalibrary.org/research/government/tulsa-area-faqs (last visited Dec. 4, 2024)

Thomas Van Hare, *The Bombing of Tulsa*, HIST. WINGS (Feb. 27, 2017), https://fly.historicwings.com/2017/02/the-bombing-of-tulsa/

Michael K. Velchik & Jeffery Y. Zhang, *Restoring Indian Reservation Status: An Empirical Analysis*, 40 YALE J. ON REG. 339 (2023)

The Tulsa Race Massacre, OKLA. HIST. SOC'Y, https://www.okhistory.org/learn/trm1 (last visited Dec. 20, 2024)

Tulsa Race War, OKLA. EAGLE, Nov. 2, 1978, at E1

Richard "Dick" Warner, *Computations as to the Deaths from the 1921 Tulsa Race Riot* (Jan. 10, 2000), Tulsa Historical Society & Museum, Accession No. 2006.126.001, https://ppolinks.com/tulsahistory/2006_126_001_pdf.pdf

Ed Wheeler, *Profile of a Race Riot*, OKLA. IMPACT MAG. (1971), https://www.si.edu/object/nmaahc_2011.60.18

History, Northern District of Oklahoma, DEPT. OF JUST. (June 26, 2024), https://www.justice.gov/usao-ndok/history

Victor Luckerson, *Black Wall Street: The African American Haven That Burned and Then Rose From the Ashes*, THE RINGER (June 28, 2018) https://www.theringer.com/2018/06/28/national-affairs/black-wall-street-oklahoma-greenwood-destruction-tulsa

C. Documentaries

DREAMLAND: The Burning of Black Wall Street (The SpringHill Co. for CNN Films 2021), https://www.imdb.com/title/tt13450602/

Tulsa Burning: The 1921 Race Massacre (The History Channel 2021), https://www.imdb.com/title/tt14252496/

Tulsa: The Fire and the Forgotten (Saybook Productions Ltd. for PBS 2021), https://www.imdb.com/title/tt14378152/

The Legacy of Black Wall Street (Trailblazer Studios 2021), https://www.imdb.com/title/tt14688474/

Rise Again: Tulsa and The Red Summer (Trilogy Films for National Geographic 2021), https://www.imdb.com/title/tt14673732/

D. Podcasts

American History Tellers: The Tulsa Race Massacre: Pt 1 – The Promised Land, WONDERY (May 29, 2019), https://wondery.com/shows/american-history-tellers/episode/5279-encore-tulsa-race-massacre-the-promised-land/

American History Tellers: The Tulsa Race Massacre: Pt 2 – The Powder Keg, WONDERY (June 5, 2019), https://wondery.com/shows/american-history-tellers/episode/5279-encore-tulsa-race-massacre-the-powder-keg/

American History Tellers: The Tulsa Race Massacre: Pt 3 – The Invasion, WONDERY (June 12, 2019), https://wondery.com/shows/american-history-tellers/episode/5279-encore-tulsa-race-massacre-the-invasion/

American History Tellers: The Tulsa Race Massacre: Pt 4 – Rebirth, WONDERY (June 19, 2019), https://wondery.com/shows/american-history-tellers/episode/5279-encore-tulsa-race-massacre-rebirth/

American History Tellers: The Tulsa Race Massacre: Pt 5 – Bearing Witness, WONDERY (June 26, 2019), https://wondery.com/shows/american-history-tellers/episode/5279-encore-tulsa-race-massacre-bearing-witness/

E.   Forensic Reports

Kary Stackelback & Phoebe Stubblefield, *Archaeological and Forensic Research in Support of the 1921 Tulsa Race Massacre Graves Investigation* (Mar. 2022), https://www.cityoftulsa.org/media/18119/sensitivecontentarchaeologicalandforensicresearchinsupportofthe1921tulsaracemassacreinvestigation.pdf

City of Tulsa, *1921 Graves Investigation*, https://www.cityoftulsa.org/1921graves

F.   Timelines

Chronological Maps of the Tulsa Race Riot, in TULSA RACE RIOT: A REPORT BY THE OKLAHOMA COMMISSION TO STUDY THE TULSA RACE RIOT OF 1921 (Feb. 2001), okhistory.org

I. Marc Carlson, *Timeline of the Tulsa Race Massacre*, https://www.jhfcenter.org/_files/ugd/9bd760_6869ca9a385646acbdaa125b7165bbc4.pdf (as posted on the John Hope Franklin Center for Reconciliation website)

Timeline: The 1921 Tulsa Race Massacre, TULSA WORLD (last updated May 29, 2021), https://tulsaworld.com/news/local/racemassacre/timeline-the-1921-tulsa-race-massacre/collection_1c02a7b4-86ce-11e8-b63d-c3bbb45d4a6c.html

Timeline: The Questions That Remain, TULSA WORLD (2009), https://www.tulsaworld.com/app/race-riot/timeline.html

PHOTOGRAPHIC EVIDENCE

Tulsa City-County Library Digital Collection, *1921 Tulsa Race Massacre*, https://digitalcollections.tulsalibrary.org/digital/collection/p15020coll6/search/page/1

Yuliya Parshina-Kottas et al., *What the Tulsa Race Massacre Destroyed*, N.Y. TIMES (May 24, 2021), https://www.nytimes.com/interactive/2021/05/24/us/tulsa-race-massacre.html

National Museum of African American History and Culture, *Remembering Tulsa Before the Massacre*, https://nmaahc.si.edu/explore/stories/remembering-tulsa-before-massacre

CONTEMPORANEOUS NEWS ARTICLES

A.   Tulsa Articles

- *Signal to Call Tulsa for Duty*, TULSA DAILY WORLD, Nov. 18, 1917, at 1

- *Grand Ball New Year's Eve Is Planned by Tulsa Home Guards to Raise Funds*, TULSA DAILY WORLD, Dec. 14, 1917, at 7
- *Tulsa Home Guards Are Imposing Company of Fighters*, TULSA DAILY WORLD, Feb. 17, 1918, at 42
- *Program*, TULSA DAILY WORLD, Sept. 25, 1918, at 39
- *Mob Rule and the Law*, TULSA STAR, March 6, 1920, at 8
- *Air Police Sworn in by Mayor*, TULSA TRIB., May 1, 1920, at 1
- *Make Tulsa Decent*, TULSA TRIB., May 13, 1921, at 24
- *30 Witnesses on Stand in Probe*, TULSA DAILY WORLD, May 21, 1921, at 17
- *Whites Advancing Into 'Little Africa'; Negro Death List Is About 15*, TULSA DAILY WORLD, June 1, 1921, at 1
- *Many Shots Are Fired in Clash at the Frisco*, TULSA TRIB., June 1, 1921, at 7
- *Many More Whites Are Shot*, TULSA DAILY WORLD, June 1, 1921, at 1
- *Negroes Fleeing from City: List of Dead Mounts*, TULSA DAILY WORLD, June 1, 1921, at 1
- *Scores Badly Wounded Removed to Hospitals; Three Die on the Way*, TULSA DAILY WORLD, June 1, 1921, at 1
- *Arrest of Young Negro on Statutory Charge Causes Battle Between the Races*, TULSA DAILY WORLD, June 1, 1921, at 1
- *Race War Rages for Hours After Outbreak at Courthouse; Troops and Armed Men Patrol[l]ing Streets*, TULSA DAILY WORLD, June 1, 1921, at 1
- *Fire Razes Black District; All Negros Interned as Guardmen Patrol City*, TULSA TRIB., June 1, 1921, at 1, 3
- *Seven Battles Rage During War of Races*, TULSA TRIB., June 1, 1921, at 5
- *Barrett Placed in Full Command, Governor Comes*, TULSA TRIB., June 1, 1921, at 1
- *Girl Attacked by Negro Not at Home Today*, TULSA TRIB., June 1, 1921, at 6
- *Civic Workers Care for Negroes Held in Concentration Camps*, TULSA TRIB., June 1, 1921, at 6
- *Trains Held Up; Negroes Ordered Off*, TULSA TRIB., June 1, 1921, at 6
- *Many Shots Are Fired in Clash at the Frisco*, TULSA TRIB., June 1, 1921, at 7
- *Fire Fighters Are Helpless; Flames Raging*, TULSA TRIB., June 1, 1921, at 8
- *Blacks Carry Belongings as They Vacate*, TULSA TRIB., June 1, 1921, at 8
- *Dick Rowland Is Spirited Out of City*, TULSA TRIB., June 1, 1921, at 8
- *Hundreds Flee to Country as Fighting Rages*, TULSA TRIB., June 1, 1921, at 10
- *Negroes Shuffle to Safe Retreat Hands Held High*, TULSA TRIB., June 1, 1921, at 11
- *Panic in Lobby of Hotel Tulsa When Negroes Cut Loose*, TULSA TRIB., June 1, 1921, at 11
- *Civic Club Plans Immediate Relief for All Negroes*, TULSA TRIB., June 1, 1921, at 11
- *Assistant Fire Chief First City Official Wounded*, TULSA TRIB., June 1, 1921, at 14
- *New Battle Now in Progress*, TULSA DAILY WORLD, June 1, 1921, at 1
- *Final Edition*, TULSA DAILY WORLD, June 1, 1921, at 1

- *The State in Action*, TULSA TRIB., June 2, 1921, at 1
- *Strict Martial Law Lifted*, TULSA TRIB., June 2, 1921, at 1
- *Martin Blames Riot to Lax City Hall Rule*, TULSA TRIB., June 2, 1921, at 1
- *Jury Inquiry Is Demanded by Governor*, TULSA TRIB., June 2, 1921, at 1
- *Search Cuts Known Death List to 27*, TULSA TRIB., June 2, 1921, at 1
- *Free Interned Negroes; Red Cross Is in Charge*, TULSA TRIB., June 2, 1921, at 1
- *Vandals Sack Burned Area of Valuables*, TULSA TRIB., June 2, 1921, at 2
- *Tulsa Closed Last Night by State Militia*, TULSA TRIB., June 2, 1921, at 2
- *The Injured*, TULSA TRIB., June 2, 1921, at 2
- *Negro Officer Is Heavy Loser in Race Riots*, TULSA TRIB., June 2, 1921, at 3
- *Air Observers Watched Blacks for the Police*, TULSA TRIB., June 2, 1921, at 3
- *Negro Finds $600 In Melted Gold in Ruins of His Home*, TULSA TRIB., June 2, 1921, at 3
- *5000 Negros Held in Fairground Camps*, TULSA DAILY WORLD, June 2, 1921, at 2
- *When Riot Stalked in Tulsa*, TULSA DAILY WORLD, June 2, 1921, at 7
- *No Graves Dug, Bodies of 18 Negroes Held*, TULSA TRIB., June 2, 1921, at 4
- *Niles Blames Lawlessness for Race War*, TULSA TRIB., June 2, 1921, at 4
- *Insurance Men Say Policies Won't Be Paid*, TULSA TRIB., June 2, 1921, at 4
- *Negroes From Tulsa Flee to Other Towns*, TULSA TRIB., June 2, 1921, at 5
- *The Disgrace of Tulsa*, TULSA DAILY WORLD, June 3, 1921, at 2
- *Agitators Were Cause of Riots: Propaganda Responsible for Ill Feeling Among Races Mouzon Says*, TULSA DAILY WORLD, June 3, 1921, at 2
- *Martial Law*, TULSA DAILY WORLD, June 3, 1921, at 4
- *Heavy Losses Sustained by Gun Store Men*, TULSA TRIB., June 3, 1921, at 4
- *Blacks Forced to Leave State They Declare*, TULSA TRIB., June 3, 1921, at 5
- *Realtors Start Task of Listing All Losses*, TULSA TRIB., June 3, 1921, at 11
- *Militia's Reign Brought to End*, TULSA DAILY WORLD, June 3, 1921, at 1
- *Plan to Move Negros into New District*, TULSA TRIB., June 3, 1921, at 1
- *City to Meet Demands Out of Its Own Purse*, TULSA TRIB., June 3, 1921, at 1
- *U.S. Orders Race Riot Inquiry*, TULSA TRIB., June 3, 1921, at 1
- *Governor to Lift Martial Law at Once*, TULSA TRIB., June 3, 1921, at 1
- *C. of C. Asks Martial Law Be Continued*, TULSA TRIB., June 3, 1921, at 1
- *Police Say They Knew of War Plans*, TULSA TRIB., June 3, 1921, at 1
- *Tulsa Will*, TULSA TRIB., June 3, 1921, at 20
- *Sheriff Says Telephone Call Started Riot*, TULSA TRIB., June 3, 1921, at 1
- *Police Seize 30 in Riot Wake*, TULSA TRIB., June 4, 1921, at 1
- *Blood Shed in Race War Will Cleanse Tulsa*, TULSA TRIB., June 4, 1921, at 1
- *One Held on Charge of Inciting Riot*, TULSA TRIB., June 4, 1921, at 1
- *Red Cross in Field Until All Are Well*, TULSA TRIB., June 4, 1921, at 1

- *Negro Tells How Others Mobilized*, TULSA TRIB., June 4, 1921, at 1
- *Red Cross to Spend Months Aiding Blacks*, TULSA TRIB., June 4, 1921, at 6
- *Hostess House for Negroes Is Being Erected*, TULSA TRIB., June 4, 1921, at 6
- *Jury Summons Being Issued for Riot Quiz*, TULSA TRIB., June 4, 1921, at 6
- *Sub-Station of Post Office Is Razed by Fire*, TULSA TRIB., June 4, 1921, at 6
- *It Must Not Be Again*, TULSA TRIB., June 4, 1921, at 8
- *Bad Ni**ers*, TULSA DAILY WORLD, June 4, 1921, at 4
- *Warning Against Further Trouble*, TULSA DAILY WORLD, June 4, 1921, at 1
- *Weapons Must Be Returned*, TULSA DAILY WORLD, June 4, 1921, at 3
- *Mob Held Back by Mayor Daley for Two Hours*, TULSA TRIB., June 5, 1921, at 7
- *Press Scolds Tulsa; Editors Blame Police*, TULSA TRIB., June 4, 1921, at 11
- *The End of Argonaut Days*, TULSA TRIB., June 4, 1921, at 18
- *Total Loss in Fire Is Fixed at $1,500,000*, TULSA DAILY WORLD, June 5, 1921, at 10
- *Mob Held Back by Major Daley for Two Hours*, TULSA TRIB., June 5, 1921, at 7
- *Mayor Warned of Uprising Negros*, TULSA TRIB., June 6, 1921, at 1
- *Race Riot in Tulsa*, STATE SENTINEL, June 6, 1921, at 1, 4
- *Black Agitators Blamed for Riot*, TULSA DAILY WORLD, June 6, 1921, at 1
- *Notice*, TULSA DAILY WORLD, June 7, 1921, at 2
- *Notice*, TULSA TRIB., June 7, 1921, at 1
- *Charges filed against 32*, TULSA TRIB., July 7, 1921, at 1
- *Police Order Idle Blacks to Fair Camp*, TULSA TRIB., June 7, 1921, at 4
- *City Is Not Liable, Says Legal Board*, TULSA TRIB., June 7, 1921, at 1
- *Negro Section Abolished by City's Order*, TULSA TRIB., June 7, 1921, at 1
- *All Blacks Must Wear Green Tags*, TULSA DAILY WORLD, June 7, 1921, at 9
- *Jury Probe of Riot Blocked; Inquiry Is On*, TULSA TRIB., June 8, 1921, at 1
- *Get a Green Card*, TULSA TRIB., June 8, 1921, at 13
- *White Dead Are Forgotten, Rev. Cooke Charges*, TULSA TRIB., June 9, 1921, at 11
- J.H. Welch, *Unquestionably So*, TULSA DAILY WORLD, June 9, 1921, at 4
- *All Idle Blacks to be Arrested by Zero Hour Tonight*, TULSA TRIB., June 10, 1921, at 1
- *Bye Bye Tulsa Is Song of Many Blacks Without Jobs Here*, TULSA TRIB., June 11, 1921, at 2
- *It Must Be Stopped*, TULSA TRIB., June 11, 1921, at 4
- *Black Camp at Fairgrounds Is Nearly Empty*, TULSA TRIB., June 12, 1921, at 13
- *Grand Jurors Probe Takes a New Angle*, TULSA TRIB., June 13, 1921, at 1
- *Public Welfare Board Vacated by Commission: Mayor in Statement on Race Trouble*, TULSA TRIB., June 14, 1921, at 2
- *Grand Jury Gives Report to Court*, TULSA DAILY WORLD, June 16, 1921, at 1
- *Propaganda of Negros Is Blamed*, TULSA TRIB., June 18, 1921, at 1
- *Finish the Job*, TULSA TRIB, June 23, 1921, at A19

- *Official Heads Named in Probe*, TULSA TRIB., June 25, 1921, at 1
- *M'Cullough to Face Charges Freeling Hints*, TULSA TRIB., July 23, 1921, at 1
- *Police Order Negro Porters Out of Hotels*, TULSA TRIB., June 14, 1921, at 1
- *Roundup of 64 Indicted Blacks Is On: No Warrants Issued for Whites*, TULSA TRIB., June 17, 1921, at 1
- *Gustafson Eager for Trial, Certain of His Vindication; Commissioners Back Him Up*, TULSA DAILY WORLD, June 26, 1921, at 1
- *Curiosity Drew Mob, No Violence from Whites Until Armed Negroes Arrived*, TULSA DAILY WORLD, July 19, 1921, at 1, 7
- *Home Guard Chooses Rooney for Captain*, TULSA TRIB., June 19, 1918, at 6
- *38 Indicted in Race Riot Probe*, TULSA DAILY WORLD, June 19, 1921, at 2
- *Police Head Hit on Five Counts; 11 Others Named*, TULSA TRIB., June 25, 1921, at 1
- *Grand Jury Blames Negroes for Race Rioting; Whites Clearly Exonerated*, TULSA DAILY WORLD, June 26, 1921, at 1, 8
- *Arsenal For City Hall*, TULSA TRIB., June 29, 1921, at 1-2
- *Smitherman, Held for Inciting Riot, Released on Bond*, TULSA TRIB., July 11, 1921, at 2
- *Legal Fight Waged Over Riot Evidence*, TULSA TRIB., July 13, 1921, at 1
- *State Elects to Try Gustafson First on Riot Action Charge*, TULSA DAILY WORLD, July 14, 1921, at 1, 2
- *State Elects to Try Gustafson First on Riot Action Charge*, TULSA TRIB., July 14, 1921, at 1
- *Sheriff Offers No Aid to Gustafson*, TULSA DAILY WORLD, July 15, 1921, at 8
- *Sheriff Slept Through Tulsa Riot*, TULSA DAILY WORLD, July 15, 1921, at 1, 8
- *Instruction Is Denied by Court*, TULSA DAILY WORLD, July 16, 1921, at 1
- *World's Sunday Sermon: Tulsa's Race Riot and the Teachings of Jesus*, TULSA DAILY WORLD, July 17, 1921, at C7
- *Chief Tells Own Story of Race Riot*, TULSA TRIB., July 19, 1921, at 1
- *Chief and Officers Take Witness Stand*, TULSA DAILY WORLD, July 20, 1921, at 1
- *Verdict Returned After Six Hours of Deliberation*, TULSA DAILY WORLD, July 23, 1921, at 1, 11
- *Jury Convicts Gustafson on Both Counts*, TULSA TRIB., July 23, 1921, at 1
- *Inefficiency of Police Is Denied*, TULSA DAILY WORLD, July 29, 1921, at 1
- *City Not Liable for Riot Damage*, TULSA DAILY WORLD, Aug. 7, 1921, at 1, 2
- *City May Not Appeal Fire Zone Ruling*, TULSA TRIB., Sept. 2, 1921
- *Cannot Enforce Fire Ordinance: Court Holds Unconstitutional Act Against the Burned District*, TULSA DAILY WORLD, Sept. 2, 1921
- *Mobs Lynch White Boy at Tulsa and a Colored at Oklahoma City*, TULSA STAR, Sept. 4, 1920 at 1, https://gateway.okhistory.org/ark:/67531/metadc72815/m1/1/?q=riot
- *Misguided Oklahoma Patriots*, TULSA STAR, Sept. 4, 1921, at 4, https://gateway.okhistory.org/ark:/67531/metadc72815/m1/4/?q=riot

- *Six Tulsa Negroes Will Not Be Tried at Present Term of Court; Dick Rowland Also Freed,* TULSA DAILY WORLD, Sept. 29, 1921, at A16
- *Romance of War Told in Court Trial,* TULSA TRIB., Oct. 1, 1921, at 6
- *Await Action of County Board: Red Fork Officials Still Have Several Days of Grace,* TULSA DAILY WORLD, Oct. 22, 1921, at 18
- *You Tell the World,* TULSA DAILY WORLD, Feb. 12, 1922, at 3

B. Non-Tulsa Articles

- *War Council to Get Behind Home Guards,* OKLA. WEEKLY WORLD, Sept. 6, 1917, at 1
- *Autos Circle Slowly Around Negro Section in Indian War Style,* ST. LOUIS POST DISPATCH, June 1, 1921, at 1
- *Bitter Race War Rages in Oklahoma,* EVENING HERALD, June 1, 1921, at 1
- *3 Die In Riot; Call Troops,* CHI. DAILY TRIB., June 1, 1921, at 1, https://www.proquest.com/historical-newspapers/3-die-riot-call-troops/docview/174859399/se-2
- *56 Slain in Race Riot in Streets of Tulsa, Okla.,* PHIL. EVENING PUB. LEDGER, June 1, 1921, at 1
- *Races at War in Tulsa,* THE KANSAS CITY STAR, June 1, 1921, at 1
- *Men Returning to City Tell Story of Riot,* OKLA. CITY TIMES, June 1, 1921, at 33
- *Nine Whites, 65 Negroes Killed In Tulsa Race Riot,* ST. LOUIS POST DISPATCH, June 1, 1921, at 1, https://www.proquest.com/historical-newspapers/nine-whites-65-negroes-killed-tulsa-race-riot/docview/578367214/se-2
- *Partial List of Killed and Injured In Tulsa Race Riots,* ST. LOUIS POST DISPATCH, June 1, 1921, at 2, https://www.proquest.com/historical-newspapers/partial-list-killed-injured-tulsa-race-riots/docview/578377991/se-2
- *Fire Adds Horror in Racial Clash; Troops in Charge,* ATLANTA CONST., June 2, 1921, at 1, https://www.proquest.com/historical-newspapers/fire-adds-horror-racial-clash-troops-charge/docview/498073765/se-2
- *25 Whites, 60 Negroes Toll In Tulsa Race War; 1,500 Homes Are Burned,* SUN, June 2, 1921, at 1, https://www.proquest.com/historical-newspapers/25-whites-60-negroes-toll-tulsa-race-war-1-500/docview/537200855/se-2
- *Tulsa Dead Total 85, Nine of Them White,* BOS. DAILY GLOBE, June 2, 1921, at 1, https://www.proquest.com/historical-newspapers/tulsa-dead-total-85-nine-them-white/docview/504151890/se-2
- *Race War Renewed, Death Toll Mounts: From 85 To 175 Slain In Tulsa, Estimates Indicate,* WASH. POST, June 2, 1921, at 1, https://www.proquest.com/historical-newspapers/race-war-renewed-death-toll-mounts/docview/145906584/se-2

- *Neglect By Peace Force Blamed For Tulsa Riot*, ST. LOUIS POST DISPATCH, June 2, 1921, at 1, https://www.proquest.com/historical-newspapers/neglect-peace-force-blamed-tulsa-riot/docview/578393768/se-2
- *The Reproach of America*, ST. LOUIS POST DISPATCH, June 2, 1921, at 20, https://www.proquest.com/historical-newspapers/reproach-america/docview/578366565/se-2
- *Race Riot Drama, Wild West Scenes in U.S. City*, THE NORTH STAR, June 2, 1921, at 1
- *Soldiers Subdue Big Race Riot*, CHICAGO DAILY TRIB., June 2, 1921, at 1, https://www.proquest.com/historical-newspapers/soldiers-subdue-big-race-riot-77-known-dead/docview/174875792/se-2
- *85 Killed In Race Riots At Tulsa; Ten Blocks Are Burned*, N.Y. TRIB., June 2, 1921, at 1, https://www.proquest.com/historical-newspapers/85-killed-race-riots-at-tulsa-ten-blocks-are/docview/576458845/se-2
- *Blame Red Propaganda for Tulsa Race Riots*, L.A. TIMES, June 2, 1921, at 11, https://www.proquest.com/historical-newspapers/blame-red-propaganda-tulsa-race-riots/docview/160984003/se-2
- *10 Blocks of Tulsa Homes Prey to Fire; 25 White Men Dead*, PHILA. INQUIRER, June 2, 1921, at 1, https://www.proquest.com/historical-newspapers/june-2-1921-page-1-22/docview/1830730680/se-2
- *Series of Fierce Combats: Angered Whites Surround Negro Quarter and Set It On Fire*, N.Y. TIMES, June 2, 1921, at 1, https://www.proquest.com/historical-newspapers/series-fierce-combats/docview/98408421/se-2
- *Boy Started Fire to Avenge Mother Shot by Negroes*, MUSKOGEE DAILY PHOENIX &TIMES-DEMOCRAT, June 2, 1921, at 1
- *Guard Chief Leaves Riot Scene Today*, SAPULPA HERALD, June 2, 1921, at 1
- *Tulsa Race Riot Will Be Probed: Cause of Battle Attributed to Impudent Negro, Hysterical Girl and "Yellow Journal" Reporter*, ATLANTA CONST., June 3, 1921, at 1, https://www.proquest.com/historical-newspapers/tulsa-race-riot-will-be-probed/docview/498073876/se-2
- *First Detailed Story of How the Tulsa Race Riot Started: Statements by Chief of Police and Sheriff of Happenings After Arrest of Negro Tuesday*, ST. LOUIS POST DISPATCH, June 3, 1921, at 21, https://www.proquest.com/historical-newspapers/first-detailed-story-how-tulsa-race-riot-started/docview/578372524/se-2
- *Guards Return with Governor*, THE DAILY OKLAHOMAN, June 3, 1921, at 1
- *Blacks Tied Together*, THE BLACK DISPATCH, June 3, 1921, at 5
- *Tulsa Race Riot Charged to Cowardice of Officials*, N.Y. TRIB., June 3, 1921, at 1, https://www.proquest.com/historical-newspapers/tulsa-race-riot-charged-cowardice-officials/docview/576403256/se-2

- *Riot Charged to Official Neglect: Citizens of Tulsa Hold Local Authorities Responsible For Outbreak*, WASH. POST, June 3, 1921, at 1, https://www.proquest.com/historical-newspapers/riot-charged-official-neglect/docview/145903506/se-2
- *Blame for Riot at Tulsa to Be Fixed By Jury*, SUN, June 3, 1921, at 1, https://www.proquest.com/historical-newspapers/blame-riot-at-tulsa-be-fixed-jury/docview/537216760/se-2
- *Tulsa Death Toll Now 30*, BOS. DAILY GLOBE, June 3, 1921, at 12, https://www.proquest.com/historical-newspapers/tulsa-death-toll-now-30/docview/504148257/se-2
- *Tulsans at Work on Two Plans to House Negroes*, ST. LOUIS POST DISPATCH, June 3, 1921, at 2, https://www.proquest.com/historical-newspapers/tulsans-at-work-on-two-plans-house-negroes/docview/578374927/se-2
- *The Lesson of Tulsa*, CHI. DAILY TRIB., June 3, 1921, at 8, https://www.proquest.com/historical-newspapers/lesson-tulsa/docview/174856356/se-2
- *Jury Riot Quiz Set for Tulsa: Governor Orders It, Declares City, County Officers Had "No Nerve,"* DETROIT FREE PRESS, June 3, 1921, at 1, https://www.proquest.com/historical-newspapers/jury-riot-quiz-set-tulsa/docview/566753825/se-2
- *Tulsa*, N.Y. TIMES, June 3, 1921, at 11, https://www.proquest.com/historical-newspapers/tulsa/docview/98414103/se-2
- *Race Riots*, DETROIT FREE PRESS, June 3, 1921, at 6, https://www.proquest.com/historical-newspapers/race-riots/docview/566659075/se-2
- *Attorney General's Office Wires to Federal Officers Here to Conduct Thorough Probe to Fix Blame; Governor Gives Directions to Freeling*, OKLA. CITY TIMES, June 3, 1921, at 33
- *Refugees Declare Peonage Prevalent: Eight Who Fled From Oklahoma Before The Riot Tell of Warnings Given To Quit The State*, N.Y. TIMES, June 3, 1921, at 2, https://www.proquest.com/historical-newspapers/refugees-declare-peonage-prevalent/docview/98425979/se-2
- *Tulsa In Remorse To Rebuild Homes*, N.Y. TIMES, June 3, 1921, at 1, https://www.proquest.com/historical-newspapers/tulsa-remorse-rebuild-homes-dead-now-put-at-30/docview/98428838/se-2
- *Radical Leaders Blamed for Riot*, ATLANTA CONST., June 4, 1921, at 12, https://www.proquest.com/historical-newspapers/radical-leaders-blamed-riot/docview/498077091/se-2
- *Negro Agitators Caused Race Riot, Witnesses Say*, ST. LOUIS POST DISPATCH, June 4, 1921, at 3, https://www.proquest.com/historical-newspapers/negro-agitators-race-riot-witnesses-say/docview/578376294/se-2
- *Tulsa Begins Hunt for Riot Agitators*, PHILA. INQUIRER, June 4, 1921, at 2, https://www.proquest.com/historical-newspapers/june-4-1921-page-2-22/docview/1830720954/se-2

- *Civil Law Rule Is Restored in Tulsa: State Troops Withdrawn As City Quiets Down After Outbreak*, WASH. POST, June 4, 1921, at 1, https://www.proquest.com/historical-newspapers/civil-law-rule-is-restored-tulsa/docview/145901553/se-2
- *U.S. Inquiry in Tulsa Race Riots Ordered: Daugherty To Learn If Federal Laws Were Violated*, N.Y. TRIB., June 4, 1921, at 4, https://www.proquest.com/historical-newspapers/u-s-inquiry-tulsa-race-riots-ordered/docview/576404823/se-2
- *Military Control Is Ended at Tulsa*, N.Y. TIMES, June 4, 1921, at 1, https://www.proquest.com/historical-newspapers/military-control-is-ended-at-tulsa/docview/98420285/se-2
- *Probe of Tulsa Riot Ordered by Daugherty*, THE SUN, June 4, 1921, at 3, https://www.proquest.com/historical-newspapers/probe-tulsa-riot-ordered-daugherty/docview/537251757/se-2
- *Lee Not Yet Advised*, MUSKOGEE DAILY PHOENIX & TIMES-DEMOCRAT, June 4, 1921, at 1
- *Smoldering Aftermath of Tulsa's Carnival of Race Rioting*, CHI. DAILY TRIB., June 4, 1921, at 3, https://www.proquest.com/historical-newspapers/smoldering-aftermath-tulsas-carnival-race-rioting/docview/174808760/se-2
- *Martial Law at Tulsa Ends; City to Atone In Full: Prominent Negroes Put Blame On Own Race*, CHI. DAILY TRIB., June 4, 1921, at 3, https://www.proquest.com/historical-newspapers/martial-law-at-tulsa-ends-city-atone-full/docview/174793498/se-2
- *U.S. to Probe Tulsa Rioting: Daugherty Orders Inquiry to Find If Federal Laws Were Violated*, DETROIT FREE PRESS, June 4, 1921, at 8, https://www.proquest.com/historical-newspapers/u-s-probe-tulsa-rioting/docview/566659903/se-2
- *Military Control Is Ended at Tulsa*, N.Y. TIMES, June 4, 1921, at 1, https://www.proquest.com/historical-newspapers/military-control-is-ended-at-tulsa/docview/98420285/se-2
- *Negro Reds Started Riots: Members of Own Race in Tulsa Make the Accusation*, L.A. TIMES, June 4, 1921, at 11, https://www.proquest.com/historical-newspapers/negro-reds-started-riots/docview/160928871/se-2
- Oklahoma Historical Society, *The Tulsa Race Massacre: The Aftermath* (last visited Dec. 20, 2024), https://www.okhistory.org/learn/trm5
- *Troops Withdraw from Tulsa City*, ATLANTA CONST., June 5, 1921, at A10, https://www.proquest.com/historical-newspapers/troops-withdraw-tulsa-city/docview/498072224/se-2
- *Citizens of Tulsa Tell of Conditions There Preceding the Race Riot*, ST. LOUIS POST DISPATCH, June 5, 1921, at A1, https://www.proquest.com/historical-newspapers/citizens-tulsa-tell-conditions/docview/578385761/se-2
- *Denies Negroes Started Tulsa Riot: Head of Blood Brotherhood Defends the Purpose of The Organization*, N.Y. TIMES, June 5, 1921, at 21, https://www.proquest.com/historical-newspapers/denies-negroes-started-tulsa-riot/docview/98409569/se-2

- *Soldiers Quit Tulsa as City Grows Normal*, N.Y. TRIB., June 5, 1921, at 10, https://www.proquest.com/historical-newspapers/soldiers-quit-tulsa-as-city-grows-normal/docview/576406014/se-2
- *Tulsa Resolves to Clean House and Redeem Name, Says Editor*, SUN, June 5, 1921, at 8, https://www.proquest.com/historical-newspapers/tulsa-resolves-clean-house-redeem-name-says/docview/537200523/se-2
- *Tulsa Rioting Blamed on Negro Secret Order*, SUN, June 5, 1921, at 8, https://www.proquest.com/historical-newspapers/tulsa-rioting-blamed-on-negro-secret-order/docview/537220002/se-2
- *Thirty Whites Held for Tulsa Rioting*, N.Y. TIMES, June 5, 1921, at 21, https://www.proquest.com/historical-newspapers/thirty-whites-held-tulsa-rioting/docview/98409403/se-2
- *Tulsa To Make Up Fire Losses: Negroes Will Have Better Homes*, DETROIT FREE PRESS, June 5, 1921, at 12, https://www.proquest.com/historical-newspapers/tulsa-make-up-fire-losses/docview/566725489/se-2
- *Memorial Services for Dead in Tulsa Race Riot*, BOS. DAILY GLOBE, June 6, 1921, at 3, https://www.proquest.com/historical-newspapers/memorial-services-dead-tulsa-race-riot/docview/504151696/se-2
- *Urges Negroes Here to Arm Themselves: Colored Leader at Meeting on Tulsa Riots Intimates There Will Be Three More Riots*, N.Y. TIMES, June 6, 1921, at 7, https://www.proquest.com/historical-newspapers/urges-negroes-here-arm-themselves/docview/98350627/se-2
- *Chats With Visitors: Blames Tulsa Riot On Criminals*, WASH. POST, June 6, 1921, at 6, https://www.proquest.com/historical-newspapers/chats-with-visitors/docview/145898192/se-2
- William Howard Taft, *Taft Charges Riot at Tulsa Was Due Largely To Whites*, WASH. POST, June 6, 1921, at 1, https://www.proquest.com/historical-newspapers/taft-charges-riot-at-tulsa-was-due-largely-whites/docview/145900833/se-2
- *The Responsibility for Race Hostility*, SUN, June 7, 1921, at 8, https://www.proquest.com/historical-newspapers/responsibility-race-hostility/docview/537210929/se-2
- *Harding Exhorts Negroes to Study*, N.Y. TIMES, June 7, 1921, at 3, https://www.proquest.com/historical-newspapers/harding-exhorts-negroes-study/docview/98448549/se-2
- *Harding Denounces Fatal Tulsa Riots*, WASH. POST, June 7, 1921, at 1, https://www.proquest.com/historical-newspapers/harding-denounces-fatal-tulsa-riots/docview/145899872/se-2

- *Harding Voices Regret Over Tulsa Rioting*, N.Y. TRIB., June 7, 1921, at 2 https://www.proquest.com/historical-newspapers/harding-voices-regret-over-tulsa-rioting/docview/576454647/se-2
- *Rioting Charged to Tulsa Negroes*, ATLANTA CONST., June 8, 1921, at 9, https://www.proquest.com/historical-newspapers/rioting-charged-tulsa-negroes/docview/498072756/se-2
- *What Race Riots Cost*, ST. LOUIS POST DISPATCH, June 8, 1921, at 28, https://www.proquest.com/historical-newspapers/what-race-riots-cost/docview/578362232/se-2
- *Begin Prosecution of Tulsa Rioters: Charges Filed Against Four Negroes as Attorney General Starts State Investigation*, N.Y. TIMES, June 8, 1921, at 7, https://www.proquest.com/historical-newspapers/begin-prosecution-tulsa-rioters/docview/98448132/se-2
- J. Merrill, *Rioting at Tulsa Shames the Nation*, DETROIT FREE PRESS, June 8, 1921, at 6, https://www.proquest.com/historical-newspapers/rioting-at-tulsa-shames-nation/docview/566730350/se-2
- *Official Investigates Tulsa Race Riots*, L.A. TIMES, June 8, 1921, at 11, https://www.proquest.com/historical-newspapers/official-investigates-tulsa-race-riots/docview/160910419/se-2
- *Rioting Charged to Tulsa Negroes*, ATLANTA CONST., June 8, 1921, at 9, https://www.proquest.com/historical-newspapers/rioting-charged-tulsa-negroes/docview/498072756/se-2
- *Tulsa After the Riots*, N.Y. EVENING POST, June 9, 1921, at 6, https://www.proquest.com/historical-newspapers/what-other-papers-say/docview/145896096/se-2
- *Jury Is Completed in Tulsa Riot Trial*, ATLANTA CONST., June 10, 1921, at 9, https://www.proquest.com/historical-newspapers/jury-is-completed-tulsa-riot-trial/docview/498060702/se-2
- *Jury Probes Tulsa Riots: Investigators Include Minister, Banker and Business Men*, WASH. POST, at 1, https://www.proquest.com/historical-newspapers/jury-probes-tulsa-riots/docview/145895655/se-2
- *Tulsa Grand Jury Begins Inquiry Into Race Riot*, ST. LOUIS POST DISPATCH, June 10, 1921, at 1, https://www.proquest.com/historical-newspapers/tulsa-grand-jury-begins-inquiry-into-race-riot/docview/578374377/se-2
- *Personal Experiences of Those Who Came Out from the Shambles of Loot, Arson and Murder*, THE BLACK DISPATCH, June 10, 1921, at 8
- *Letters From the People: The Negro in Oklahoma*. ST. LOUIS POST DISPATCH, June 12, 1921, at A2, https://www.proquest.com/historical-newspapers/letters-people/docview/578369963/se-2

- *Negro Says Greed of Tulsa Whites Started Rioting*, N.Y. TRIB., June 13, 1921, at 4, https://www.proquest.com/historical-newspapers/negro-says-greed-tulsa-whites-started-rioting/docview/576451745/se-2
- *Nation Not of Races but of Individuals*, DETROIT FREE PRESS, June 17, 1921, at 6, https://www.proquest.com/historical-newspapers/nation-not-races-individuals/docview/566654017/se-2
- *Extradition Warrant for Negro*, ST. LOUIS POST DISPATCH, June 17, 2021, at 16, https://www.proquest.com/historical-newspapers/cant-pronounce-clients-name/docview/578378965/se-2
- *Dick Rowland in South Omaha; No Trace of Girl*, The BLACK DISPATCH, June 17, 1921, at 1
- *Negroes Indicted for Tulsa Rioting*, DETROIT FREE PRESS, June 18, 1921, at 7, https://www.proquest.com/historical-newspapers/negroes-indicted-tulsa-rioting/docview/566734536/se-2
- *Many Thousands Leave Tulsa*, BLACK DISPATCH, June 18, 2021, at 1, https://gateway.okhistory.org/ark:/67531/metadc152337/m1/1/
- *64 Negroes Indicted for Riot at Tulsa*, PHILA. INQUIRER, June 18, 1921, at 18, https://www.proquest.com/historical-newspapers/june-18-1921-page-24/docview/1830751547/se-2
- *Grand Jury Puts Blame for Tulsa Riot on Negroes*, ST. LOUIS POST DISPATCH, June 25, 1921, at 1, https://www.proquest.com/historical-newspapers/grand-jury-puts-blame-tulsa-riot-on-negroes/docview/578358759/se-2
- *Tulsa Police Chief and Others Indicted for Riot*, N.Y. TRIB., June 26, 1921, at 3, https://www.proquest.com/historical-newspapers/tulsa-police-chief-others-indicted-riot/docview/576400936/se-2
- *Tulsa Police Chief Indicted in Probe: Four Other Officers Also Charged in Connection With Recent Race Riots*, SUN, June 26, 1921, at 5, https://www.proquest.com/historical-newspapers/tulsa-police-chief-indicted-probe/docview/534419338/se-2
- *Police Chief Is Indicted During Tulsa Riot Quiz*, CHI. DAILY TRIB., June 26, 1921, at 13, https://www.proquest.com/historical-newspapers/police-chief-is-indicted-during-tulsa-riot-quiz/docview/174843136/se-2
- *Tulsa Race Riot Jury Indicts Police Chief*, N.Y. TIMES, June 26, 1921, at 16, https://www.proquest.com/historical-newspapers/tulsa-race-riot-jury-indicts-police-chief/docview/98391321/se-2
- *Oust Tulsa Chief on Jury's Advice: Race Riot Investigators Indict Five of Police, Seven Civilians*, WASH. POST, June 26, 1921, at 4, https://www.proquest.com/historical-newspapers/oust-tulsa-chief-on-jurys-advice/docview/145912732/se-2
- *Negroes Blamed for Race Riot By Tulsa Grand Jury: Police Chief, Four Policemen And Seven Civilians Are Indicted Following the Investigation*, ST. LOUIS POST DISPATCH, JUNE 26,

1921, at 2, https://www.proquest.com/historical-newspapers/negroes-blamed-race-riot-tulsa-grand-jury/docview/578371230/se-2

- *Red Circulars, Urging Negro Revolt, Seized*, N.Y. TRIB., June 29, 1921, at 2, https://www.proquest.com/historical-newspapers/red-circulars-urging-negro-revolt-seized/docview/576411224/se-2

- Walter F. White, *The Eruption of Tulsa*, THE NATION, June 29, 1921, https://www.thenation.com/article/society/tulsa-1921/

- *Alleged Red Arrested*, LOS ANGELES TIMES, June 30, 1921, at 111, https://www.proquest.com/historical-newspapers/new-chief-justice-may-be-named-soon/docview/160852325/se-2

- *Tulsa Race Riot Victims Aided by $1,012 Fund*, CHI. DAILY TRIB., July 10, 1921, at 12, https://www.proquest.com/historical-newspapers/american-legion-notes/docview/174805688/se-2

- *Sheriff Takes Stand in Tulsa Police Trial*, CHICKASHA DAILY EXPRESS, July 14, 1921, at 1

- *Sheriff Testifies in Trial of Chief Gustafson, Tulsa*, DAILY ARDMOREITE, July 14, 1921, at 1

- *Tulsa to Pay Guard for Expenses During Riot*, DURANT WEEKLY NEWS, July 15, 1921, at 6

- *Indications Are that Gustafson Trial Will Last All Next Week*, DAILY ARDMOREITE, July 15, 1921, at 1

- *Sheriff Sleeps Through Big Riot at Tulsa*, DURANT DAILY DEMOCRAT, July 15, 1921, at 3

- *Express Packagettes: Sheriff McCullough testified*, CHICKASHA DAILY EXPRESS, July 16, 1921, at 4

- *Tulsa Police Aided Riot*, SUN, July 16, 1921, at 7, https://www.proquest.com/historical-newspapers/tulsa-police-aided-riot-report/docview/534403252/se-2

- *Tulsa Chief, Lax in Riots, Guilty of Theft Plots*, CHI. DAILY TRIB., July 23, 1921, https://www.proquest.com/historical-newspapers/tulsa-chief-lax-riots-guilty-theft-plots/docview/174777930/se-2

- *Tulsa Police Chief Guilty: Jury Finds He Failed To Act To Protect Public In Riots*, N.Y. TRIB., July 23, 1921, at 1, https://www.proquest.com/historical-newspapers/tulsa-police-chief-guilty/docview/576421434/se-2

- *Tulsa Chief Is Found Guilty on Two Counts: Woman Assistant Attorney-General Stresses Failure to Disarm Negroes Before Riot*, ST. LOUIS POST DISPATCH, July 23, 1921, at 2, https://www.proquest.com/historical-newspapers/tulsa-chief-is-found-guilty-on-two-counts/docview/578383436/se-2

- Roscoe Dunjee, *Ask Federal Investigation of Use of Air Planes and Machine Guns in Tulsa Race Massacre*, BLACK DISPATCH, Aug. 26, 1961, at 1, https://gateway.okhistory.org/ark:/67531/metadc152347/?q=%22machine%20guns%20in%20tulsa%22

- *President Harding at Lincoln University*, LINCOLN UNIV. HERALD, Aug. 1921, at 11

- *Ex-Police Bares Plot of Tulsans: Officer of Law Tells Who Ordered Aeroplanes to Destroy Homes*, CHI. DEFENDER, Oct. 14, 1921
- *Dick Rowland Is Freed of All Charges: Man For Whose Life Mob Fought Is Found Innocent of All Charges*, CHI. WHIP, Oct. 15, 1921, at 1, https://idnc.library.illinois.edu/?a=d&d=TCW19211015-01.1.1&e=-------en-20--1--txt-txIN---------

SURVIVOR ACCOUNTS

A. Survivor Accounts Provided to the Cold Case Unit by J4G Clients

VIOLA FORD FLETCHER & IKE HOWARD, DON'T LET THEM BURY MY STORY: THE OLDEST LIVING SURVIVOR OF THE TULSA RACE MASSACRE IN HER OWN WORDS (Mocha Media, 2023)

Depositions of Viola Ford Fletcher, Hughes Van Ellis, and Lessie Benningfield ("Mother") Randle, *Randle v. City of Tulsa*, No. CV-2020-1179 (Okl. Dist.) (provided by J4G)

Continuing Injustice: The Centennial of the Tulsa-Greenwood Race Massacre May 19, 2021, Hearing Before the H.R. Subcomm. on the Const., Civil Rights, and Civil Liberties, 117th Cong. (2021) (statements of Viola Ford Fletcher, Hughes Van Ellis, Lessie Benningfield ("Mother") Randle), available at https://www.govinfo.gov/content/pkg/CHRG-117hhrg48273/html/CHRG-117hhrg48273.htm and https://www.c-span.org/video/?c4963668/1921-tulsa-race-massacre-survivors-testify-congress

B. Firsthand Accounts Authored by Survivors in the Decade Following the Massacre

Buck Cobert Franklin, *The Tulsa Race Riot and Three of Its Victims* (Aug. 22, 1931), https://nmaahc.si.edu/object/nmaahc_2015.176.1

MARY E. JONES-PARRISH, THE NATION MUST AWAKE: MY WITNESS TO THE TULSA RACE MASSACRE OF 1921 (Trinity University Press, 2021)

MARY E. JONES PARRISH, EVENTS OF THE TULSA DISASTER (1922)

Survivor testimonials given to Mary E. Jones Parrish and included in *Events of the Tulsa Disaster*:

- James T.A. West
- Jack Thomas
- Richard J. Hill
- Mrs. Roseatter Moore
- P.S. Thompson
- Dr. R.T. Bridgewater
- E.A. Loupe (Plumber)
- Mrs. Carrie Kinlaw
- J.P. Hughs

- A.J. Newman
- Anonymous/"Name Withheld"
- C.L. Netherland
- M.D. Russell
- J.C. Latimer
- "A.H."
- Dimple L. Bush
- R.A. Whitaker
- Richard J. Hill

C.   White Witness Accounts Given Contemporaneously

Letter of Thomas James Sharp to Joseph Anthony Sharp (June 28, 1921) [2021.170.001], Tulsa Historical Society & Museum, Tulsa, OK, https://www.tulsahistory.org/wp-content/uploads/2018/11/2021.170.001.pdf

Amy Comstock, *"Over There:" Another View of the Tulsa Riots*, SURVEY, July 2, 1921, https://digitalcollections.tulsalibrary.org/digital/collection/p16063coll1/id/5850/

D.   Survivor Accounts Collected Since 1980

1. The Eddie Faye Gates Tulsa Race Massacre Collection, Gilcrease Museum, available at https://collections.gilcrease.org/anthology/eddie-faye-gates-tulsa-race-massacre-collection

   - Alfred Stanley Dennie
   - Eunice Jackson
   - George Monroe
   - Iola Streeter Jackson
   - Veneice Dunn Sims
   - Kinney Booker
   - Elwood Lett
   - Theodore Porterfield
   - Ernestine Gibbs
   - Ruby McCormick
   - Wes Young
   - Otis G. Clark
   - Genevieve Elizabeth Tillman Jackson
   - Willie Mae Thompson
   - Julia Bonton Jones
   - Eldoris McCondichie
   - Georgia Walker Hill
   - Samuel Walker

2. Accounts collected by the Tulsa Reparations Coalition, available at https://tulsareparations.z19.web.core.windows.net/Vignettes.htm

- John Melvin Alexander
- Juanita Delores Burnett Arnold
- Kinney I. Booker
- Binkley Wright
- Other eyewitness accounts (short summaries)

3. Oklahoma Historical Society Oral History Collection Interviews, available at
   https://www.okhistory.org/learn/tulsaracemassacre

   - Ethelyn Gimlin (H1983.109)
   - Thomas and Mary Hamilton (H1984.019)
   - Ruth Powers (H1983.101)
   - Zola Faye Sells (H1982.052)
   - Earkysee Sutton (H1982.029)
   - Mary Magdaline Wyatt (H1982.061)
   - Thomas Edward Gage Jr. 06/12/1987

4. Tulsa Race Riot (Massacre) Commission Interviews, available at
   https://www.okhistory.org/learn/tulsaracemassacre (conducted in 1999; collected by the
   Oklahoma Historical Society Audio and Oral History Archives)

   - George Monroe, Tape 1 (1999.069.01)
   - Lola Streeter-Jackson, Tape 1 (1999.069.01)
   - Veneice Dunn-Simms, Tape 1 (1999.069.01)
   - Kinny Booker, Tape 1 (1999.069.01)
   - Edward Lett, Tape 1 (1999.069.01)
   - Ernestine Gibbs, Tape 1 (1999.069.01) - Tape 2 (1999.069.02)
   - Ruby McCormick, Tape 2 (1999.069.02)
   - Wes Young, Tape 2 (1999.069.02)
   - Otis Clark, Tape 2 (1999.069.02)
   - Joe Burns, Tape 2 (1999.069.02)
   - Elizabeth Cooley Chappelle, Tape 3 (1999.069.03)
   - Annie Birdie Beard, Tape 3 (1999.069.03)
   - Augusta Mann, Tape 3 (1999.069.03)
   - George Monroe, Tape 3 (1999.069.03)
   - Eldoris McCondichie, Tape 3 (1999.069.03)
   - Jobie Elizabeth Holderness, Tape 4 (1999.069.04)
   - Eunice Jackson, Tape 4 (1999.069.04)
   - Myrtle Rollerson, Tape 4 (1999.069.04)
   - Beulah Loree Smith, Tape 4 (1999.069.04)

5. Accounts in HANNIBAL B. JOHNSON, BLACK WALL STREET 100, 233-237 (Eakin, 2020)
   (taken from Eddie Faye Gates interviews (above))

- J.B. Bates
- Kinney I. Booker
- Otis Grandville Clark
- Ernestine Gibbs
- Leroy Leon Hatcher
- Wilhelmina Guess Howell
- Simon R. Richardson
- Veneice Dunn Simms
- Wess H. Young, Sr.

6. Accounts in Tulsa Historical Society and Museum Online Collection, available at https://tulsahistory.pastperfectonline.com/

- John Zink, Sr. (white witness), Catalog No. 1971.001.002 (Jan. 29, 1971) https://tulsahistory.pastperfectonline.com/archive/D41E4300-7B95-4B47-B76D-416752805357
- Gertrude Winterringer Carr (white witness), Catalog No. 1979.085.001 (March 20, 1979) https://tulsahistory.pastperfectonline.com/archive/4742E741-DF87-431A-A135-317655104335
- Joan Agnes "Johnnie" Coe (white witness), Catalog No. 2005.146.001 (Feb. 3, 2005) https://tulsahistory.pastperfectonline.com/archive/B0B9DD66-6045-44CD-B77C-531578412262
- William Danforth Williams, Catalog No. 1977.072.001 (March 29, 1977), https://tulsahistory.pastperfectonline.com/archive/0337EA50-379B-4BE3-8660-404844825836

7. *We Are Greenwood Oral History Project*, Justice for Greenwood, available at https://www.justiceforgreenwood.org/oral-history-project/

- U.D. Emerson
- Jack and Daisy Scott
- Wilbur and Zola Stephens
- Lessie Benningfield-Randle
- John R. Emerson, Sr.
- Simeon Neal
- Joe E. Burns
- Marciano and Josefina Villareal
- J.B. Stradford
- Theodor Porterfield

8. Ruth Sigler Avery Collection, *Collection Series 1: Tulsa Race Massacre of 1921*, OSU-Tulsa Library (July 2021)

- Bob Forsman (Box 2, Folder 16)

- S.M. Jackson (Box 2, Folder 16)
- Helen Donohue Ingraham (Box 3, Folder 6)
- Robert L. Fairchild, Jr. (Box 2, Folder 12)
- James Leighton Avery (Box 1, Folder 10)
- Andre Wilkes and Margaret Wilsey (Box 7, Folder 3)
- W.R. Holway (Box 3, Folder 2)
- William D. Williams (Box 7, Folder 6)
- L.C. Clark (Box 1, Folder 21)
- Cecelia Nails Palmer (Box 14, Folder 38)
- Elsie Gubser (Box 2, Folder 26)
- Edward L. Goodwin (Box 2, Folder 24)
- Marguerite Griffith Allstrom (Box 1, Folder 3)
- Ruth Wingfield (Box 7, Folder 7)

9. Other Accounts

- *Survivor Olivia J. Hooker recalls the 1921 Tulsa race riots*, USA TODAY (June 11, 2020), https://www.usatoday.com/videos/news/2020/06/11/survivor-olivia-j-hooker-recalls-1921-tulsa-race-riots/5345617002/
- Video Compilation (Olivia Hooker, Eldoris McCondichie, Jimmie Lily Franklin, Eunice Jackson, Clyde Eddy, and John Hope Franklin), from *Tulsa Objects in the National Museum of African American History and Culture (NMAAHC) Online Collection*, NAT. MUSEUM OF AFRICAN AM. HIST. AND CULTURE, SMITHSONIAN INST., https://nmaahc.si.edu/explore/search-collection/tulsa-objects-nmaahc-collection
- *Tulsa Greenwood Race Riot Accountability Act of 2007: Hearing Before the Subcomm. on the Const., Civil Rights, and Civil Liberties of the H.R. Comm. on the Judiciary*, 110th Cong. 24-46 (2007), https://www.govinfo.gov/content/pkg/CHRG-110hhrg34924/pdf/CHRG-110hhrg34924.pdf (testimony of Olivia Hooker and John Hope Franklin)
- Margarett Zulpo, *Remembering When the Sky Rained Death // 95-Year-Old Wom[a]n Recalls 1921 Riot*, TULSA DAILY WORLD, May 18, 1994 (account of survivor Rosa Davis-Skinner), https://tulsaworld.com/archive/remembering-when-the-sky-rained-death-95-year-old-women-recalls-1921-race-riot/article_35d47882-6d91-5395-b92f-7acb73c0f8c4.html
- Charlene Scott Warnken, *Tulsa riot is burned into her memory*, EASTERN OKLAHOMA CATHOLIC, May 29, 1983 (account of witness Ruth Sigler Avery)
- Interview with Beatrice Campbell-Webster, *Guide to the 1921 Tulsa Race Massacre Oral History Collection, 2004-2007*, NAT. MUSEUM OF AFRICAN AM. HIST. AND CULTURE, SMITHSONIAN INST., https://mads.si.edu/mads/view/NMAAHC-A2014_240_9_1_1_PM

APPENDIX B

APPENDIX B

Interviewees

Historians, Journalists, Scholars, and Authors

The following scholars of the Tulsa Race Massacre shared their time and expertise with us or provided us with materials we used in compiling our report.

Chief Egunwale Amusan[1]

Dr. Raymond Doswell

Dr. Kimberly C. Ellis

Dr. Scott Ellsworth

John W. Franklin[2]

Dean Oren Griffin, Esq., Ph.D.

Dr. Karlos K. Hill

Randall Hopkins, Esq.

Hannibal B. Johnson, Esq.

Quraysh Ali Lansana

Victor Luckerson

Suzette Malveaux, Esq.

Larry O'Dell

Dr. Kristen T. Oertel

---

[1] Chief Amusan is also the descendant of a massacre survivor. Our discussion with him was during a tour he provided of the Greenwood District.

[2] Mr. Franklin is also the descendant of a massacre survivor. Mr. Franklin provided us information both in an interview and during a tour of massacre-related exhibits at the National Museum of African American History and Culture.

Oklahoma Commission to Study the Tulsa Race Riot of 1921

We spoke to the following Commissioners from the Oklahoma Commission to Study the Tulsa Race Riot of 1921.

Jimmie White

Vivian Clark Adams

Jim Lloyd

Advocates and Community Organizations

We spoke to one or more members of the following organizations. Names of individuals have been withheld for privacy except for those who requested publication.

Greenwood Chamber of Commerce, https://tulsachamber.com/member_directory/active/greenwood-chamber-of-commerce/

Greenwood Cultural Center, https://www.greenwoodculturalcenter.org/

Historic Vernon AME Church, https://www.historicvernoname.church/

John Hope Franklin Center for Reconciliation, https://www.jhfcenter.org/

Justice for Greenwood,[3] https://www.justiceforgreenwood.org/, including Damario Solomon-Simmons, Professor Eric J. Miller, SolomonSimmonsLaw, and Schulte Roth & Zabel LLP

Archives, Universities, Libraries, and Museums

We visited, consulted, or used resources from the following archives, and met with many archivists and librarians. Names of individuals have been withheld for privacy except for those who requested publication.

Greenwood Rising Black Wall Street History Center, https://www.greenwoodrising.org/

Helmerich Center for American Research (Gilcrease), Eddie Faye Gates Collection, https://collections.gilcrease.org/anthology/eddie-faye-gates-tulsa-race-massacre-collection

National Archives, College Park, MD, https://www.archives.gov/

---

[3] Justice for Greenwood and its founder and executive director, Damario Solomon-Simmons, and Professor Eric J. Miller, also assisted in arranging a tour of the Greenwood District, participated in interviews of those descendants who are clients of Justice for Greenwood's law firm, identified and assisted in identifying and interviewing other interviewees, and provided massacre-related information to us.

National Museum of African American History and Culture (Smithsonian),
https://nmaahc.si.edu/

Oklahoma Department of Libraries, Tulsa Race Massacre Collection, https://libguides.osu-tulsa.okstate.edu/tulsaracemassacre

Oklahoma State University, Tulsa Campus, Ruth Sigler Avery Collection,
https://library.okstate.edu/search-and-find/collections/digital-collections/tulsa-race-riot-of-1921-collection/, particularly Lynn Wallace and Sheena Perez.

The University of Tulsa, McFarlin Library, Department of Special Collections and University Archives, https://libraries.utulsa.edu/speccoll

The University of Tulsa, College of Law, B.C. Franklin Collection,
https://utulsa.edu/academics/law/legal-clinics/buck-colbert-franklin-legal-clinic/

The City of Tulsa

Members of the Tulsa Police Department and other city employees spoke to us during the evaluation.

Survivors

Names of living survivors, redacted in the January 9 Report pursuant to the Privacy Act, have been unredacted pursuant to a written request.

Hughes Van Ellis

Lessie Benningfield Randle ("Mother Randle")

Viola Ford Fletcher ("Mother Fletcher")

Descendants

We met with the following descendants and community members. Names of living descendants, even those identified in other sources, have been withheld for privacy except for those who requested publication.[4]

1. XXXXXX

2. XXXXXX

3. XXXXXX
   XXXXXX, XXXXXX, XXXXXX, XXXXXX, XXXXXX, XXXXXX

---

[4] Any individual who participated in the investigation who affirmatively wishes to be identified in this report can make a written request to have his or her name unredacted.

4.   Dr. Tiffany Crutcher

5.   XXXXXX

6.   XXXXXX

7.   XXXXXX

8.   XXXXXX

9.   XXXXXX

10.   Ike Howard

11.   Heather Nash

12.   XXXXXX

13.   Michael Eugene Penny

14.   LaDonna Penny

15.   XXXXXX, XXXXXX & XXXXXX

16.   XXXXXX

17.   XXXXXX

APPENDIX C

REPORT FORM NO. 1

58260-8

REPORT MADE BY: James G. Findl.	PLACE WHERE MADE: Oklahoma City	WHEN MADE: 6-3-1921	WHICH MADE: 3-X1921

TITLE OF CASE AND OFFENSE CHARGED OR NATURE OF MATTER UNDER INVESTIGATION:

TULSA, OKLAHOMA RACE RIOT   Tulsa, Okla.

Possible Radical Matter.

STATEMENT OF OPERATIONS, EVIDENCE COLLECTED, NAMES AND ADDRESSES OF PERSONS INTERVIEWED, PLACES VISITED, ETC.

At Oklahoma City, Okla.

Beginning investigation of above entitled matter, the news-papers of June first carried the account of rioting in Tulsa, and that a number of people were killed; that during the night, at the urgent request of the Citizens Committee at Tulsa, the Governor had called out the State Militia, two companies at Tulsa, and three companies at Oklahoma City, one from Wagoner and one from Bartles-ville, to quell the riot.

Agent sent Agent Weiss to Tulsa on the first train, to inves-tigate this matter, along with other matters at Tulsa, as Agent be-lieved that such a condition should be reported on, even though there possibly could not be any violation of any Federal law con-nected therewith.

At noon June 2nd Agent received the following telegram from the Chief of Bureau:

"Press carrying account race riots Tulsa. Desire immediate investigation; wire all facts."

Agent got into communication with Agent Weiss at Tulsa over the long distance telephone, and instructed him to send a long tele-gram direct to the Chief of the Bureau, giving a short statement of the facts and conditions as they existed.

On the morning of June 3rd Agent is in receipt of a copy of the following telegram which Agent Weiss dispatched to the Chief of Bu-reau:

COPY OF THIS REPORT FURNISHED TO:

2 to Washington.

-1-

REPORT FORM NO 2
James G. Findlay.   June 1 to 3, 1921.   -2-

"Tulsa, Okla., June 2, 1921.

Chief Bureau of Investigation,
    Dept. of Justice, Washington, D. C.

Stop five. Race riots Tulsa, Okla. May thirty-first negro Deck
Rowland charged by white elevator girl with attempted assault.
Rowland jailed in county jail. Same evening white mob of about
twenty-five armed men go to county jail to lynch Rowland. About
same sized mob of armed negroes go to jail to protect Rowland.
Sheriff refuses to disarm or arrest any of either mob. Negro mob
starts to leave but returns shortly and some one, apparently white
man, fires a shot. Negroes flee, shooting as they run and make a
stand at Frisco tracks and Boston street. White mob augmented by
several crooks and follow negroes to negro section. Both sides
shooting but negroes retreating.

Whites invade negro section, shooting at fleeing negroes and
setting negroes residences, church and business buildings on fire
until 7 A. M. next day, looting as they go. National Guard arrive
about then and martial law proclaimed. Rioting ends suddenly and
everything now normal. Known dead are ~~indubitably are~~ nine whites
eighteen blacks. Undoubtedly many dead negroes in burned houses.
Property damage in negro section about one million five hundred
thousand.

Sheriff and Police Department apparently made no effort to
preserve order. Sheriff accused of calling armed negroes to jail
in first instance. Everything now quiet, National Guard still on
duty. State Grand Jury probe ordered by Governor with State attorney General to conduct same which is set for June eighth. No Federal violation appears. Trouble started spontaneously and due to
fact that County and city officers have been for years notoriously
crooked and inefficient.
                            Weiss."

Before the writing of this report, the afternoon of June 3rd,

official reports from Tulsa state that there are ten whites and

twenty-one negroes dead, and about three hundred injured, and it is

believed that about ten of the injured are fatally injured.

A complete report from Agent Weiss will be forwarded as soon

as possible.

Continued.

44

REPORT MADE AT: Oklahoma City	DATE WHEN MADE: 7-5-1921	PERIOD FOR WHICH MADE: 7-2-1921	REPORT MADE BY: T. F. Weiss

TITLE AND CHARACTER OF CASE: *African*
NEGRO ACTIVITIES (BLOOD BROTHERHOOD) : Possible Radical Matter.

FACTS DEVELOPED:
At Tulsa, Okla.

Referring to report, this title, by Agent Sausele, dated Wichita, Kansas, June 25, 1921.

Interviewed CHARLES DALEY, police inspector, Tulsa, Oklahoma, who said he had heard some rumors that such an organization was being formed in Tulsa, Sapulpa and vicinity, but MR. DALEY had nothing definite, and had heard of no literature or organizers.

MR. DALEY stated that he had heard that HENRY COX, negro, 200 block North Hickory, Sapulpa, Oklahoma, and HENRY LEE, negro, Sapulpa, had attended a meeting at Sapulpa a couple of weeks ago and that a negro named LON JOE, living five miles west of Tulsa, had also attended a meeting of negroes at Sapulpa; that the purpose of these meetings was said to be to organize the negroes and march on Tulsa and fire the residence section and wage war on the whites; that the purpose of this proposed march on Tulsa was retaliation for what the negroes suffered May 31st; that the march on Tulsa was to begin on the night of July 3rd and plan to take advantage of the fireworks being set off in various parts of the city to cover up the first reports of the attacking negro shots, etc.

MR. DALEY stated that he had charge of the proper defense of Tulsa, and had seven machine guns and experienced gunners.

REFERENCE:	COPIES OF THIS REPORT FURNISHED TO: 3 Washington; 2 Kansas City.

ORIGINAL

45

REPORT FORM No.2 T. F. Weiss. _____ July 2, 1921. _____ -2-

with them, fifty or more minute-men, airplanes, militia and police in readiness; that all the roads leading into Tulsa from outside, especially from Muskogee, Okmulgee and Sapulpa would be well-guarded on the nights of the 2nd and 3rd, and no strange negroes allowed to pass without identification.

Agent inquired closely from MR. DALEY and others, but could find no one who had any information of any literature or any traveling organizers for this "BLOOD BROTHERHOOD" organization. From all rumors and information Agent could get, the object of the alleged negro plant to attack Tulsa was to avenge the killing and destroying of property of the negroes at Tulsa May 31st, and June 1st.

Agent, however, arranged with MR. DALEY to be notified immediately by wire or long distance, in the event any disturbance between whites and blacks broke out at Tulsa or in that vicinity, and also arranged with MR. DALEY to be furnished with the names and addresses of all informants in the future who have or claim to have definite information as to any radical organization or organizers among the negroes, and also to be furnished promptly with all literature along that line secured by the police department of Tulsa.

Open.

7—871

REPORT FORM NO. 1

REPORT MADE BY	PLACE WHERE MADE	DATE WHEN MADE	PERIOD FOR WHICH MADE:
T. F. Weiss	Oklahoma City	6-5-1921	6/1-3/1921

TITLE OF CASE AND OFFENSE CHARGED OR NATURE OF MATTER UNDER INVESTIGATION:

RIOTING AT TULSA, Oklan   May 31st and June 1st, 1921

STATEMENT OF INFORMATION OR EVIDENCE COLLECTED, NAMES AND ADDRESSES OF PERSONS INTERVIEWED, PLACES VISITED, ETC.

At Tulsa, Okla.:

Beginning. Agent arrived at Tulsa June 1st at 5:45 P. M. on other business, but finding the amount of damage done, and lives lost, began at once to quietly gather data with the view of ascertaining the true cause and origin of the trouble, and as to whether any violation of Federal Law was involved, or facts committed warranting the Federal Government to take a hand.

During June 1st, 2nd and 3rd Agent talked with more than a hundred, blacks and whites, having personal knowledge of some phases and stages of the trouble, and went through and inspected the devastated negro section. All whom Agent conversed with agreed that the whole affair was practically spontaneous, and not due to any preliminary organized ill feeling between blacks and whites, and that neither blacks nor whites had any leaders or organization and that premeditation was also plainly absent.

The plain uncolored truth is as follows:

On May 31st a white woman, named MRS. SARAH PAGE, running the elevator in the Drexel Building, Tulsa, complained to the police department that a negro boy, named DICK ROWLAND, about fifteen or sixteen years old, had grabbed her by the arm, in said elevator, during business hours; that she screamed and ROWLAND ran away.

Chief of Police Gustafson stated to Agent the above, and added that the woman bore no scratches, bruises, or disarranged dress, and that she stated the boy had made no bad remark of any kind;

3 copies Washington.   -1-   7-677

T. F. Weiss.   June 1 to 5, 1921.   -2-

that she just got scared. That the negro boy admitted at the police
station to taking hold of MRS. PAGE'S arm, but insisted he and she had
been joking and playing and he meant no harm, but got scared and ran
when she screamed.

GUSTAFSON states that his investigation did not justify any charge
against the negro, and none was filed; that the same afternoon the
"Tulsa Tribune", (a sort of yellow sheet) printed an untrue and inflam-
atory story with the result that by 4 P. M. rumors were current on the
streets that a mob of whites were going to lynch ROWLAND that night;
that he, GUSTAFSON, then had ROWLAND put in the county jail for safety,
and told Sheriff WILLIAM McCULLOUGH of the lynching rumors; that about
7:30 P. M. a white mob, including white women, began gathering at the
county jail, and later a bunch of about twenty-five armed negro men came
also to the county jail; that he, GUSTAFSON, had heard that Sheriff Mc-
CULLOUGH had called these armed negroes by phone to come to the jail
armed to protect ROWLAND.

WILLIAM ELLIS, Deputy United States Marshal, Tulsa, stated to Agent
that May 31st he heard rumors that ROWLAND was to be lynched that night,
and took his wife with him in his car to the jail about 6 P. M. to see
the lynching, but to take no part; that there were forty or fifty white
men and their wives at the jail when he got there and twenty-five or
thirty heavily armed negroes, standing off to one side, muttering and
cursing; that Sheriff McCULLOUGH was also present, but the white mob did
not seem to be seriously intending to lynch anybody; that he, ELLIS,
urged the Sheriff to disarm everybody at once, and before the tension
became dangerous, offering to assist him; that the Sheriff refused to
disarm any ones but did talk to the negroes, whom he called by their

T. F. Weiss.   June 1 to 5, 1921.   -5-

first names, to go home and avoid trouble; that the negroes did start
away, but in a few minutes, they or others returned, stood around and
cursed; that when the negroes came back the second time a large, tall
white man stepped up to McCULLOUGH, and said: "Bill, why did you call
those armed niggers up here?"; that McCULLOUGH replied, "I didn't call
them", and the white man said, "You are a God damned liar, for I heard
you do it". ELLIS states that McCULLOUGH then said nothing but went inside the jail and shut the door; that Chief of Police GUSTAFSON, and a
policeman named BLAINE were present during all this, and made no move
to prevent trouble, so that he, ELLIS, took his wife and drove away,
as it was apparent Hell was going to break loose.

ELLIS states that he drove home, six or eight blocks, and about
ten minutes after he got home, heard a noise in the street in front of
his house; that he looked out and saw about sixteen niggers, with guns,
holding up two autos of whites, that the whites, some of whom were women, were standing in the cars with their heads high in the air, and the
niggers cursing them vilely; that the niggers, however, did not harm the
whites, but let them drive on in a few minutes, after which the negroes
fired about thirty shots in the air and ran. (This shows the purpose-
lessness of the negroes.

ELLIS states that he stayed home that night, but was down town
next morning; that the whites were stealing and pillaging in the negro
section, which was on fire, and continued to do this till noon; that
they thus stole Victrolas, sewing machines, clothes, furs, autos, furniture, etc. and that he has helped recover some stuff thus stolen; that
in one white man's house were found three Victrolas and nine silk

49

T. F. Weiss.   June 1 to 3, 1921.   -4-

shirts--all admitted as being stolen from the negroes.

ELLIS states that there was no unusual race feeling prevailing; that the trouble just started on a small scale, and grew out of bounds; that at 8 P. M. three good officers could have controlled the situation and avoided all trouble, but neither the police nor Sheriff's office at any time made the least effort to preserve order; that these officers seemed to have no sense, no interest, and no guts.

Chief of Police GUSTAFSON also assured agent that there was no apparent premeditation, or unusual race feeling on either side; that neither side had leaders or organization, and that it all was a spontaneous growth, mainly due to the many crooks and transients who took advantage of the conditions from midnight on, broke into hardware stores, pawn-shops, and sporting goods shops, and stole hundreds of guns and a lot of ammunition, and then began about daylight to loot the negro houses, after driving the negroes out; that probably the burning of property was to cover up this, as many houses were looted before being set afire.

MR. HALL, Secretary to Chief of Police GUSTAFSON, stated that he, HALL, was present at the County Jail, "from start to finish", and that no effort was made by any county or city peace officer, to disarm the members of the mob. HALL indignantly declared that to have attempted that would have been bad judgment, as it would surely have lead to shooting.

L. W. CRUTCHER, attorney, Mayo Building, Tulsa, stated to agent that he was with white mob at jail until about 9 P. M. He described the facts about same as ELLIS, and as to time after ELLIS had left, CRUTCHER stated the tension became higher and higher, the armed niggers

T. T. Weiss.   June 1 to 3, 1921.   -5-

getting bolder and more insulting; that finally a white man remarked
that as he had a gun he would show the niggers about cursing whites, or
words to that effect, whereupon another white man handed the first one
a gun and remarked, "There is a gun, brother"; that a few seconds later
a shot rang out, evidently by the man who had just been given a gun,
whereupon the niggers started to run back towards their own section of
town, shooting aimlessly as they ran, but killing two whites within the
next four blocks; that the whites pursued the blacks to the Frisco
track, on Boston Street. These tracks are a sort of dividing line between the white and negro sections; that the negroes made a stand at
the tracks, but the shooting died down.

CRUTCHER states this was about 10 P. M. and that things were quiet
till 2 A. M. at which time a negro business building was set on fire,
and more shots fired; that this died down till about 5 A. M. when fires
again started in the negro section, starting in five or six places,
blocks apart, at one time; that shooting continued and a mob of several
hundred whites invaded the negro section, setting fire as they went,
that this continued till about noon, by which time the entire negro
section, business and residence, was in flames.

CRUTCHER states that the burning was mostly by the criminal white
element of Tulsa, and that he did not believe there was any agitation
or premeditation by either side; that the Sheriff's force and Police
Department simply made no effort to enforce law; though it could have
easily been done any time up to 2 A. M.; that the lower element of
whites simply seized the opportunity to pillage, burn and shoot the negroes without interference from the authorities. CRUTCHER was of the

T. F. Weiss.   June 1 to 3, 1921.   · -6-

opinion that many dead negroes were in the debris of the burned houses,
and mentioned the case of a negro maid whose bullet riddled and burned
boyd was found in the ashes of her burned home by her employers.

TOM DYER, Jenks, Oklahoma, stated to agent that a Tulsa policeman
named RIGNON came to Jenks, near Tulsa, in a car the night of May 31st
and invited several white men to go to Tulsa, intimating a raid on the
negroes; that he, DYER, did not go that night, but that ROBERT HANSKON,
an oil driller, quit work and did drive over after midnight, at RIG-
NON'S invitation; that HANSKON'S dead body was found June 1st in the
negro burned section, near where RIGNON afterward told DYER he, RIGNON,
had stationed himself.

DYER stated that he did drive to Tulsa next morning and watched th
white mob burn and sack the negro section; that he got there about
10:30 A. M. and saw hundreds of whites, including white women and white
girls, carrying Victrolas, trunks, clothing, furs, etc., out of negroes'
houses before they were burned, and hauling or carrying the plunder off;
that there was absolutely no effort made by the country or city officers to preserve order or enforce the law, and that this continued till
about 1 P. M., when the militia took charge.

DYER also states that this policeman RIGNON, bragged to him, DYER,
of being part of the white mob, and personally killing four niggers, as
they sat in an auto DYER also states that he saw a neighbor, who
lives in Jenks, take two Victrolas from negro houses, put them in a
word and drive away, presumably for home.

(DYER was very indignant, and stated he was going before the Grand
Jury and tell all he knew.)

T. F...Biss.   June 1 to 5, 1921.   -7-

All the above named are withes, who are really a little prejudiced toward negroes, but state they cannot condone the actions of the county and city officers, and the white mob, that invaded the negro section.

By June 2nd the whites and blacks were mingling amicably on the streets of Tulsa and in the devastated negro section. Many of the negroes were searching in the ruins of their homes for valuables and keepsakes. Agent talked to them, and found no bitterness but a suprising amount of optimism and resignation. They nearly all told the same story of hearing shots, seeing houses set on fire, and fleeing for their lives, some of their members, who had guns, shooting as they fled. "The Tulsa World" and "Tribune" were advocating making good the property losses by private donations, and were distributing blanks to the losers, to file their claims by. This probably had much to do with the negroes' optimistic attitude.

A real estate and insurance firm estimated the total loss at $1,500,000.00. R. G. DUNN estimated the loss in merchandise alone at $250,000.00. Agent inspected the destroyed area, and is of the opinion that above estimates are conservative. The area is about two miles long and from two to six blocks wide; a few houses are left standing, but those burned are most completely consumed. The residences ran from shacks to $6,000.00 and $7,000.00 homes.

The business buildings included several hundred one to three-story brick and frame stores, garages, hotels, rooming houses, cafes, picture shows, churches, etc. One church alone, that cost $85,000.00 is completely destroyed. The negroes saved almost absolutely nothing when they fled, and between four thousand and five thousand of them were rendered homeless.

The police department and many good citizens are recovering considerable of the stolen property, and some arrests are being made--but not many. A number of good xxxx autos are known to have been stolen by the mob, including a Peerless limousine, belonging to a white man, and a Marmon.

The known dead to datex are ten whites, twenty-one blacks, wounded about 125. At first it was feared that many blacks would be found to have been shot, and burned, but after talking with the negroes who fled, Agent believes that but few dead bodies will be found in the debris, as must of the negroes fled as soon as the first fires started about daylight.

In response to phone message from Agent in Charge Findlay on June 2nd, Agent sent night letter, Mackay, to Chief of Bureau, which has already been submitted in Agent Findlay's report, this titled, dated June 1 to 3, 1921, and need not be copied here.

To sum up, Tulsa for years has been notoriously lax in law enforcement and has had both crooked and inefficient county and city officers (see our reports for three years back).

The present trouble was really not a race riot, nor was it the result of racial feeling, or agitators. It began in a small half-hearted attempt to lynch a negro youth--who is apparently innocent--and grew to an armed clash between whites and blacks, brought on by the Sheriff's crazy calling of armed negroes to the county jail. (Two Deputy Sheriffs are negroes, and one, BARNEY CLEAVER, can, if he will tell about this call.)

54

DEPARTMENT OF JUSTICE
Box 455
Chicago,
Ill.

OFFICIAL BUSINESS
PENALTY FOR PRIVATE USE, $300.

CHICAGO
ILL.
JAN 9.
8 PM
18

Chief,
Bureau of Investigation
Dept. of Justice,

Attention
Mr. J.E. Hoover
Intelligence Division

Washington,
D.C.

APPENDIX D

DEPARTMENT OF JUSTICE

MAIL AND FILES DIVISION

SCREENED
BY *WQR* DATE: *1/10/66*

File No. *158260*

Sub. *8*

See also Nos.

T—1148

158260 — 8

PRESIDENT
R. Rev. SAMUEL FALLOWS, D.D., LL.D., Bishop

1ST VICE-PRES AND SUPT
JOHN BUTLER CALDWELL

TREASURER
Rev J. G. LAWSON

International Purity Association

International
Purity Journal
ESTABLISHED 1897. PUBLISHED BY THE
International Purity Association
50 CENTS PER YEAR
JOHN BUTLER CALDWELL, Editor

Acked
7/25/21

INCORPORATED, ILLINOIS, 1854-1911
DEVOTED TO
RACE IMPROVEMENT, EUGENICS, CONSCIOUS EVOLUTION, PRE-NATAL
INFLUENCES, AND THE RIGHT OF EVERY CHILD TO BE WELL-BORN
LONG DISTANCE TELEPHONE FRANKLIN 85

OFFICE OF
MME. LOZANTO, VICE-PRES.
SAINT JOSEPH, MO.

3020 Penn St.

HEADQUARTERS
127 N. WELLS ST.
CHICAGO, ILL.

AUG 2 21

158...8...

My Dear Mrs. Harding,

I am so grateful

for the reply to my former letter.

I have gained ____ information very recently that I want to put before you, in an informal way, as I deem we are one great family with Mr. Harding (and yourself) at the head. I further more believe that you, each, are interested in the highest good of every citizen and community — hence, enclose the information that will show you more fully what the Tulsa Oklahoma disaster means to our people in black. And to ask for aid for these from the government, as Mr. Harding may determine, and personally as you each can decide in

PRESIDENT
Rt. Rev. SAMUEL FALLOWS, D.D., D.LL.D., Bishop

1st VICE-PRES AND SUPT
JOHN BUTLER CALDWELL

TREASURER
Rev J. G. LAWSON

Internatiomal Purity Association

INCORPORATED, ILLINOIS, 1894-1911

DEVOTED TO

RACE IMPROVEMENT, EUGENICS, CONSCIOUS EVOLUTION, PRE-NATAL
INFLUENCES, AND THE RIGHT OF EVERY CHILD TO BE WELL-BORN

LONG DISTANCE TELEPHONE FRANKLIN 88

International
Purity Journal
ESTABLISHED 1897. PUBLISHED BY THE
International Purity Association
60 CENTS PER YEAR
JOHN BUTLER CALDWELL, EDITOR

OFFICE OF
MME. LOZANTO, VICE-PRES.
SAINT JOSEPS, MO.

HEADQUARTERS
197 N. WELLS ST.
CHICAGO, ILL.

us to best mode of procedure — but in
each case to give us your influence
for better things for them.

I am in touch with Mr. G. A. Gregg, who
is well known here. Quoting from his
letter to me under date of July 11, '21,
is this: "We are doing what we can in
our behalf. We must have an advocate.
We can not have our burdens alone, —
The saddest observation and memory is,
that amid all the suffering of our people
not a person stood but in Tulsa and
gave voice in our behalf."

Knowing existing conditions as I
do, both of church and state, yes, and
press, I fully realize why 'twas so.
They simply lack the "sand" to carry
out what they can't help but know
to be the correct attitude and action.

PRESIDENT
Rev. SAMUEL FALLOWS, D.D., Ph.D., LL.D., Bishop

1st VICE-PRES. AND SUPT.
JOHN BUTLER CALDWELL

TREASURER
Rev J. G. LAWSON

International
Purity Journal
ESTABLISHED 1887. PUBLISHED BY THE
International Purity Association
60 CENTS PER YEAR
JOHN BUTLER CALDWELL, EDITOR

International Purity Association
INCORPORATED, ILLINOIS, 1884-1911
DEVOTED TO
RACE IMPROVEMENT, EUGENICS, CONSCIOUS EVOLUTION, PRE-NATAL
INFLUENCES, AND THE RIGHT OF EVERY CHILD TO BE WELL-BORN
LONG DISTANCE TELEPHONE FRANKLIN 88

OFFICE OF
MME. LOZANTO, VICE-PRES.
SAINT JOSEPH, MO.

HEADQUARTERS
197 N. WELLS ST.
CHICAGO, ILL.

toward the colored race. I have mingled
with the public too much studying
conditions to _not_ know where I stand.
Tulsa, in the sight of God can _not_
deny those colored people the rights of
citizenship in the fullest sense, nor
refuse to see that the desolation shall
be made as good for them as it
was before the riot. It is their duty—
morally, legally,— our government should
see that it is done. I realize that Mr.
Harding's hands are _extremely_ full,
but from biblical standpoint— "one of
the least of these" is the Tulsa ~~riot~~
colored people in their distressed condition at this time, ignored by the Christian
people of that city seemingly, and in helping
them at this crisis, would be doing it
unto Christ. What a changed world

this would be if proposed, which would be practical, and not prostitute the earth and its fullness for individual selfishness.

The enclosures explain the situation, which to the wise is sufficient.

Thanking you and Mr. Harding, for your interest in those people, both for myself and them, and hoping they can be returned for all this, &c. (The strain if the action will not out) I am

Very Sincerely
Mme. Lozant

St. Joseph
July 18 - 1921

▲PPEAL!

TULSA'S COLORED PEOPLE

have not the earnest attention of the nation,
because the associated press reports do not state in a manner,
that will stimulate a desire to give relief, the cruel conditions that
have and do exist.

Official Tulsa and therefore Tulsa at large
*Is NOT helping in proportion to
the appalling need.*

People are without stoves, cooking utensils, quilts and bedding of
all kinds—the merest necessities of existence—

and ready money

*All they have left is courage to face
the future*

Mr. James L. Fieser, Southwestern Division Manager of the
Red Cross said: "Winter's approach worries the Red Cross." Unless Tulsa wishes to have a tent colony on its hands in the fall and
face a more serious problem, it should SPEED UP its reconstruction program. He sees a big job ahead here for Tulsans and that
now the financial end of the undertaking is the most important
feature. *Money is needed for relief and needed badly.*

We appeal to you for help

Tulsa Colored Citizens Relief Committee

S. D. Hooker, Chr.; G. A. Gregg, Executive Sec'y.; Rev. R. A.
Whitaker, Sec'y.; Hon. E. I. Saddler, Legal Advisor; J. Tyler
Smith, Treas.; E. A. Troupe, Rev. H. T. S. Johnson, Rev. Jas. A.
Johnson, Rev. J. R. McClain, Dr. J. M. Keys, S. G. Smith, Mrs. A.
Bankhead, Hon. J. H. Goodwin.

The Gear Printing Company, Kansas City, Kansas

#1026 Kenyon, Street, N.W.

Washington, D.C.,
July, 2nd., 1921.

Mrs.█ ██████.██████.████████.
████████████ulder Avenue,
Tulsa, Oklahoma,

Dear Madam:—

Your cousin Mr. Jordan, who formerly lived in Tulsa, and who now works with me, told me this morning that he had gotten a letter from you, stating the facts concerning the whole-sale murder of the colored people of Tulsa. I am writing to ask you if you will at your convenience, write me concerning the same. I want to know first-handed of the trouble. It would be more than criminal in me to divulge the name of my informant. I will tell you what we of the East think of this affair:—We learn from reliable sources that the up-shot of the whole matter was that the white people wanted the land on which the colored people had their homes, stores and the like, and that this murder was started for this reason—and no other.

The colored man who stepped on the foot of the white department store girl elevator operator, was charged with this simple thing and nothing else.

We learn that the colored men went to the sheriff and asked for protection. He told them that the man would be protected. When the white mob came to storm the jail, the colored men came too. There were 200 of each. The colored men told the mob that there was not going to be any lynching, and the sheriff, asked the white men if they were going to take that from "These niggers"? Then the lower regions opened. The police tried and only disarmed the colored people. When the houses were set on fire the police refused to let the firemen, put it out. Then the militia was called and they surrounded the colored section, and the white mob having protection, they fired all the buildings. They looted the department stores, and shot down women and children in their burning homes. The real estate companies who insured these homes had a riot clause, in all their policies to colored people. The colored people lost all their holdings in oil, and their homes and property, as well as all their books. Their receipts and the like were destroyed in the flames, except what was not stolen by these white fiends. They say they are going to build. Yes! Some shacks, three miles further out. We know the truth and the hearts of the Race everywhere in America, bleeds for thee. Let me know what I can do and I will thank my God, that I have the priveledge. Shall earnestly await your reply.

Have written a poem "TULSA—HOW OUR HEARTS BLEED FOR THEE". Haven't a copy here at work. Will send you one when I write again. May God bless all of you.

Good-bye,

Respectfully Yours——

Rev. J. Luther Martin

Rev, J. Luther Martin.

⌐outh Boulden, Ave.   Tulsa, Oklahoma,
                                                       July, 6th., 1921.

Rev .J.Luther Martin,
#1026, Kenyon, St.,N.W.,
Washington, D.C.,
Dear Sir & Brother:-

Yours of the 2nd., inst. to hand and contents noted. I am more than glad to answer such a manly, sympathetic and heart-felt letter. First I will say that every word in your letter is true. The gathering at the jail is said to have been about 500 whites and 200, colored. When this trouble began they held a battle from 10:30 o'clock, Tuesday morning/ night until 9:00 o' clock Wednesday morning.
As near as I can say the militia arrived here somewhere about 9:00 O'clock or 9:30. But let me say that the fire had been started before, and the police would not let the firemen put out the fire. They killed two of the firemen because they were trying to do their duty. The whites drove trucks up to the doors of the colored homes and loaded them before setting fire,while the poor people were running for their lives. Some had only one or two pnices on;no shoes nor the like. The whites took all/ their belongings;they took the colored peoples' victrolas, beddding,wearing materials, watches, rings —in fact everything that they could get their hands on.
One of the saddest things that happened ,was that they took$800;00 from an old woman, beat her and then threw her out into the street, and then set her house on fire. Many crimes like that were committed. They took over $700;00 from one woman and then pitched her out of the window on her head. After they had disarmed the colored people;then they rounded them up like Texas cattle,searching them all the time, and taking all the money they found. A man told me--- and I know that it is true,that where tehy carried them , they had all the colored people shot to pieces, lying across the door where the people had to go in,and as they would go into the place they would demand "hands up", He said that the guards took, #11:00 from him, and $20:00off the man just in front of him. The man asked the. guard, "are you going to credit me for my money ?"With this he said, "you-son-of -a-gun, and you---- ----- ----- ----- don't ask again. The colored man then threw down his book. The white guard commanded, him to pick it up,or he would put him in the same fix, the dead man in the door was. In some fo the homes they.ndressed up in the colored peoples' clothes, leaving what they had on when they went in their, and then would burn the homes.
Sad but true;-there were babies burned in these homes,when there were thousands of men, women, and children, with no place to hide nor anything to lie upon. One woman gave birth to a child that night in a truck,exposed and couldn't hide.
white men cursing her for a cow and other things. Now as to the building, the homes again for the colored people,these white people don't intend to do nothing of the kind. They said that they were going to and when they raised the money,for that purpose,they said that they were going to put it in the bank. Now listen I know that the colored didtrict was still burning, when I read in the papers that they were going to move "the niggers", farther out N.E., and biuld for. them out there, and take their land and not allow them to build on it. But thank God; the colored people were too wise to let them do that. Now they think that they can bar them out by saying that nothing can go up but fire-proof buildings. Now as what you aan do I can't say, but I hope that you can do something for the protection of our people. Now there is a Committee,of three man here fromWashington, as you know, looking after this affair, and they are to be here for three weeks. They say that theses whites have got to place every thing back, and that if they didn't that the Government would and take it from the Tulsa whites. Oh! I am about to forget to tell you that some of the colored peoplesm clothes are being taken off those white men and women righthon the street and they are being sent to jail in their under-clothes.
I am told that there has been a car-load of the colored peoples' belongings, brought from Texas. I could write all day and something would be untold. Now listen!
One of our finest surgeons, Dr. Namely, a friend of Dr. Jackson,came out of his house with both hands up, and the whites, shot him to death, and then robbed him in the presence of his wife. God only knows and He only, will know untill , the day will come when all things will be made known!
            I will be glad to hear from you at any time,

                    Respectfully Yours,

                        Mrs. *********.***********.************.

#1026, Kenyon, Street, N.W.,
(In reHPS. (script)WCH.
158260-8-
Dictated,WCH-EOT.)

Washington, D.C.,
July, 12th., 1921.

158260-8

To the Honorable,
The Attorney-General, of the Unites States,
Washington, D.C.,
Dear,Sir:-

Your letter of June, 8th., 1921, as noted above, was received in due course of mail. In reply I should like to state that I have been active, in trying to get data, so: as to in a small way ,assist your Department, in asortaing the truth in reference to the "rape of Tulsa" ! You will please note in paragraph three(3),of my letter too Mrs. ****,****,****, of Tulsa,(a copy of which is enclosed),as of July 2nd., 1921, that I state that it would be more than criminal in me to divulge the name of my informant". It is for this very reason that I with-hold her name. This letter is over my signature,consequently,,the Department can hold me responsible for all statements contained therein. I may state however that the information I wrote, Mrs.John Doe, was gained from no less a source, than one sponsored by the great Methodist Episcopal Church,in the person of the Rev. Dr.W.A.C.Hughes,Field Sectoy, Board of Home Missions and Church Extension. The M.E.Church, him and a white man there to investigate.
He personally told us these facts at a Mass Meeting, held recently in one of our representive Churches. He also read letters from Tulsa. There were several white men present. As to whether or not they represented your Department, I do not know.
In the attached letter from Mrs. X., there is made mention of "the guards". Does this imply, the National Guard of Oklahoma? My letter to her suggests that this is what is meant. Your Department can however verify the same. If these were men in the uniform sanctioned by the United States Government, then the crime is not only against the colored people of Tulsa, but against the Sovergein Dignity of the United States of America. As a matter of fact, the crime does strike at the cardinal principals of Americanism, which to the rest of the world stands for, Liberty, Justice and Right! I am not a lawyer, but I think I learned when I was in school, something that goes as follows:-The Constitution of the United States say:- "ALL persons born or naturlized in the United States of America or its Territories, and subject to the jurisdiction thereof are citizens of the United States. No state shall make or enforce any Law which shall abridge the rights, priviledges or immunities of any citizen thereof, neither shall ANY STATE, deny any citizen the right to equal protectin of the Law". I think the Declaration of Independence says:-"We hold these truths to be self-evidento, that ALL men are************endowed by their Creator, with certain inalienable rights; that among these are the right,LIFE, LIBERTY and the persuit of happiness I can hardly beleive that "mob-law", will supplant the Law of the Land".
I cannot beleive that the so-called question of "States Rights",is more dominant than "The Powers that be",---which is the United States, centralized in Washington. It seems to me that the question of"States Rights", was settled at Appomattox, when Lee surrendered to Grant. *****************While I know that the colored people of the country are doing all they can to help the Tulsa sufferers; yet I DO want to beleive that the Committe, mentioned in the letter from there, has been sent out by your Department. I want to beleive that the Government for which we have bled and died, and have ever been ready to defend, also the Flag, dyed by Negro blood from Chrispus Attucks, to Metz, will protect us from criminals and murderers at all times.
We trust that your Department, will not cease its vigilance(and I have no reason to beleive otherwise), until every one of theses Tulsa, murderers are brought to justice and paid the penalty of their crimes.
    Again thanking you for your prompt reply,
    I wish to subscribe myself,
    Yours-for Justice and Right-------

Rev. _____

158260-8

TELEPHONE XW 25

POST OFFICE BOX 183

Already Proven to be the
Greatest Remedy in
the World.

HOTTENTO
DISCOVERED, MANUFACTURED AND DISTRIBUTED BY
C. DEARMAN
MEDICAL RESEARCH SCIENTIST

Will Relieve, Assuage, Conquer
and Cure More Different Con-
tagious, Infectious and bad
Chronic Diseases than
any Other Remedy in
the World.

OFFICE: NORTHEAST OF CITY

Box 183.

TULSA, OKLA.

6/38/21

1921

Honorable, Warren G.Harding. President of the United States of America.
White House.
Washington, D.C.
Most Honorable

Secy. to the President

I am a Negro man forty seven years of age, I
manufacture a medicine, I am a Baptist Minister of the Gospel, I have lived
in Tulsa, Oklahoma, for the past fourteen years I knew not whether you have
recieved a special report of the horrible affair that happened in our city
some weeks ago, Howbeit feeling that you for some reason may not be fully
acquainted with conditions as they exist, I thought it not amiss to submit
for your consideration, a report which you will find enclosed.

I am indeed your humble servant

C. Dearman,

LLT

158260-8-18

6/28/21.
Tulsa, Oklahoma.
Box 183.

Honorable, Warren G.Harding, President of the United States of America.
White House
Washington, D.C.
Most Honorable Sir.

On behalf of ten thousand Negroes that live in our city of Tulsa, I am asking that you through your Department of Justice or any other of your Departments that you deem necesary, give consideration by investigation or otherwise of the herrible affair that happened in our city on the first day of June 1921. I am asking for Federal action because I believe that it is the ond only agency that is capable of getting at the bottom of this affair.

The local grand jury has met and adjourned some white people and some negro people have been indicted for inciting riot, looting etc, be that as it may I feel sure that the bottom of the affair has not been reached. My belief borne out by some facts is that Foreign propaganda or some other propaganda equally as dangerous was responsible for the whole affair,For instance upon making inquiry among my people the Negroes, a woman told me that her son-in-law who was in Texas before this affair happened ever heard a long distance telephone conversation stating that a white mob was going to form for the purpose of lynching a Negro in Tulsa, and that a Negro mob was going to oppose the white mob and that then the white mob would enlarge itself and kill Negroes loot and burn their homes and use their land for industrial purposes. Upon making further inquiry I found that some white man telephoned certain Negroes in our part of the city and advised them to form a Negro mob and oppose the white mob.

Now Mr, President I am very much of the opinion that the man or men that advised the white mob to form was the same man or men that advised the Negro mob to form and urged them to oppose the white mob, and that the same man or men urged the white mob to enlarge itself and kill Negroes, loot and burn their homes etc, and that the same man or men are responsible for the handicapping the work of the Red Cross among our people and that the same man or men refused to accept outside aid for us when itmwas preffered and that the same man or men persistently refused to aid us themselves causing hundreds of our people here at the present time to be in a condition worse than any condition of slavery that ever existed in this country, And now whenwe say that we want food, clothing and shelter they answer us by saying thatnwe want your land where your houses were burned.

The Red Cross under the direction of Mr, Maurice Willows is doing a commendable and most wonderful work among our people which is highly appreciated by all of our people,, and were it not for the Red Cross many of our people would have died from exposure, disease and starvation long before this hour, In all the good work that the Red Cross has accomplished among our people it has been done in the face of a hidden hand of opposition,you can better understand when I tell you that in many instances high officials of the Red Cross have had to lay aside their ink and pens and take up the saw and hammer and build temporary refuges for some of our people.

I am very much inclined to the opinion that the final aim of these that were responsible for the crimes committed against our people here was for the specific purpose of embarrassing the United States Government for the reason that the saying is now being spread abroad that the United States cannot again talk about the atrocities of any other nation because the crime committed here was the worst in the history of the world.

Mr, President it seems as but yesterday that ten or fifteen thousand white people armed with pistols, shotguns, rifles, army rifles, machine guns, tegather with four or five armed airplanes murderously sweeped down upon us on that fatal wednesday morning of June the first 1921. and almost the entire ten thousand colored people were killed wounded or made prisoners after which hundreds and hundreds of automobiles driven by white men and white women came into our section of the city and stolen and taken our goods from our stores and from our homes about fifteen hundred of our homes were robbed and about one thousand of our homes And business houses, churches, undertaking parlors school houses and hospitals were both robbed and burned. immediately after this horrible crime press reports went out from Tulsa that she would make good all our losses but to date not one dollar of our losses have been made good by either the city, cokkty or state. and no plans as far as we are able to learn are on foot for that purpose about all that we can hear is that they are going to compel the railroads to build a Union Station here and that they are going to compel us to sell our lands for that purpose.

(2)

All the help that we have ever been able to get came from the Red Cross and a
few private individuals both white and colored. Our condition beggars description and all that I can say Mr, President is that if it is not beneath your
dignity and that if you can lend your attention from matters of greater
importance to you than our affair that you come to our city and see for your
self our ruins, our desolation, our despair. But if you cannot come, We trust,
We hope, We believe Mr, President that you will act in the matter that will
insure us succor, aid and protection and also that you will bring to the surface
the propagandist that is responsible for this terrible affair, that he or they
may recieve the punishment that the laws of our United States Government
decrees will be swift, sure and certain.

I am subject to your command.

C. Dearman,

158260-S

WWG-AC

-16

July 11, 1921.

Arthur T. Tallman, Esq.,

35 Bullman Street,

Phillipsburg, N. J.

Dear Sir:

Receipt is acknowledged of your letter of the 3rd instant in which you enclosed a copy of the circular entitled "The Tulsa Massacre", issued by the Central Executive Committee of the Communist Party of America. Although this matter had already been brought to our attention, I desire you to know that your action in calling it to the attention of the Government is appreciated.

Respectfully,

For the Attorney General,

RECORDED Herron

Attorney.

THE STANDARD SILK CO.
PHILLIPSBURG, N. J.

$1 \cdot 572 \cdot 1 \cdot C \cdot 8$

July 3" 1921

Department of Justice
Washington

D. C.

Gentlemen;

I enclose two copies of "The Tulsa Massacre" put out by the Central Executive Com. Communist Party of America. It shows to what lengths they will go, and their shrewdness in picking up anything that can foment trouble. I picked up these pamphlets on the street this morning. I think the hot bed of these people in this section is Easton Pa just across the river from Phillipsburg N.J.

yours Resp.

Arthur D. Dallman
35 Buchanan St.

Circular attached.
7/6/21 F.D.W.

Added. 7/11/21

$158260-8-16$

The Tulsa Massacre!

By the time this leaflet is in your hands all the horrible details of the mass murder of the helpless Negro population of Tulsa, Oklahoma will be known to the entire world.

There are no words vivid enough to describe the action of the well dressed armed mob of business men who, with automobiles and airplanes, surrounded the Negro quarter in Tulsa on June 1st, setting fire to their homes, destroying ten city blocks and rendering homeless more than ten thousand Negro workers; ruthlessly slaying men, women and children killing over 90 and wounding more than 200.

There is only one appeal that will stop these fiendish and bloody outrages—that is the appeal to organized force. The only language that the bloodthirsty capitalist of America can understand 'is the language of ORGANIZED POWER. Only by reprisals—by answering force with force —will the business mobs and their White Guards, the Klu Klux Klan etc., be restrained from continuing their brutal and cowardly assaults upon the Negro and working class population of this country.

If there is any red blood in the veins of the working class of America it will come to the defense of its colored brothers; who are the victims of the same bloody capitalist class that exploits and murders the workers regardless of color or race.

In their own interests, the white workers of America, must come to the aid of the exploited Negro masses. Their skins are darker-hued than ours, but the interests are the same. Black and White, we, the workers, have but ONE enemy—THE CAPITALIST CLASS—which uses its GOVERNMENT to suppress us.

There are more than ten million Negroes in this country. Almost all of them are of the working class. These Negro wage workers, whom we have refused to admit into our trade unions, are rapidly being reduced to serfdom and peonage—to a condition of slavery worse than chattel slavery before 1861. Shall we, the white wage slaves, stand by idly and permit the CAPITALISTS to murder, rob and crush ten millions of our fellows? The crushing of ten million Negro workers can mean nothing but the beginning of a system of peonage and degradation for the entire working class of America. For the breaking of the spirit of these ten million Negro wage workers will enable the WHITE CAPITALISTS to use these colored men and women against the white wage workers as strike breakers in order to crush the resistance of the entire working class. Already there are five million wage workers walking the streets of the cities and towns of America in search of work—unemployed, desperate, hungry—and the CAPITALISTS are making a general assault upon our unions, through the open shop movement, in the effort to destroy our unions and break our resistance. •

If the Negro worker can be used against the White worker, who is to blame? We have refused to allow our colored brothers to join our unions. We have repeated all the idiotic accusations against their ace. We have foolishly allowed ourselves to be swayed by race prejudice. We have failed to ORGANIZE the Negro workers. We have refused to treat him as our own, our equal BROTHER in the CLASS STRUGGLE. WE ARE TO BLAME.

BREAK DOWN THE BARRIERS IN THE UNIONS. WIPE OUT THE "COLOR LINE." There is only ONE line that we can draw—that is the CLASS LINE. White and Black, Jew and Gentile, ALL THE

71

WORKERS, the exploited masses, must be organized on the basis of their CLASS interests.

Our Negro fellow workers were supposed to have been "emancipated" during the American Civil War. The Constitution of the U. S. is supposed to guarantee their "freedom." Since then they have been herded into separate districts, segregated in Jim Crow cars, their women subject to the assaults of white men, their children deprived of elementary education, their men denied the right to acquire trades or professions, their whole race kept in ignorance and degradation. They have been burned alive, lynched, murdered and brutally assaulted upon the slightest provocation. The hideous accusation of rapine has been fastened upon their entire race. This is the kind of "freedom" that CAPITALIST CONSTITUTION guarantees to the working class. This is the only kind of "freedom" that the WORKERS can expect from the CAPITALIST GOVERNMENT of the United States. For the Government of the U.S. is nothing but the organized expression of the WILL of the CAPITALIST CLASS. The Government of the U. S. is nothing else but a ruthless DICTATORSHIP of the RICH over the POOR.

It is in the interest of both the Negro and the White WORKERS to destroy this CAPITALIST GOVERNMENT, root and branch. Shoulder to shoulder, and heart to heart, the workers of ALL races must UNITE to establish in this country a WORKERS' GOVERNMENT—THE SOVIET REPUBLIC OF AMERICA.

THE COMMUNIST PARTY OF AMERICA calls upon our colored comrades to ORGANIZE, and with arms in their hands, to resist the murderous armed assaults upon their homes, their women and their children.

THE COMMUNIST PARTY OF AMERICA calls upon the White workers to assist their colored brothers and with arms in their hands, to help them to repel such armed attacks upon them by the wealthy business men, as occured in Tulsa, Oklahoma and in hundreds of other places.

THEIR FIGHT IS OUR FIGHT. THE COMMUNIST PARTY OF AMERICA recognizes no artificial division between the WORKING CLASS. We call upon ALL workers of ALL races to UNITE against their COMMON ENEMY—the Capitalist Class and the CAPITALIST STATE.

Both Negro and White workers must by this time realize the kind of "democracy" they fought for in France. This is the only kind of "democracy" that the workers can get under the capitalist government of the United States.

In Russia, under the Tzar's Government, the Jews were the victims of race riots and pogroms. In Russia the workers and peasants overthrew the CAPITALIST Government of Russia and established a WORKERS' GOVERNMENT—THE SOVIET REPUBLIC OF RUSSIA. The workers of all races in Russia are UNITED. Race prejudice and race wars have disappeared.

Only by following our Russian Comrades' heroic example and by establishing in this country the SOVIET REPUBLIC OF AMERICA will White and Black workers be able to live and work in peace and enjoy the fruits of their labor.

WORKERS OF AMERICA—ORGANIZE! WIPE OUT THE "COLOR LINE"!

HAIL TO THE PROLETARIAN REVOLUTION!

DOWN WITH THE CAPITALIST SYSTEM AND THE CAPITALIST STATE!

LONG LIVE THE WORKERS' REPUBLIC OF AMERICA!

CENTRAL EXECUTIVE COMMITTEE
COMMUNIST PARTY OF AMERICA

DUANE MOWRY
LAWYER
COLLECTIONS
2442 CHESTNUT ST.   TELEPHONE WEST 1821
MILWAUKEE, WISCONSIN

DEPT OF THE INTERIOR
RECEIVED
JUN 27 1921
SEC'Y'S OFF.-MAILS AND FILES

Milwaukee, Wis., June 28, 1921.

Hon. Warren G. Harding,
President of the United States,
White House,
Washington, D.C.

My dear Mr. President:-

Herewith is my recent contribution
to the subject of MOB RULE, which appeared this morning in
our local newspaper, The Milwaukee Sentinel. It is suggestive,
mainly. But I am hoping that it may interest you, and, perhaps,
assist you in arriving at some practical solution of this
inexcusable national disgrace.

But as you have other letters from me bearing on
this subject, it is not necessary for me to refer to the
matter further at this time.

I beg, my dear sir, to be,

Your most obedient servant,

LLT

158260-8-

once,
proc-
o long
ay back
for pe-
elcomes

ns busi-
ving the
iwes for

founding his colony of Rhode Island.

The Puritans of Boston allowed no one to vote unless he belonged to their church.

The Pilgrims permitted any well behaved citizen to exercise that privilege. Miles Standish, the great military captain, never belonged to their church, yet he held the highest offices in the colony except that of govrnor.

One of your correspondents a while ago said the Pilgrims "burned witches." The fact is, there never was but one trial for witchcraft at Plymouth. The accused was acquitted and thereupon the whole witchcraft craze was ridiculed out of that colony. The Puritans hung some witches—they did not burn them.

Any reader who wishes to verify these statements is referred to "The Pilgrim Republic," by John Goodwin, the most thorough and authentic history of that colony.

FAIRPLAY.

Oshkosh, Wis., June 15, 1921.

MOB VIOLENCE IN OKLAHOMA.

To the Editor of The Sentinel:

tion and
ception,
iren are
ent, dis-

n in his
n asso-

requir-
schools
to work
w gives
pend its

ce as a
ny boys
ter they
ome but
t work,
success.
wasted.
resent-
hich do

requir-
s a wise
en who
tions to

e more
action
permit

is cases
y would
the irk-
entments
ake up

dge of
careful

ent and
iren" at
ieteenth

There

The recent lawless outbreak in Tulsa, Okla., which furnishes the subject for the leading article in the current issue of the Literary Digest, is additional evidence of the utter hopelessness of the present social order to cope successfully with this national disgrace. No one will be punished for this inexcusable crime, and lynch law will be again inflicted whenever any community, in its lawlessness, feels so inclined to do.

And yet "there is no evidence to show that punishment of negroes by mob violence tends to decrease lawlessness among the negroes, or even tends to restrain the vicious element from committing offenses against the whites. On the contrary, lawlessness seems to beget lawlessness, and the publicity given to revolting crimes by lynching the perpetrators of them, seems really to incite others to commit similar crimes, or at least suggests to others like crimes when opportunity offers."

But the writer quoted says that "the problem of finding a remedy for lynching is really a problem of increasing and maintaining a popular reliance on the formulation and the administration of the law. Every measure which will in any way promote such a reliance, either by invalidating the excuses offered in justification of the practice, or by developing a strong public sentiment against it, deserves serious consideration, and every such measure, unless likely to be productive of other evils possibly greater, should be immediately adopted and put into operation."

It would seem, therefore, that "strict and impartial law enforcement" would do much to deter the commission of crime by whole communities. The difficulty seems to be and is that there is no law enforcement for the rule of the mob. The due administration of the law has totally failed to administer justice to those guilty of mob violence.

President Harding has held out hope that the subject of lynch law will receive consideration at his hands and by the present congress. Let us hope so, for there is great and pressing need for constructive legislation, which will render the rule of the mob the act of criminals and to be dealt with as such. DUANE MOWRY.

Milwaukee, Wis., June 18, 1921.

FILES

50 Years Ago — Workmen are engaged in putting a new gilded cross on the spire of the Spring Street Methodist Episcopal church to take the place of the one wrenched off some time ago by the wind ...The State Medical society will close its annual session here today...s. There will

Today. — be a fair and festival at the Unitarian church this evening.s..."The Jolly Tailor" is the name of the attractive play which will be given at Kurz's theater tomorrow evening.

+ + +

25 Years Ago — The entire property of the Oberman Brewing company was sold yesterday to Philip Jung....Beginning next Saturday, open air concerts will be given at Lake park every Wednesday and Sat-

158260 - 8 - JUN 25 1921

B.J

June 16, 1921.

Hon. Horace Porter,
Mayor of Riverside,
Riverside, Calif.

My dear Mayor:

I have your letter of the 9th instant and thank you for writing me with reference to the subject mentioned. I can assure you that I at all times want to see the Federal laws enforced and I shall be very happy to cooperate with you and see that all citizens of the United States have guaranteed to them their constitutional rights.

I have instructed the United States Attorneys in Oklahoma to report any violations of the Federal laws in connection with the recent race riots, and I am in hopes of having their report. With reference to your local cities I shall be very happy at any time to have reports of any violations in your community.

I can not let the opportunity go by to wish you well, and it is gratifying to know an Ohioan, who has wandered westward, is still imbued with political activities.

Yours truly,

Attorney General.

M

RECORDED

158480- 3- 13	Misc.	6-18-21.

Will Green,
   Haskell Okla.

n Writes re- race riots in Tulsa Okla.

   Stewart Herron Kr   5-23-21.

158260 - 8 11

158260 - 8 - 13

JUN 28 1921 A. M.

Hash Okla

June 18 - 1921

R. J. B.

To the Attorney General.

Daughter

Dea sir. I

thought I would write to

you concerning the Race

Riote in Tulsa. Okla.

I will say in just.

that it most Thatto

the entire Business

district of the negroes

woes wiffe out with.

Fire. the Home Guards

woos helping Burn

Houses and shooting

negroes as they was

121

Running out of Amunition.
The Home Guards it
was [illegible] [illegible] the
[illegible] Oath when they
Could have Stopped
the mob from Burning
the House. 4 airplanes
were Flying over the
[illegible] Belt dropping
[illegible] missiles on
buildings [illegible] [illegible]
and [illegible] it was
white men were fighting
negroes life gas [illegible]
on the firing line
in [illegible] it a
Coward that would
do such. the negro

12

hase no P_____ in
America right or wrong
this goverment is going
to stop, not fall of
we are going to die
by the thousand
ing to Protect our
Rights in the united
State. did you git that.
if the Folk of Oklahoma
allowes airplanes to
estroy ~~_____~~
Negroes Homes,
and Rem Homes by
hundreds. some white
people is going to
die with ours that
all the Negroes of
Tulsa

had a Right to eVade
the down town
district to Protect
their Race. a white
man would have did
the same thing if
a Negro mot- was
going to lynch a
white man
the White Man have
Protection. they were
a made up thing
between the mob and
the High Sheriff and
the Police department
to not stopped the
mob. that wore the
reason.

They also rule two
mikhi guns in the
negrows. If this government
doht need any more
negrow if they dont
stop them in the
army.
Read and
act
Will Green

WCH-ECT

150260-8-11

June 16, 1921.

Mr. E. C. Branch,

127 River St.,

Troy, New York.

Dear Sir:

Your letter of June 9th to the President of the United States, enclosing a clipping from the Troy, New York, Times, relative to the Tulsa race riot, and giving your views upon the matter, has been referred to this Department, and I beg to assure you that what you say will receive due consideration.

There is not, however, in the matter sent by you, the slightest indication that the airplane referred to was a government airplane, and therefore this Department does not feel that it should investigate that aspect of the matter.

Respectfully,

For the Attorney General,

(Signed) Annette Abbott Adams

Assistant Attorney General.

RECORDED

158260-8

Troy, N. Y.

June the 9th, 1921

Mr. Warren G. Harding, President of U. S. A.

White House,

Washington, D. C.

My Dear Sir:-

I am sending you a clipping from the Troy, N. Y., Times,
June the 7th, 1921 for your information, relative to the Tulsa,
Okla. Race Riot.   I see from this article, that an aeroplane
dropped bombs on Negro Apartment Houses, in the Negro settlement.
If this was a U. S. Aeroplane, did this pilot have the authority
to make the attack upon these Negroes?   My race would appreciate
it very much, if you would have the War Department to investigate
the allegation.

You can see from this report the Negro was not aggressive
from the very fact the negroes was in the church, and apartment
house, and both of was in a negro settlementn   The negroes in the
church and apartment could not make much of a fight in a church.
I am of the opinion the negroes in the church especially was hiding,
and possibly those in apartment also.   If the negroes met the attack
they did so in the negro settlement.   It was a strange thing to
see so many white men in a negro settlement.   Their business there?

The writer of this Press Article was once a northern man,
but he is now a Southern man.   I doubt his brief narrative being

- 2 -

real facts.   The Tulsa Riot will not stand an honest investigation.
If the soldiers was not compelled to turn the machine guns on God's
Church, God himself will take care of the incident in due time, in his
righteous supreme court of heaven.   God the Supreme Judge, I believe in
the divine act of Sowing and Reaping Gal. 6-7.

God does not at all times handle cases swiftly, of injustice,
only where justice is weak and the principle of justice is a joke,
God takes up the case in a righteous gigantic way!

I only ask justice for my race.   As citizens under the U.nS.
Constitution my race is entitled to justice.   The blood of our
negro boys upon foreign fields was the price of justice!   What may
our race expect from the American Government and Flag?

Thanking you in advance for consideration of my race.

Yours respectfully,

E. L. Branch
127 River St
Troy N.J.

Enc-

Troy N. Y. Times
June the 7th 1921

TROJAN SAW TULSA RIOT.

Well-Known Trojan's Vivid Account of Personal Observation of the Difference Between Whites and Blacks at Southern Hys

*Editorial, of
the same issue,
June 7, 1921*

One of the finest cases of the Color die... there of the flood disaster was the negro porter of a Pullman car which formed part...

City of Riverside

HORACE PORTER, MAYOR

Riverside, California,
June 9, 1921.

158260-8-14

ATTORNEY GENERAL

Attorney General Daugherty,

Washington, D. C.

My dear Sir:-

I am enclosing you a clipping from the
Los Angeles Times, June 4th, stating that you have
as Attorney General ordered the investigation of
the Tulsa race riot.

What especially interests me is the re-
mark in this telegram that the Tulsa situation is "purely local". But I desire as the Mayor of the City of
Riverside, California, to urge upon you that the Tulsa
riots disclose a national situation, as well as a local.
Similar agitators to those at work at Tulsa are at work
to my personal knowledge, in Riverside, California, and
probably in every community in the United States.

I urge upon you that the investigation should
be nation wide. ~~The situation is serious and fast bring-~~
ing a crisis between the colored and white races in our
country. I suggest that your investigation include the
teachings of the National Society for Improvement of the
Colored People, headquarters in New York City, and their
organ The "Crisis". I know personally some of the leaders
in this movement and am personally acquainted, on the basis
of personal conversations, with their extremely radical
views, demanding social equality in the sense of social in-
termingling and marriage.

I am myself a northern man, a native of our state
of Ohio, born at old Marietta. My people were abolitionists,
I have myself always championed the colored people and am
their true friend. As Mayor of the City of Riverside, I
have been striving to quiet certain negro agitations similar
to those of Tulsa caused by personal visits of the representatives of the New York Society and by the reading of The Crisis.

My conviction is that we have escaped riot in
Riverside, California only by extreme care, tact and firmness
in dealing with these colored agitators.

I beg of you, and of President Harding, most serious
attention to the national situation. I can give you more
light and testimony in the matter if you so desire it.

Very sincerely yours,

Mayor.

TULSA THEN --AND NOW

G. A. GREGG, A.B.
Executive Secretary, Hunton Branch Y. M. C. A.
Tulsa, Oklahoma

Graduate of University of Kansas
Teacher of Mathematics in Western Universty Several Years.
Prominent in Fraternal and Religious Organizations in
Kansas and Missouri
Brother of Dr. John A. Gregg, President of Wilberforce
University
A Safe, Sane Christian Leader, in whom the People Have
Confidence.

Detailed to direct the relief work for the
Tulsa Riot Victims

S. D. HOOKER
CHAIRMAN, COLORED CITIZENS RELIEF COMMITTEE
TULSA, OKLAHOMA

Marked by Mrs. Logan Ti.

FOREWORD

An earnest appeal for the helpless,
destitute, law abiding, city building,
innocent of offense colored citizens
of Tulsa, who face extreme suffering
if help of all kinds is not immediately given.

G. A. GREGG.

Leaving Tulsa as I did on May 26th, 1921, to be present at the graduation of my two daughters, Ruth and Eunice, the latter from the Eighth grade, May 27th, and the former from Western University, June 2nd, found me away from Tulsa on the dates of the riot, May 31 and June 1,

But the Tulsa that I left and the Tulsa that I found on my return, June 5th.

I left a Tulsa throbbing with life and high hopes, people who were happy, people who in the main were prosperous, a wide awake, alert, active, forward-looking folk. Some who had come in the early day when it tried men's souls, and now were resting and beginning to enjoy the fruits of their years of toil. People who were singing the praises of Tulsa, prosperous.

No man, be he millionaire or pauper, had more pride in Tulsa than her upstanding, forward-looking colored citizens. None clamored harder against the overbearing police system and the evils of the underworld.

Ten months in Tulsa, ten active constructive months of human hopes and aspirations; ten months of a vision of a better day and then on platform and in press the phrase "The Dawn of a New Day" was in actual use. This in Tulsa colored.

Tulsa's colored citizens settled in the north end of the city, separating themselves at right angles to the Tulsa white.

Standpipe hill jutted out into the colored section like the state of Florida extends into the ocean. This hill is owned by a white man. From it one can get a fine panoramic view of Tulsa and the surrounding country. The white people would not buy it and the colored could not, although they lived on three sides of it.

The good people of color were building magnificent church structures. One, Mt. Zion Baptist, had merged into completion at a cost of $85,000—hard-earned and frugally kept. It was a consolation to the old members who had labored many years and now, in a home comfortable, were ready to worship God and patiently serve until He called them home.

Paradise Baptist church was a cozy brick building situated on the north side of standpipe hill, while Mt. Zion was on the south side of it. The members of this church were building on the pay-as-you-go plan.* It was completed with the exception of interior furnishings. The Methodist Episcopal and African Methodist Episcopal churches had their first story completed and money in the bank for the superstructure.

There were four well equipped drug stores, many grocery stores, Elliott & Hooker, men's and women's furnishing store carried as high a grade of goods as any in the city; two fine hotels accommodated the traveling public; Welcome grocery was a model, modern barber shops and two shoe shops with uptodate machinery. Dreamland theatre catered to the pleasure

4

and entertainment of the people. The physicians were equipping themselves with all the modern apparatus required to alleviate human suffering. Young men as dentists had invested heavily in preparing to take care of the distressed in their line. Women had invested in beauty parlors and dressmaking establishments. Cafes were prepared to feed satisfactorily the many patrons. In fact the people were so industrious and put in so much time at work that they did not prepare their food at home but patronized the cafes. Four upholstered jitney busses carried the people from their homes to their work. An undertaking establishment equipped with caskets ranging from $50 to $1000, all for the accommodaton of the colored people. A $10,000 limousine for the accommodation of the bereaved families was the latest addition.

The Tulsa colored people in every sense of the word were building a modern, up-to-date business city.

They were constantly handicapped as to public utilities, which were managed and controlled by the white man. They constantly prayed him to extend and furnish the same. Procrastination, political promises and hope deferred was the final result. The colored section of Tulsa was insufficiently lighted. And if evil did hold sway and the bad Negro did exist he had the cover of a neglected city darkness in which to ply his evil trade. They have "cried "Let there be light" and there was no

light. The kerosene lamp, the tallow dip or darkness prevailed in their city. In Tulsa white night had been turned into day.

The unsanitary condition, the surface tub-toilets, the stench therefrom increased the wonder that the health of the community was as good as it was.

The colored man of Tulsa built his home not upon sand, but upon an exceedingly great faith, for when fire does break out all he can do is to stand by and see all his earthly possessions go down in ashes. Water protection was insufficient.

In spite of all the physical and mental handicaps he has wrought well, and though a part of his city lies in ashes, the carpenter's hammer is heard and new lumber in the form of a house flares up in every direction. The Tulsa attitude of the black man is to build and rebuild.

The Young Men's Christian Association was the latest addition to civic betterment. This is an inspiring chapter in the city's history.

Conscious of the unwholesome moral trend of the life of the young people, a few active wide awake, progressive citizens, on their own initiative and the friendly counsel and co-operation of that fine Christian gentleman, Mr. C. E. Buckner, general secretary of the Tulsa "Y" set about the organization of the Hunton Branch Y.M.C.A. They raised their own budget of $3,012 for the first year's work. The central association stood ready to furnish $1,000 of

5

it, but the board of managers, led on by that prince of men Mr. S. D. Hooker, raised the full amount themselves. The membership was more than 500 men and boys.

In like manner they raised the budget for the next year's work, notwithstanding the tightness of the times they increased the budget to $5,207 and had the pleasure on Tuesday evening before the Tuesday of the riot, of rejoicing over the fact that the entire amount had been pledged.

Shortly before that a community institute was held. For the first time in the history of the University of Oklahoma, the Extension Division, consisting of seven white men and women, experts in their line, carried on a three-day session in the colored community of Tulsa. They touched and stimulated the church school, civic and home life of the people in a most encouraging manner. It gave our people a new hold on the cheering possibilities of life. The workers were pleasantly informed as to the inner life and cravings of the colored people. The latter did not know that white people could be so kind, helpful and interested in their personal problems. The institute cost $1,000. The people thought it worth many times the cost.

These are some of the evidences of the new attitude of mind developing in Tulsa's colored citizens.

Just another fact showing the desire for civic improve-

ment wholesome ideals and better things for Tulsa.

Just a week before the riot, the board of managers of Hunton Branch Y. M. C. A., together with the mayor and city commissioners invited President King of the Republic of Liberia to be Tulsa's guest. President King accepted.

This would have heartened the colored citizens of Oklahoma to make more of their opportunities. The $1,000 cost to the colored citizens of Tulsa for this visit of President King and his party was no deterrent.

The houses of Tulsa's colored citizens ranged from the temporary floorless box house to modernly equipped ones of the latest and best interior and exterior furnishings.

This, in brief, and in brief only, for much can be said of the high hopes and aims of the colored citizens of Tulsa. This is the Tulsa that I left on the night of the 26th of May 1921.

And the Tulsa that I found on my return the 4th of June. What a contrast!

Tulsa had turned a page to run parallel with the Huns and Goths—vandals of Europe or the Indians in Custers last charge.

An awkward colored boy steps on the toe of a white elevator girl—she slaps him—a retort discourteous on his part —arrested on the charge of assault and battery—newspaper omits "and battery" — public thinks rape — threatening groups of whites gather about jail—colored men fearing the

6

usual happening; gather to prevent a lynching—a careless, reckless shot—and the restraints of civilization are thrown aside and men became brutish beasts.

The boy ought to have apologized. The girl ought to have recognized the accident. The paper ought not to have garbled the story with false emphasis. White men ought not to have gathered about the jail. They should be willing to let the law have the right of way. The colored men ought to have trusted those whose sworn duty it was to protect the prisoner.

A cordon of police could have surrounded the first groups, white and black. But these are sad words "It might have been." But nothing that happened can justify the driving of twelve thousand innocent sleeping colored people, clad in their night clothes, out into the streets, marched to convention hall and elsewhere, then loot, rob and steal the hard, laborious earnings of a struggling people, handicapped at best.

I have worked ten months, with these people. I have had a deep sympathy for them in their struggle against great odds.

Loot — they backed auto trucks up to the vacated (by force) Negro homes and loaded everything movable and of value. One colored woman went to eleven different white homes and in each recovered portions of her household goods.

Rob—Every bit of money

found on their persons was taken. Masonic rings were removed from thier fingers, watches and chains from their persons. In fact, everything of a material nature, etc., preparatory to the cruel initiation which has not yet ended was taken from them. And so in their penniless, destitute condition they were corralled, first one place and then another.

Thanks to the good people who took them into their homes, fed and clothed them, housed them until the cruel police order compelled even the white people to give up and send to the fair grounds those whom they had befriended. Kind offers were thwarted by the police regulation.

With homes looted, homes and stores burned to ashes, with the sick, aged and enfeebled carried out or left to perish in the flames; mothers giving birth to children in the open, herded, corralled and guarded like prisoners of war, and before the smoke of a thousand homes had blown away the trembling, homeless learn that the city fathers have passed an ordinance "making it forever impossible for them in their destitute condition to go back and rebuild on their own home place.

While their hearts are bleeding, their homes and all the relics that make the memory of life's past sustaining with shocking realization that their families and broken and scattered and fearing that they may be slain by the cruel bullet of the

7

mob, with trembly, weak, tired, hungry and hungerless bodies, compelled to be in the stalls of the fair grounds under a heavy, cruel guard of home-guards—guards who greet them with harsh orders and vulgar language—while suffering all this and more, the mayor and commissioners, the Real Estate Exchange, the Welfare Board are like those who crucified Christ, casting lots for the Negro's hard-earned land.

Aht if they would only stop and think how long it required those poor struggling people to own that little portion of earth! Yet by every method known and being discovered by the combined trained minds of the best legal talent that the city and state affords, not one loop hole is being left through which or by means of which the colored citizen can ever again re-build on his own land.

We appeal to the conscience and good judgment of the American people, where is the line separating the lower element that cleared the way and the higher element that sat at noon luncheon under the cool of the electric fans and carefully and judiciously planned that this "never again would be a Negro section."

And immediately proceeded to publish without the owner's consent or offering a cent:

"Wanted, Wholesale Houses in Tulsa."

"New Walfare Committee in active campaign to Better City."

"Through the reconstructon committee appointed by the

mayor and city commissioners Tuesday (June 14), Tulsa extends a welcoming hand to wholesale houses and industrial plants which are to be located on the trackage property in Little Africa swept by fire and which is now within the city fire limits restricted to the erection of fire-resisting buildings".

"The committee also expressed a sentiment in favor of using a part of the burned area for a union station whenever such a project is ready for consideration by the railroads entering Tulsa."—Tulsa World, June 15, 1921.

Think of it! A union station where the races of men pass through, built upon the blood stained soil of the Negros' property. What an approach to the "Magic City" of the Great Southwest." A symbol of greed and blood!!

And added to this anguish of soul comes quick and fast the police regulation that all Negroes to have the freedom of Tulsa's streets must wear a green tag stating age, residence, name, and name of employer, who must be white. Men who did business for themselves had to find a white man to sign their cards. If not employed, a red card must be worn. This readst "If the bearer is on the streets after 7 o'clock he will be arrested and taken to the fairground"—By some called the "bull-pen."

The guards are placed at all roads entering the colored section. Men, women, boys and

8

girls are held up by these guards, many of whom are rough, rude and discourteous.

Every step from the sudden awakening by the firing of guns and the buzzing of airoplanes to the present moment evidences in increasing humiliation. Those who were privileged to return to their homes found their contents gone or mutilated. Everything from a shoe a piano to an automobile was found in the homes of white folks.

I left a happy, hopeful, progressive people; I found a crushed, humiliated, discouraged humanity. I left a praying people; I found them wondering if God is just. I left a Young Men's Christian Association with bright and promising prospects, just ready to jump into a $150,000 building campaign; I found a budget destroyed, resources consumed a board of managers in despair.

Tulsa has destroyed the homes, taken the lives and maimed the bodies of the best friend the white man has in American sea, the world.

There is no man in the world that has stood by and will stand by the white man like the Negro.

There is no justification for the wholesale destruction of property and resources of the thousand of innocent, law abiding, home building Negroes. We do not condone the wrong deeds of the bad Negro. We deplore his existence. We pray the co-operative influences of all people to help reform or restrain him as well as his co-partners in white. We find it difficult to reach him. You find it difficult to reach his white partner. They clash. You and we are thrown into a whirlpool of human rage. We who emerge with bloody bruised bodies, and the savings and buildings of a lifetime smouldering in ashes must face each other and realize how trivial and avoidable the cause and how deplorable and lasting the results.

Is the spirit of America dead? Shall the color of a man's skin be the symbol for adverse sentiment?

Mine is a Christian program. Am thoroughly convinced that an active wide-awake Christianity will cure this human ill.

There come times in a Christian program when it becomes necessary to "drive out the money changers" and land grafters.

Unhappily Tulsa has worked into that stage.

Tulsa is not all bad. There are good citizens in Tulsa. They, as much as any, deplore the spot that will not out.

We need a nearer approach to the principles and teaching of the Golden Rule. The hammer and claw, pistol and gun, create hate. And hate hurries us on to destruction.

There is no place in a Christian program for hate.

Let's make America safe for her own citizens and courteous to others.

9

PARTIAL LIST OF LOSSES

Sustained by Victims of the Tulsa Riots.

PROPERTY OWNERS	LOSSES
Mr. Jim Cherry	$ 50,000
Mr. O. Gurley	65,000
J. H Goodwin	30,000
Mr. John Gat	25,000
Dea R T Bridgwater	32,000
Mrs. Lula T. Williams	85,000
Mrs Annie Porine	35,000
Mrs. Jennie Wilson	25,000
Mr. A. Brown	15,000
Mr J. B. Stradford	125,000
Mr. A. J. Phillips	40,000
Mr. W. H. Smith (Welcome Grocery)	40,000
Elliott & Hooker, Clothers and Dry Goods	45,000
Dr. A F. Bryant	50,000
Mr. C. W. Henry	35,000
Jackson Undertaking Co	15,000
Mr T. R. Gentry	25,000
Prof J. W. Hughes	15,000
Mr S. M. Jackson	15,000

NORTH GREENWOOD STREET.

RESIDENCE	SIZE	BUSINESS	VALUE
2-Story Brick			
101— Wood'd	70x 80	Earl Real Estate Co	$ 15,000
103		Bayers & Anderson, Tailors	
103½		R. T Bridgwater, Physician	
103½		T. R. Gentry, Real Estate	
105½		Wesley Jones, Physician	
105½		James M. Key, Physician	
105½		Mrs Mary E J Parrish, School	
105½		Two Apartments	
105½		Oklahoma Sun Office, Theo Baughman.	
WILLIAM'S BLDG	35x 55		$ 12,500
2-Story Brick			
102		Dr J. J. McKeever.	
102		Mrs. Lulu Williams, Confectionary.	
102—Second Floor		Apartments	
102—Third Floor		Offices	
MRS. E. G. HOWARD'S BLDG	35x 80		$ 5,000
2-Story Brick			
107		Barber Shop	
107½		Safety First Loan Co.	
107½		Mrs. Sarah Whitaker. Rooms.	
BRYANT BLDG	50x 90		$ 15,000
2-Story Brick.			
108		Bryant's Drug Stores Dra A. F. Bryant	
108½		Rooming Rooms	
110		C. L. Netherland, Barber Shop	
PHILLIPS			$ 15,000
2-Story Brick.			
111		Hardy & Hardy, Restaurant.	
111½		Hardy & Hardy, Rooms.	
GURLEY BLDG	60x140 80 Rooms		$ 15,000
2-Story Brick.			
112		Brunswick Billiard Parlor.	
112½		Gurley Hotel	
112½		Dock Eastman & Hughes, Cafe.	
PHILIP'S BLDGs	50x 80		12,500
2-Story Brick			
115		Carter's Barber Shop.	
115½		E. A. Hardy, Furnished Rooms.	
116		Gentry, Nealy & Vadel, Billiards.	
117		Osawaka Cigar Store.	

10

11

GURLEY BLDG. O. W. Gurley
25x50 .... $10,000
1-Story Brick
119 .... A S Newkirk, Photographer
119½ .... S G Smith, Insurance
119¾ .... Seabaugh & Franklin, Attorneys and Oil Deal.
119¾ .... Smith's Apartment.
DIXIE BLDG Redfern 50x130 .... $50,0
1-Story Brick
120 .... Dixie Theatre
120½ .... Samuel Stradenberg, Shoe Shiner
125 .... J R. Bell
GIST BLDG Gist 25x50 .... $12,500
2-Story Brick.
121 .... J P. Gist, Barber.
121 .... Nails Brothers, Shoe Repair Shop
121½ .... Gist Rooms
SMITH BLDG 50x125 .... $50,000
2-Story Brick.
122 .... Welcome Grocery
122½ .... Smith's Apartment
122¾ .... Dr Wells
122 .... Dr Robinson
122½ .... Dr P. Travis
122½ .... Das Smitherman
122½ .... Attorney E I Sadler
122½ .... Y M. C A. Rooms
124 .... Elliott & Hooker, Clothing and Dry Goods
GOODWIN BLDG. 25x50 .... $7,000
2-Story Brick.
123 .... Union Grocery, Duncan & Clinton
123½ .... Rooms
WILLIAMS' BLDG. No. 2 25x140 .... $30,000
2-Story Brick.
129 -133 .... Dreamland Theater.
129½ .... A J. Whitley, Physician.
129½ .... Alexander Hotel.
MRS. TITUS BLDG 20x 50 .... $1,500
1-Story Brick
127 .... Little Pullman Cafe.
MRS. PARTEE BLDG.
(?) 15x 40
1-Story Frame
201 .... Cain's Cafe. $1,500
203 .... Dr. R. T Motley, Office
HILL'S BLDG. 25x 70 .... $8,000
2-Story Brick.
124 .... Star Printing Co , A. J Smitherman.
124½ .... Morgan Rooms.
REDWING BLDG. 25x100 .... $30,800
2-Story Stone
205 .... Wm. Kyle, Druggist.
204 .... Red Wing Cafe, J. L. White.
206 .... Abbie Funche, Tailor.
206½ .... Red Wing Hotel, Mrs. J T. Prensley.
208 .... Barber Shop, Ahner & Hutton, Prop.
STRADFORD BLDG. 50x140 .... $50,000
"A"
301 Stradford Hotel .... Stradford Hotel
301 "A" .... A L. Ferguson, Drugs.
CLEANER & CHERRY BLDG.
25x 80.
2-Story Brick. .... Anderson & Person, Groceries $8,000
501 .... Knights of Pythias.
501½ .... Odd Fellows Hall.

FRANKFORT AVENUE, NORTH.

BUILDING	SIZE	BUSINESS	VALUE
BURNETT'S BLDG. 1½-Story Brick	40x 80		$6,000
302		T. J Wineman, People's Tailoring Co	
BAKER'S BLDG. 2-Story Brick.	40x 80		$4,500
304½		W A. Baker, Grocery.	
MRS. MEEKS' BLDG.	25x 40	Apartment.	$750

1-Story Frame
502 .... W M Curry, Grocery
(2) 1-Story Stones 25x100
525 .... Johnson's Plumbing Office $3,000
527 .... Bell & Little Cafe
529 .... Cold Drinks and Cream Parlor
1-Story Frame 15x 30
CAMERON EAST
525 .... Bluejacket's Shop
529 .... Loup's Plumbing Office
STRADFORD BLDG
Facing Cameron St Included in Hotel Bldg
Waffle House

ARCHER EAST.

BUILDING	SIZE	BUSINESS	VALUE
1-Story Brick		H A Wayne, Physician	
1-Story Frame		Golly Huff, Confectionery	$2,500
206 1-Story Brick	18x 30	A J Douglas, Barber Shop	$1,200
210 1-Story, 4-Room Stucco		B F Smith, Physician	
214 1-Story Frame		H A Guess, Attorney	$750
205		Rev W H. Twine, Real Estate	750
207		Charles Allen, Tailor	750
201 1-Story Frame		Friedman Bros Grocery	$800
214½ 1-Story Frame		R J Clark, Tailor	$500
216		J L Locard, Restaurant	800
316½		Wm. Bunn, Shoe Shine Parlor	250
218 1-Story Frame		Ray Smith, Barber Shop	$300
228 1-Story Frame		Woodard & Tillman, Confectionery	$400
328		Grace & Warren, Restaurant	300
402 G		G W. Hutchins, Attorney.	
410½		C. W. Williams, Restaurant	$1,200
418		B L Neal, Tailor	1,200
421 2-Story Frame		Midway Hotel	$4,000
421		Grace Johnson, Restaurant	800
429 1-Story Frame		Public Library	$750
501 1-Story Frame		Mrs Grace Johnson, Rooms	3,500
505 1-Story Frame		R Roland, Rooms	$5,000
514 1-Story Brick		Steam Laundry, Mrs Pastel	3,500
MRS. PARTEE'S BLDG. 1-Story Brick	25x 40		
516		L Grier, Shoe Maker	$2,500
516		Mrs. Luis Lacy, Restaurant	900
516½		Rooms	1,000
608		W. D Kelley, Lunch Counter	400
MRS. DORA WELLS' BLDG			
613		Mrs Dora Wells, Garment Factory.	$2,500
614 1-Story Stone	50x120	East End Garage, Mr Williams	$8,500
617 1-Story Frames		R. R. Robinson, Physician	1,500
419 1-Story Frame		Louira White, Fun Rooms	4,000
MYERS BLDG. 2-Story Brick			
622		Jackson Und Co., S M Jackson	$40,000
622½		Mrs N O. Smith, Beauty Parlor	
622½		Dr. L N. Neal, Chiropractor	
622½		Beauty Parlor.	

CINCINNATI STREET, NORTH.

RESIDENCE	SIZE	BUSINESS	VALUE
1-Story Frame			
4		T D Jackson, Barber	$700
6		Cavr French Dry Cleaners	700
10		T B. Carter, Billiards	800

14

512—Arthur Scott 800
514—James Yates 1,300
515— 800
516—Abe Yates 1,000
517—J. H. Hodnett, 1-Story Frame, 6 rooms   Mrs. Emma Works
519—Mrs. Emma Works, 1-Story Frame, 6 rooms Mrs. Emma Works ... 2,000
529—Edward Jones 2,350
522—C. M. Mathews 800
531—J. H. Smith 1,200
535—M. C. Allen 4,500
537—C. H. Perkins, 1-Story Frame, 3 rooms   C. H. Perkins 1,000
.... 1,000

RESIDENCE   NO. ROOMS   PROPRIETOR   VALUE
BRADY EAST.
208—Wm Jones 1,500
210—Garfield Dixon 800
211—Emma Dixon 800
316—M. S. Jones 1,200
319—Mrs. Margaret Davis 5,000
404—Leon Homer 3,000
412—J. J. Jones 600
502—Benjamin Blythe —House moved 750
539—Albert Vernon—House moved
516—John Williams

RESIDENCE   NO. ROOMS   PROPRIETOR   VALUE
DAVENPORT EAST
416—Dr. B. A. Wayne, 1-Story Frame, 6 rms. Dr. B. A. Wayne ... 1,200
HASKELL EAST.
RESIDENCE   NO. ROOMS   PROPRIETOR   VALUE
401—J. H. Goodwin, 2-Story Frame, 9 rms. J. H. Goodwin 4,000
407—1-Story Brick, 5 rooms   J. H. Goodwin 1,000
409—1-Story Brick, 6 rooms   J. H. Goodwin 3,500
   —2-Story Frame, 5 rooms   J. H. Goodwin 2,000
   —Garage   J. H. Goodwin 500

RESIDENCE   NO. ROOMS   PROPRIETOR   VALUE
FRANKFORT AVENUE NORTH
208—Haney Van Dyke, 1-Story Brick   Brockman Bros 2,500
210—C. W. Drummond, 5 rooms 1,750
212—J. Bell, 4 rooms 1,230
214—Frannie Hood, 3 rooms 400
218—Thomas Johnson, 3 rooms 400
220—Rufus Allen, 5 rooms 1,200
221—Edward Richardson, 3 rooms 450
224—Edward Howard, 5 rooms 2,250
300—James Jefferson, 4 rooms 1,500
302—G. A. Arush, 5 rooms 3,000
304—Samuel Perkins, 4 rooms 1,000
306—Hap Watson 5,000
309—Catherine Jackson 1,256
338—S. E. Easley 2,000
313—Al Young .... Edgewater
314—Floyd Gilkey
316—F. W. Waddell 2,500
317—Rev. A. W. Brown, 8 rooms   M. Jackson 1,250
318—Alice Haggler, 6 rooms   M. Jackson 2,000
319—Elmer Williams 2,000
320—Theodore Baughman 1,500
320½—W. Devrow, 2 houses on lot Stovall 860
321—Wright Jones   Bridgewater 3,500
322—Jessie C. Vann   Bridgewater 1,000
23—C. C. Nimley   Mrs. Watson 750
401—Toby Campbell   Bridgewater 2,500
402—Hinie B. Blackman 500
403—Robert Robertson 750
403½—Victor Visher 1,000
404—A. W. Tindall 1,250
406—L. T. Johnson 1,250
408—Willie Connor 2,500
407—John Hampton 1,000
408—Charles Berry   . Watson 1,000
409—W. L. Hicks 1,500
410—H. J. Green 900
   —Emma Anderson 500
413—Swears Nebles 1,000
414—Mrs. Mary Mitchell, 1-Story Frame M: Mary Mitchell 1,700
416—Mrs. Aurelia E. Watson 1,000
427—Amy Hawkins 2,000
498—Mrs. Mary Simms 1,500
500—Wm. Dysart 1,000
.... 1,000

15

506—Olive Dupree 700
508—Mrs Sophia Smith 700
511—Mrs Bonnie Whipple 1,500
513—W. M. Henderson 500
513—Len Jenkins 850
514—Mandy Lincoln 1,500
515—Mrs. Emma Swinger 1,000
516—Mrs. Margaret McKeever 2,000
519—O W Hawkins 850
521—M K Randler 2,500
622—Mrs. Ella (Wesley) Meeks, 2-Story frm. Mrs Ella Meeks ... 2,000
                                             Staley Webb
624—Staley Webb, 1-Story Frame   Staley Webb
GREENWOOD AVENUE NORTH.
RESIDENCE   NO. ROOMS   PROPRIETOR   VALUE
303—Deck Eastman 1,200
304—Alvin Graves 2,500
306—"A"—B. W. Vadet 1,900
307—Daniel Black 2,500
308—Rev. J. A. Johnson, 2-Story Frame Rev J A Johnson 1,200
309—Harry Hearn 1,500
310—J. E. Fields 1,500
336—Wm Cherry 1,600
312—Joseph Saunders 1,000
314—Mack Bergman 1,750
315—Sallie Grayson 1,750
316—C. D Turner 1,500
31—G L Gasper 1,000
318—Anderson Parker 750
319—M. A. Byers 1,000
321—W. M. Hawaid 2,000
400—W. M. Bruner 950
401—Frank Gaylord 1,250
402—Perkin & Wood, Physician 960
403—E. T. Waters 850
404—Seward Cooper (Laundry) 900
406—Wm. Clark 1,000
406—Mrs. Ida Berry 1,000
407—Wm Young 1,000
408—Mrs. Munroe L. Sanders 250
408½—W. H. Cohn, Physician 1,000
406—Mrs Fannie White 700
411—Mrs. Martha A. Newman 950
413—Henry Johnson 950
415—E. G. Carter 1,000
414—James King 1,750
416—Reed Thomas 3,000
417—Nathaniel Dorset 3,000
418—Mrs. Samuel Mackley, 1-Story Frame   Mrs. Samuel Mackley . 1,000
421—Mrs Brpella Randle 1,000
502—Mrs May Thompson 500
505—A. C. Jackson 500
6—Love Williams 350
06—A. W Williams 1,000
06—Mrs Jannie Russell
507—Mrs. Carrie Barner 2,000
508—Barney Cleaver, 2-Story Frame   Barney Cleaver 2,000
509—W. M. Luper 2,000
510—J. B. Burton 1,000
511—Mrs. Carrie Colbert 1,000
512—J. H. Golden 1,000
512—E. Winning 2,000
51—M. C. Edwards 2,000
515—Jane Daniels 850
516—Mrs. Josie Daniels 350
519—James Thomas 868
520—Julius Muckroy ....
524—Mary Amanda
604—Rev. J. R. McClain   James Cherry 4,000
705—James Cherry   A. L. Phillips 4,000
716—A. L. Phillips, 1-Story Frame   A. L. Phillips
HARTFORD AVENUE NORTH.
RESIDENCE   NO. ROOMS   PROPRIETOR   VALUE
12—L. F Gross 500
21—L. F Gross 300
22—Nelson Talbert 1,000
104—Frank Taylor 800
104—Mrs Lottie 750
106—Henry Richmond 1,200
108—Jack Seoti ....

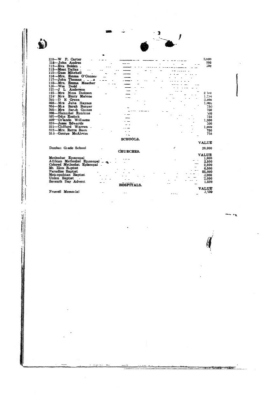

			VALUE
110—W. P. Carter			2,000
114—John Andres			500
112—Eva Bolden			50c
113—Mont Dallas			
115—Gus Mitchell			
116—Mrs. Emma O'Conner			
117—John Thomas			
119—Mrs. Emma Meacher			
120—Wm Dodd			
121—J L Anderson			
122—Mrs Nina Dickson			2 5cc
124 Mrs Emry Malone			1,750
301—D E Green			3,000
303—Mrs John Haynes			1,000
304—Mrs Sarah Burger			750
305—Mrs Sarah Gaines			750
306—Hannibal Rankins			500
307—Odd Reaick			750
309—Orlando Williams			1,500
310—Jesse Edwards			500
311—Clifford Warren			1,000
312—Mrs. Retta Boon			750
313—George McAlvin			750

SCHOOLS.

	VALUE
Dunbar Grade School	20,000

CHURCHES.

	VALUE
Methodist Episcopal	1,000
African Methodist Episcopal	2,500
Colored Methodist Episcopal	2,000
Mt Zion Baptist	6,500
Paradise Baptist	85,000
Metropolitan Baptist	2,000
Union Baptist	2,000
Seventh Day Advent	1,500

HOSPITALS.

	VALUE
Frissell Memorial	2,500

MILITARY INTELLIGENCE DIVISION
In replying refer to
10218-422-M.I.4.

158260-8

WAR DEPARTMENT
OFFICE OF THE CHIEF OF STAFF
WASHINGTON

June 11, 1921.

GENERAL INTELLIGENCE
JUN ⸱⸱ 1921
D. VISION

Mr. L. J. Baley,
Chief, Bureau of Investigation,
Department of Justice,
Washington, D.C.

My dear Mr. Baley:-

Herewith is a photostat copy of a letter from an anonymous source, sent to the Secretary of War.

This is furnished you for your information.

Very truly yours,

For the Director, Military Intelligence Division.

MATT C. SMITH,
Colonel, General Staff,
Chief, Negative Branch.

1 incl.
bk

158260-8-10
JUN ⸱⸱ 1921
FIL. 9 R.

98

HPK

10218-422-M.I.4.

June 11, 1921.

Mr. L. J. Baley,
    Chief, Bureau of Investigation,
    Department of Justice,
    Washington, D.C.

My dear Mr. Baley:-

Herewith is a photostat copy of a letter from an anonymous source, sent to the Secretary of War.

This is furnished you for your information.

Very truly yours,

For the Director, Military Intelligence Division.

MATHEW C. SMITH,
Colonel, General Staff,
Chief, Negative Branch.

1 incl.
Mr

Grand Rapids Mich 6-1- 192_

10218-422

Chas W eck,

Sir;

I think it is time I tell you of some of the things I know to be a fact. I call your attention to Tulsa [Okla] don't for one minute let this pass as just a small race riot, that is what they want you to think. I know that for the past 8 years the negroes of the south have been taught that they are of the same blood as [...] [...] agents, mostly come in from Brazil + South America. Their [...] means of [...] harm for the [...] is [...] where they work with the lowest black and there are the [...] the white man [...] few [...] but seem to know—

(over)

At the least.
While fools in these
united states are asking
that we lay down our arms
Two of the greatest nations
on earth are getting ready to
take our country.
Any fool can see why
England grabed all the ships
from germany
The niggers of the united
states will now tell you
"We aint going to fight mexico
in Japan, they are niggers
just like our self."
I this movement is worldwide
I call your attention to the
niggers in Brittish west
africa and on other things
Who wanted the Brittish to
police our atlantic coast?

192

I know of a white man
stoping his business at
Crowley La to go to
New-orleans to get a rifel
a white man could not buy
a ~~, But the low down
they save ~~ for the niggers
and niggers buys any kind of
gun and pays the price asked
for they are getting ready to
kill the white man.

I knew one lawyer whose
made a study of the negro
and he claimed that none
had ~ come ~ this country
~ they had all~ by~
been smuggled into this
Country and that it was
possible to tell just what

In Oklahoma negroes were killed, herded in barracks to save them from murder. Some say the white men wanted their oil lands. More probably trouble started because white men out of work saw negroes working.

Senator Medill McCormick wants a committee "to report on race hatred" in this country. The committee should go to the zoological gardens, and report what it finds there. The dog hates the fox, his cousin, and doesn't hate the elephant, so different. Human beings are animals and hate their brothers, as the dog hates the fox or the wolf. They will stop that when they stop being animals—that's a long way off.

#1026 Kenyon, Street, N.W.

158260 - 8

Washington, D.C.,

June ,4th., 1921.

To the Honorable Warren G.Harding,

President of the United States,

Your Excellency:—

Enclosed please note a copy of a letter , the which I have this day forwarded
to Attorney-General Daughty. Knowing only as a layman, the burdens left you
by a former Administration, I fain would withold this letter, but for the fact
that thousands of offenseless and defenseless women and children are suffering for something for which they are not responsible.

Itseems to me that your being President of the whole country, devolves upon
you manifold duties.   I am broad enough to wish that youwill do nothing
that will make enemies for you of any section of the country,who at some other
crisis would exert all their influence to defeat your plans.

In view of the foregoingo, I shall refrain from doing the usual thing under
such circumstances viz:—asking you to rush into public print on this subject.
Your position on such matters as this is well known.

I shall however ask you to lend your weighty influence to your Attorney-General, to do justice to all concerned in the Tulsa tragedy.

I feel for these mothers, daughters, sisters and children, the same as if/
they were my very own.   our

Knowing your stand for pure Americanism, I shall rest/y case in your hands.
May God strenghten your arm.   May He ever guide you to boldlydefend the cause
of Justice and Right!

> Wishing for you a prosperous Administration,
>
> Allow me to subscribe myself,
>
> Yours -For-Pure- Americanism——
>
> Rev. J. Luther Martin
>
> Rev. J.Luther Martin.

158260-8-9

JUN 8 21

P.S. The inclosed clipping is from Mr. Bris-
bane's "Today" in Saturdays

#L026 Kenyon, Street N.W.

Washington, D.C.,

June, 4th.,1921.

To the Honorable,

The Attorney-General of the United States of America,

Dear Sir:---

Enclosed you will please find a clipping from"The Baltimore Sun", of even date.
The marked paragraph is vitally significant in placing the blame of the "why",
of the Tulsa riots.

The writer has talked to some people from this vicinity and it is the consensus
of opinion that this district was the most prosperous of all the colored
sections of the Southwest.   What valid reason can the people of Tulsa, give to the
world for deliberately destroying an entire "Little Africa"?

If your Office works on the presumption that the colored people owned too much
property, and that their holdings in oil was an incentive to the complete
destruction of an entire colored settlement, does it not occur to your Office
that this would furnish a motive?

The Negroes are going to have their homes rebuilded, but as we understand ON
ANOTHER PLOT OF GROUND,------the destroyed section is to be an industrial centre.

I submit this for what it is worth.

Trusting that a people who have ever stood ready to defend the country from the
days of Crispus Attucks, Peter Salem, and with Jackson at New Orleans, with
Roosevelt at San Juan Hill, at Carrizal, in France and elsewhere; that they, Sir,
will receive absolute justice at your hands(and we have no cause to surmise
otherwise)----------

I Am Yours,

For Justice and Right,

Rev. J. Luther Martin (signature)

Rev. J. Luther Martin.

WCH-ECT

RPS-

158260-8-7

June 13, 1921.

Mr. John E. Arnold,

    Oil & Gas Purchasing Agency,

        208 Lorton Bldg.₂ Tulsa, Oklahoma.

Dear Sir:

       Your letter of June 2d to the President of the United
States, relative to the recent race riots at Tulsa, Oklahoma, has
been referred to this Department, and I beg to assure you that the
matters stated by you will receive due consideration.

               Respectfully,

                  For the Attorney General,

                          (Signed) R. P. Stewart

                         Assistant Attorney General.

RECORDED

1 5̄8260 .78

Oil & Gas Purchasing Agency
Direct from Owners Only
Use Value Must Equal Cash Value

RESPECTFULLY REFERRED
FOR CONSIDERATION.

W. M. Christian Jr.

Secy. to the President.

June 2, 1921

158260-8-7

Mr. Warren G. Harding,
The White House,
Washington, D. C.,

My dear Warren:

Personal and Confidential

STEWART, HERRON

As a Rotarian who organized the Rotary Club of Wichita Falls, Texas, I know I can absolutely depend upon your right heartedness to serve the cause of God and humanity in this present matter:

My business has brought me to alive in Tulsa, Oklahoma, the scene of the gruesome outbreak of lawlessness described in the enclosed paper which happens to be the least sensational of our daily papers.

Our State Governor is a Democrat, and a very fine gentleman; and our State Attorney General is a Democrat, and a very fine gentleman.

Our County Sheriff is a Republican, and a gentleman.

Our Mayor and City Officials are all gentlemen regarded as being clean government citizens; but------

Our State Attorney General has already been announced as a candidate for the next Governorship of Oklahoma, and------

Local factionalism between political parties and between the city and county officials, has, I believe, led to a lack of moral courage on the part of the proper persons to sufficiently uphold the rights of our own citizens, white and black, as prescribed by the Federal and State Constitutions - possibly - I hope not, but am led by observation to believe - by their fear of the effects of their activities in behalf of righteousness upon their own chances of getting political rewards in the future. God versus politics, and you have within your personal reach the power to see to it - by proper investigation thru the Department of Justice - that Law and Order must prevail here.

Altho' we are taught that Masonic Bodies must not hold any sort

Mr. Warren G. Harding, 6/2/21 - Page #2,

of communications with Negro Masons, I feel sure that this is a time when you and I as Masons can each do our part to contribute to the relief of poor and penniless Master Masons (Negro), their widows, and orphans. You by your personal influence in the right direction in Washington to bring about a state of due respect and honor in the entire state of Oklahoma and particularly in Tulsa and county circles - for the duly constituted officers of the law in whose hands this negro rapist was held at the time this outbreak started. Me to do my share here locally. I am sure that you will cordially do anything you can legally and morally do to relieve the situation as well as to try to put "our house in order" so that "It Must Never Happen Again".

The Grand Master and Most Worshipful Potentate of Masons every where surely did not intend, in His wisdom, as per the words of His Son, Jesus Christ, that there should be one moral law or code of ethics for benefit of one color, and another - less righteous - for the negro, or other races among our citizens.

I blush with shame to think that the fair name of our city has been smutted by any such circumstances, and even tho' it was done by an element among both whites and blacks who may be claimed to be the "tougher" element, but I am sure that after due examination and strict trial, your investigators would find conditions in Tulsa and vicinity disgustingly rotten, as witness the facts brought out in the testimony of Rev. Harold G. Cooke, and Mr. C. E. Buchner in the recent investigation of Police Circles in the matter of immoral women and whiskey selling.

Courteously and Fraternally yours,

John E. Arnold

Phones Osage 9620 & 3572
208-210-213 Lorton(Old World)Bldg.
15 1-3 W. 4th St., P.O.Box 427, Tulsa, Okla.

WCH-ECT

RPS-

168260-8-4

June 13, 1921.

J. R. Coffey, Attorney at Law,

206 Love Bldg.,

Muskogee, Oklahoma.

Dear Sir:

I beg to acknowledge receipt of your letter of June 4th, relative to the recent race riots at Tulsa, Oklahoma, and to assure you that the views stated by you will receive due consideration.

Respectfully,

For the Attorney General,

(Signed) R. P. Stewart

Assistant Attorney General.

RECORDED

B

110

J. R. COFFEY
ATTORNEY-AT-LAW
206-7 LOVE BLDG.
MUSKOGEE, OKLAHOMA
June 4, 1921.

158260-4

Hon. Harry M. Dougherty,
Attorney General,
Washington, D. C.

Dear Sir:

  Should the Department of Justice of the United States decide, as I think it should, to take a part in the investigation of the cause and effect of the late race riot at Tulsa, Okla., I am sure you will undertake a route in which you can at least hope to obtain the facts desired. In this and some other parts of the country, when calamities like this occur, some times the investigators start out with the intention not to get and report the truth. The situation in this grand country is growing worse in some respects as regards race relations. The good folks of both races wiselya(?) try to make a pleasant showing; but, in many instances, the class of men who will accept the smaller offices are not the best men to act in such cases as we have on hand at this time.

  I am a colored man and I am in position to say that it will require men of both races, instead of one, and they must be honest men of high motives, to effectively do this kind of work.

  This is a delicate affair and I don't like to get mixed up in such things; but, if I can be of any service to your department in assisting your representatives here, call upon me.

        Very respectfully,

        J. R. Coffey.

RPS-

158260-8-5

WOH-FOT

June 13, 1921.

Ellwood Heacock, President,

    Spring Street Settlement (For Colored People),

        2027 North College Ave., Philadelphia, Pa.

Dear Sir:

        Your letter of June 3d to the President of the United States, calling attention to the race riot at Tulsa, Oklahoma, and expressing your views in regard to the reason and remedy for such occurrences, has been referred to this Department, and I beg to assure you that your remarks will receive due consideration.

                Respectfully,

                  For the Attorney General,

                        (Signed) R. P. Stewart
                        Assistant Attorney General.

1

158260 - 8

2027 N. College Avenue,
Philadelphia, Pa., June 3, 1921.

Hon. Warren G. Harding, President,
Washington, D. C.

Dear Sir:-

     As a citizen of our Republic which stands for so
much in the cause of human welfare and as one who is interested in the progress of the Negro Race I feel called
upon to ask your consideration of the antagonisms between
many of the white race and our colored citizens.

     The awful riot reported as having occurred in Tulsa,
Okla. is but an expression of this unfortunate condition. I
am sure that when the facts are known it will be found that
a Negro was unjustly accused of a serious crime and was in
danger of being lynched when his colored friends, probably
many of them ex-service men who had fought to make the world
safe for democracy, determined to defend him and theirs
attitude was violently resented by white men who often claim
"the black man must be kept in his place".

     In nine out of every ten race riots the fault lies
wholly with the white people and has its foundation in the
meanest kind of injustice.

     Our National Government as well as State and local
authorities should see to it that our Constitution and laws
are enforced in behalf of all of our citizens without regard
to race or color. The most searching investigation should
be made by the Federal authorities in this murderous and
wide-spread Tulsa riot and the guilty parties punished. It
is necessary as a lesson to the whole country as a matter
of justice. Many of our returned negro soldiers have highly
resolved that the lynching business must stop. No more important question is before the American people today.

     Assuring you of my appreciation of your kind attention,
I remain,

Very respectfully yours,

Edward Heacock President,
Spring Street Settlement.
(For Colored People)

158260-8-5

JUN N 99

STEWART-HERRON

113

WOH-ECT

RPS-

158260-8-6

June 13, 1921.

Hon. Channing H. Cox,

    Governor of Massachusetts,

        State House, Boston, Mass.

Dear Sir:

    Your letter of June 3d to the President of the United
States, enclosing a letter from the National Equal Rights League,
of Boston, Massachusetts, has been referred to this Department.

    The letter of the National Equal Rights League calls the
President's attention to the recent race riot at Tulsa, Oklahoma,
and requests him to cause this Department to make an immediate investigation of the matter to the end that all persons accused may
be protected in their rights under the Constitution. In your letter you state that the citizens of Massachusetts are very much stirred
by these terrible outrages and will stand behind the President in any
endeavor to punish the guilty and make such crimes forever impossible
in this country.

    The views of the National Equal Rights League and of your
honorable self will receive the due consideration of this Department. You are, however, undoubtedly aware that, under the decisions of
the Supreme Court of the United States, the Federal Government has no
jurisdiction over matters of this kind.

            Respectfully,

RECORDED

            For the Attorney General,

                (Signed) R. P. Stewart,

                Assistant Attorney-General.

158260 - 8

CHANNING H COX
GOVERNOR

THE COMMONWEALTH OF MASSACHUSETTS
EXECUTIVE DEPARTMENT
STATE HOUSE, BOSTON

RESPECTFULLY REFERRED
FOR CONSIDERATION:

Secy: to the President:

3d June, 1921.

To the President of the United States,
Washington, D. C.

Mr. President:

At the request of the National
Equal Rights League, I am forwarding an
appeal for aid to the victims of the recent
mob violence in Tulsa, Oklahoma. All the
citizens of Massachusetts are stirred to the
depths by these terrible outrages, and they
look to you for leadership in giving aid to
the afflicted, and they will stand behind you
in any endeavor to punish the guilty and to
make such inhuman and barbaric crimes forever-
more impossible in this land of freedom and
justice.

I am,

RECORDED.

Respectfully yours,

158260-8-16

JUN 9

STEWART-HERRON

JUN RJ
15 21

NATIONAL EQUAL RIGHTS LEAGUE

ORGANIZED TO SECURE EQUALITY AND JUSTICE FOR THE RACE

WILLIAM MONROE TROTTER, CORRESPONDING SECRETARY

OFFICE, 34 CORNHILL

TELEPHONE CONNECTION

BOSTON June 3, 19 21

The President, Warren G. Harding,
WMhite House, Washington, D.C.

Sir:—

The Colored citizens of Boston and vicinity and others in
sympathy, through the National Equal Rights League, appeal to you
as the Executive head of this rich and powerful government to
take note in mind and heart of the brutal slaying of dozens of
Colored American¢ citizens by white American mobists at Tulsa,
Oklahoma, and of their ruthless, wholesale attacks upon women, old
men and children by burning down all the homes and property in
the large Colored residenceaand business section. We urge you,
facing this disgrace to our country and calamity to an ethnic
group of citizens, in mercy and justice, to secure from Congress
appropriations for immediate care of sick and disabled, and for
pensions for those rendered permanently dependant by the mob's
destruction, or permanently disabled by it, and to the families
of those slain.

We request that you cause the Department of Justice to
make immediate investigation to the end that all persons accused
be protected in their rights under the constitution.

May the terrible series of lynchings which have culminated
in this message lead you to urge upon Congress speedy passage of
the Dyer Anti-lynching Bill in order that, as you said in your
message, "Barbaric lynching may be wiped from the banners of the
Republic,"

Yours for protection of life,

Matthew CU Shaw National President
Wm. Munrg Trotter, National Secretary

WOH-ECT

158250-8-12

June 21, 1921.

Mr. Oscar J. Berend,

934 Kennedy Bldg.,

Tulsa, Oklahoma.

Dear Sir:

I beg to acknowledge receipt of your letter of June 13th, enclosing a clipping from the Tulsa *Tribune* relative to alleged arming of negroes, and to advise you that the matter will receive due consideration.

Respectfully,

For the Attorney General,

W. C. Herron

Attorney.

RECORDED

117

OSCAR J. BEREND
317 WEST 9TH ST.
934 Kennedy Bl.

158260 - 8

PHONE USAGE 8841
Cedar 2528

TULSA, OKLA.,
June 13, 1921.

Attorney Generals Office,
Washington, D.C.

Gentlemen:-

      I am enclosing herewith a clipping
from the editorial page of the Tulsa Tribune. In
this editorial I have blocked out and underlined
a certain paragraph and sentences which I wish to
call to your attention.

      A timely investigation of this re-
ported condition and if found substantially correct,
immediate effective action should be taken to avoid
further occurrence similar to the Tulsa race riot,
which are the results of such agitation as mentioned
in this editorial.

Respectfully yours,

OJB:SB

Encl

RECORDED
JUN 22 21

158260-8-
JUN 16 1921 A. M.
STEWART-HERRON

118

IT MUST BE STOPPED

THE property owners, busir⁣⁣⁣⁣ss men, and righteous citizens of Tulsa hold a responsibili.t, not only to see that unnecessary suffering following the tragic hours of the race riot is prevented, but also to make sure that a sound and permanent scheme of reconstruction is worked out in which those who prize the reputation of Tulsa may participate. But in doing this there should be no false and misguiding sentiment created, no unstable standards encouraged.

The city cannot condone the looting and stealing but we must not confuse those lawless practices with the heroic defense by the white men who stood their ground and saved this city from a more serious disaster than that which we experienced. Those who suffered in defending our city from a more serious disaster should be cared for and helped and honored They defended all of us when our officers of the law, who did not suffer a scratch, failed us.

It appears to be reasonably well established that certain lawless negroes had for some time been collecting arms and ammunition. It is also well established that lawlessness was allowed to run unarrested in the old "Niggertown." The citizens of Tulsa become derelict of duty if they do not now give Attorney General Freeling the fullest support and co-operation in his investigation into officers of the law who failed to function not only during the riot but before. Tulsa, Mr. Mayor, is in no mood to witness another whitewash exhibition.

What are the officers of the law, county and city, doing NOW to get the negroes here who have advocated gun play? Many of them are doubtless now in hiding in and around the city. The people ought to have a report from the officers of the law as to what is now being done to apprehend these negroes.

The New York World accepts the uninvestigated statement of five negroes in New York City that the disaster here was the result of oil men w⁣⁣⁣⁣ were anxious to acquire the property occupied by the negr⁣⁣s and known as "Niggertown." Such a statement is not only viciously untrue but it illustrates the kind of incendiary propaganda which negro agitators spread. If the good negroes have any regard for their race they themselves will take such foes of their race in hand and stop this kind of criminal lying.

e ew York Times, in ... issue of June 6, page 7, reports that Herbert H. Harrison, president of the Liberal League of Negro Americans, at a meeting of negroes held at 135th street and Lennox avenue, New York City, urged the negroes to arm. He declared, "I should not be surprised if we saw three splendid race riots by next September." He also advises that as president of that society he is to name a committee of negroes to go to Tulsa to investigate conditions there but the names of that committee are not to be made public because if they were "then some one would be waiting for them when they got out to Tulsa."

Some one ought to be waiting for them. Because of this statement every negro arriving in Tulsa should be subjected to a rigid examination.

This is but another convincing evidence that the race riot here was planned by the bad negroes and that the law-defying negroes are planning more "splendid riots" to be delivered by September. Get that word "splendid." In all these "splendid riots" the bad negroes will trump up the lie that the whites started it.

This kind of thing is lawlessness in the extreme. This kind of thing is the repudiation of the government itself. This kind of thing is defiance of the law of the land. This kind of thing is treason.

The negroes who respect the law and who desire to be looked upon as honest and respectable Negro-Americans must suppress this thing. If they do not suppress it they condone it. America is not going to submit to any such plotted outrages. America is not going to submit to any attempt to shift responsibilities for this kind of outbreaks. The negro newspapers are full of just this kind of incendiary stuff. And IT MUST BE STOPPED. ◼ ◼ ◼ ◼ ◼ ◼ ◼

WCH-ECT

June 8, 1921.

Rev. Luther J. Martin,

    1026 Kenyon St., N. W.,

    Washington, D. C.

Dear Sir:

    I beg to acknowledge receipt of your letter of May 4th, enclosing a clipping from the Baltimore Sun relative to the Tulsa race riots.

    The Department thanks you for calling this to its attention and assures you that the matter will receive due consideration.

               Respectfully,

                    For the AttorneyaGeneral,

                        (Signed) R. P. Stewart
                        Assistant Attorney General.

#102& Kenton, reet, N.W.

15-8260 - 8

Washington, D.C.,

May, 4th., 1921.

To the Honorable,

The Attorney-General of the United States of America,

Dear Sir:-

Enclosed you will please find a clipping from"The Baltimore Sun", of even date. The marked paragraph is vital significant in placing the blame as to the "why" of the Tulsa riots.

The writer has talked to some people from this vicinity and it is the consensus of opinion that this district was the most prosperous of all the colored section in the Southwest. What valid reason can the people of Tulsa give the world for deliberately destroying an entire "Little Africa"?

If your Office works on the presumption that the colored people owned too much propery and that their holdings in oil was an incentive to the complete destruction of an entire colored settlement, does it not occur to your Office that this would furnish a motive?

The Negroes are going to have their homes rebuilded, but as we understand ON ANOTHER PLOT OF GROUND, the destroyed district is to be an industrial centre.

I submit this for what it is worth.

Trusting that a people who has ever stood ready to defend the country from the days of Crispus Attucks, Peter Salem , And with Jackson at New Orleans, with Roosevelt at San Juan Hill, at Carrizal, in France and else where ; that they Sir, will receive absolute justice at your hands(and we have no cause to surmise other wise) ———

I Am Yours ,

For Justice and Right,

Rev J.Luther Martin.

RDB

15 8 26.0 - 8 -

DEPT OF JUSTICE
JUN 6 1921 A. M.
ITS DIVISION

121

NE 4, 1921.

le

Be

PROBE OF TULSA RIOT ORDERED BY DAUGHERTY

Informal Investigation Will Be Made By Agents Of Department Of Justice.

SEARCH FOR RINGLEADERS ON

Radical Negro Leaders Blamed For Trouble—Martial Law Lifted.

Washington, June 3.—A general inquiry into the race riots at Tulsa, Okla., has been ordered by Attorney-General Daugherty, it was announced today at the Department of Justice.

The purpose of the investigation, officials said, is to determine whether the disorders were in violation of federal laws. Preliminary reports, it was added, show that the situation is purely local.

The inquiry ordered is informal and will be made by the department's agents in the field. Officials indicated that it was not probable that a special investigation would be ordered. They expressed the belief that the situation would work itself out without the intervention of the Federal Government.

Has Suspects' Names.

Tulsa, Okla., June 3.—Search for a number of alleged ringleaders of the race riots of Tuesday night and Wednesday, the lifting of martial law and progress on plans for rebuilding a negro "zone" were developments in Tulsa today.

Adjutant-General Barrett in charge of the State troops here, announced this afternoon he had the names of a number of persons suspected of being ringleaders in the trouble and that these persons when apprehended would be turned over to the civil authorities General Barrett told the Chamber of Commerce it was unnecessary to keep the troops after today, and this afternoon issued the governor's order restoring civil law.

The committee of seven at a confer-

ence, discussed the request of Gov. J. B. A. Robertson, for a searching inquiry and decided the best plan would be to handle the investigation through the grand jury. A special committee from the bar association, it was announced, will be appointed to co-operate with the county attorney's staff.

For Model Negro Section.

The committee of seven also considered the rebuilding plans and steps are to be taken to provide a well-built negro section, this to be done in part as an atonement for the harm done, and also as an example for other cities. An order was issued from military headquarters early today demanding the arrest of anyone offering for recording deed or transfers of any property in the burned district.

General Barrett, commanding Tulsa county, under the martial law proclamation, in an order asserted that irresponsible persons were seeking to obtain the property at much less than its value. Agitation by. a few irresponsible negroes was blamed for the part of the negroes in the race war here, in statements today by several prominent negroes and by Police Commissioner J. M. Adkinson.

According to Commissioner Adkins, the police were aware that negro radicals had been at work for some time. He said negro citizens had been warned several months ago that responsibility for any trouble would rest upon the negroes.

TALKS WITH TRADE BODIES

Hoover Discusses Business In Light Of Trust Laws.

Washington, June 3.—Representatives of trade associations assured Secretary Hoover in a conference today at which the collection of business information was discussed in the light of the anti-trust laws that they were in full accord with the desire of the Administration to obviate price fixing through dissemination of trade figures. The proposed publication of trade statistics by the Commerce Department in co-operation with the various industries also was indorsed.

The Secretary said he was sure only a very few associations were engaging

POSTAL TELEGRAPH-CABLE COMPANY

NIGHT LETTERGRAM

THE POSTAL TELEGRAPH-CABLE COMPANY (INCORPORATED) TRANSMITS AND DELIVERS THIS NIGHT LETTERGRAM SUBJECT TO THE
TERMS AND CONDITIONS PRINTED ON THE BACK OF THIS BLANK.
CLARENCE H. MACKAY, PRESIDENT.
RECEIVED AT

INDEPENDENT   COMPETITIVE   PROGRESSIVE

255ohkd 832am 261 collect Government NL

Tulsa Okla Jun 2-3 1921

Chief Bureau of Investigation Department of Justice washington DC

Stop five riots Tulsa Okla May thirty first negro Dick Rowland Charged
by white elevator girl with attempted assault Rowland jailed in county
jail same evening while mob of about twenty five armed men go to county
jail to lynch Rowland about same sized mob of armed negroes go to jail
to protect Rowland Sheriff refuses to disarm or arrest any of either mob
negro mob starts to leave but returns shortly and some one apparently
white man fires a shot negroes flee shooting as they run and make a
stand at Frisco Tracks and Boston Street white mob augmented by several
hundred apparently mostly crooks and follow negroes to negro section
both sides shooting but negroes retreating whites invade negro section
shooting at fleeing negroes and setting negroes residences church and
business buildings on fire until seven AM next day looting as they go
national guard arrive about then and martial law proclaimed rioting ends
suddenly and everything now normal known dead are nine whites eighteen
blacks undoubtedly many dead negroes in burned houses property damage
in negro section about one million five hundred thousand Sheriff and
Police Department apparently made no effort to preserve order Sheriff
accused of calling armed negroes to jail in first instance everything
now quiet National Guard still on duty state grand jury probe ordered by
governor with state attorney general to conduct which is set for June
eighth no Federal violation appears trouble started spontaneously and
due to fact that county and city officers have been for years notoriously
crooked and inefficient

Weis

RECORD'D

APPENDIX E

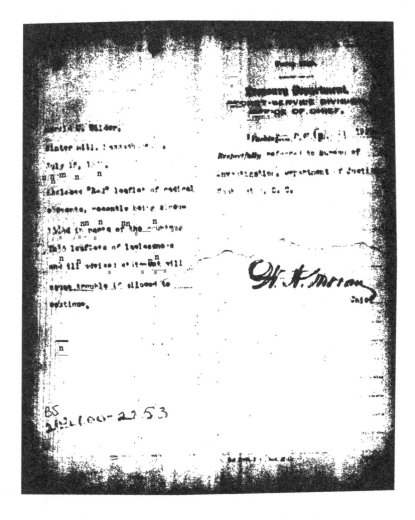

BS 2?2-6?

The Tulsa Massacre!

By the time this leaflet is in your h...ds, all the horrible details of the mass murder of the helpless Negro pop...tion of Tulsa, Oklahoma, will be known to the entire world.

There are no words vivid enough to describe the action of the well dressed armed mob of business men who with automobiles and airplanes, surrounded the Negro quarter in Tuls... June 1st, setting fire to their homes, destroying ten city blocks and rendering homeless more than ten thousand Negro workers; ruthlessly slaying men, women and children; killing over 90 and wounding more than 200.

There is only one appeal that will st..p these fiendish and bloody outrages—that is the apeal to organized fo...e, the only language that the bloodthirsty capitalist of America can understand is the language of ORGANIZED POWER. Only by repris... by answering force with force—will the business mobs and their White Guards, the Klu Klux Klan, etc. be restrained from continuing their br..t d and cowardly assaults upon the Negro and working class population of t...s country.

If there is any red blood in the ve... of the working class of America it will come to the defense of its colored brothers, who are the victims of the same bloody capitalist class that ...ploits and murders the workers regardless of color or race.

In their own interests, the white workers of America, must come to the aid of the exploited Negro masses. ...eir skins are darker-hued than ours, but the interests are the same, ... ck ..nd White, we, the workers, have but ONE enemy—THE CAPITALIST CLASS which uses its GOVERNMENT to suppress us.

There are more than ten million Negr...s in this country. Almost all of them are of the working class. The...Negro wage workers, whom we have refused to admit into our trade u...s, are rapidly being reduced to serfdom and peonage—to a condition of slavery worse than chattel slavery before 1861. Shall we, the white wage s...des, stand by idly and permit the CAPITALISTS to murder, rob and crush ...n, millions of our fellows? The crushing of ten million Negro workers ... n...ng nothing but the beginning of a system of peonage and degradation for the entire working class of America. For the breaking of the...spe...f these ten million Negro wage workers will enable the WHITE CAPITA...STS to use these colored men and women against the white wage worker...s strike breakers in order to crush the resistance of the entire work...g cl...s. Already there are five million wage workers walking the street...of the cities and towns of America in search of work—unemployed, desperate, hungry—and the CAPITALISTS are making a general assault ...n ...ur unions, through the open shop movement, in the effort to destroy our ...ons and break our resistance

If the Negro worker can be used a... ...t. White workers, who is to blame? We have refused to allow our...colored brothers to join our unions. We have repeated all the idiotic accusa...s against their race. We have foolishly allowed ourselves to be swayed ...y p...re prejudice. We have failed to ORGANIZE the Negro worker. We h...refused to treat him as our own, our equal BROTHER in the CLASS STRUGGLE. WE ARE TO BLAME.

BREAK DOWN THE BARRIERS IN THE UNIONS. WIPE OUT THE "COLOR LINE." There is only ONE line that we can draw—that is the CLASS LINE. White and Black, Jew and Gentile, Al...

WORKERS, the exploited masses, must be organised on the basis of their CLASS interests.

Our Negro fellow workers were supposed to have been "emancipated" during the American Civil War. The Constitution of the U. S. is supposed to guarantee their "freedom." Since then they have been herded into separate districts, segregated in Jim Crow cars, their women subject to the assaults of white men, their children deprived of elementary education, their men denied the right to acquire trades or professions, their whole race kept in ignorance and degradation. They have been burned alive, lynched, murdered and brutally assaulted upon the slightest provocation. The hideous accusation of raping has been fastened upon their entire race. This is the kind of "freedom" that CAPITALIST CONSTITUTION guarantees to the working class. This is the only kind of "freedom" that the WORKERS can expect from the CAPITALIST GOVERNMENT of the United States. For the Government of the U. S. is nothing but the organised expression of the WILL of the CAPITALIST CLASS. The Government of the U. S. is nothing else but a ruthless DICTATORSHIP of the RICH over the POOR.

It is in the interest of both the Negro and the White WORKERS to destroy this CAPITALIST GOVERNMENT, root and branch. Shoulder to shoulder, and heart to heart the workers of ALL races must UNITE to establish in this country a WORKERS' GOVERNMENT—THE SOVIET REPUBLIC OF AMERICA.

THE COMMUNIST PARTY OF AMERICA calls upon our colored comrades to ORGANIZE, and with arms in their hands, to resist the murderous armed assaults upon their homes, their women and their children.

THE COMMUNIST PARTY OF AMERICA calls upon the White workers to assist their colored brothers and with arms in their hands, to help them to repel such armed attacks upon them by the wealthy business men as occured in Tulsa, Oklahoma and in hundreds of other places.

THEIR FIGHT IS OUR FIGHT. THE COMMUNIST PARTY OF AMERICA recognizes no artificial division between the WORKING CLASS. We call upon ALL workers of ALL races to UNITE against their COMMON ENEMY—the Capitalist Class and the CAPITALIST STATE.

Both Negro and White workers must by this time realize the kind of "democracy" they fought for in France. This is the only kind of "democracy" that the workers can get under the capitalist government of the United States.

In Russia, under the Tzar's Government, the Jews were the victims of race riots and pogroms. In Russia the workers and peasants overthrew the CAPITALIST Government of Russia, and established a WORKERS' GOVERNMENT THE SOVIET REPUBLIC OF RUSSIA. The victims of all races in Russia are UNITED. Race prejudice and race riots have disappeared.

Only by following our Russian Comrades' heroic example, and by establishing in this country the SOVIET REPUBLIC OF AMERICA, will White and Black workers be able to live and work in peace and enjoy the fruits of their labor.

WORKERS OF AMERICA—ORGANIZE! WIPE OUT THE "COLOR LINE"!

HAIL TO THE PROLETARIAN REVOLUTION!
DOWN WITH THE CAPITALIST SYSTEM AND THE CAPITALIST STATE!
LONG LIVE THE WORKERS' REPUBLIC OF AMERICA!

CENTRAL EXECUTIVE COMMITTEE
COMMUNIST PARTY OF AMERICA.

Department of Justice

Bureau of Investigation

P.O. Box 348,
Hartford, Conn.

Hon. William J. Flynn,
Director, Bureau of Investigation,
Department of Justice,
Washington, D.C.

Dear Sir:

I have the honor to acknowledge receipt of
your letter concerning the COMMUNIST PARTY OF AMERICA
circulars entitled "THE TULSA MASSACRE", from the
Honorable Frank B. Brandegee, Senator from Connecticut.

Replying will state that the Chief Agent
of the COMMUNIST PARTY, who was handling these particular
circulars and many others, is now confined in the Hartford
County Jail, having been arrested along with two others,
for directing and distributing the COMMUNIST PARTY circulars
throughout the State of Connecticut.

An Agent of this office secured a sworn
statement from the Chief Agent of the COMMUNIST PARTY,
which is now on file in the Washington Office under the
name of HAROLD IMBATURE et al, who was sentenced for
both perjury and the distribution of circulars under the
Act concerning Sedition, Public Acts of Connecticut,
Approved May 17th, 1919, to five months in the Hartford
County Jail, and fined $100.00 and costs. The Honorable
Senator may be assured that we have the right man-serving
his sentence, along with two others for distributing the
circular "THE TULSA MASSACRE".

Very truly yours,

William P. Hazen

WILLIAM P. HAZEN
Special Agent in Charge.

BS 202 600 2058

Instruct one received from
Agent in Charge

J . P. Mooney   7/26/21   7/21 to 24/21   EDWIN C. SHANAHAN.

THE TULSA MASSACRE: Circular.

At Chicago.

Reference is made to Bureau letter dated July 19, 1921,
Initialed JEH:JPO, in regard to one ton of the above circulars
being received at 631-33 W. Huron, 631 No. ParkaAve., and 3934
Metropolitan Pl., Chicago, Ill.

Agent visited the above addresses with the following results;
631-33 W. Huron; no such address: 631 No. Park Ave., no such
address: 3934 Metropolitan Pl. is a two story red brick building;
first floor occupied by a widow and one child; name Mrs. Kubik.
Second floor occupied by John Turcan, wife and two children.
Turcan employed a laborer at C.N.&. Car Shop #5. Has first papers
only; has be n in this country for 16 years. The above information
obtained under pretext.

Agent then conferred with Asst. U.S. Attorney R.A. Milroy in
regard to the possibility of these being a violation of any feder
statute. On July 23, 1921, the following letter was received from
office of the .S.Attorney:

".... In reply to your letter of July 15, 1921, concerning
the phamplet entitled, "The Tulsa Massacre", beg to advise that
I have carefully examined this phamplet and I find in it no speci
violation of any Federal Statute.
    I suggest, however, that you take the matter up with
the State's Attorney with a view to proceeding against the author
of the phamplet under the Syndicalist Law".

Acting upon the suggestion contained in this letter Agent

JEH:JPO
7/19/21   Wash -2 U.S. Atty Milroy -1- Chgo 1   LCS.

BS-202400-2253

129

-2-

proceeded to the Deotective Bureau, Chicago Police and conferred with Sargeant McDonough about the matter. Sergeant McDonough stated that he would proceed to act on this matter under the State Syndicalist law of Illinois. Agent will make further report upon result of S. rgeant McDonough's investigation.

Continued.

TJB-AC   7C2600-2253

                                    August 12, 1921.

Wm. P. Hazen, Esq.,

    Box 548,

        Hartford, Conn.

Dear Sir:

    . A letter has been received by the Department from
Sidney Blumenthal and Company, Incorporated, at Shelton,
Connecticut, enclosing a copy of the Communist leaflet entitled "The Tulsa Massacre", which it is alleged was scattered
throughout the city of Shelton on the morning of August 7th.
The letter from Blumenthal Company was initialed G deKH;H,
and offers any assistance possible in an investigation of
the matter.

                        Very truly yours,

                            Chief.

                    202600-2253-15

REPORT MADE AT:	DATE WHEN MADE	PERIOD FOR WHICH MADE	REPORT MADE BY:
Hartford, Conn.	8-19-21	8-18-21	WILLIAM T. LYNCH

TITLE AND CHARACTER OF CASE:

THE COMMUNIST PARTY OF AMERICA.   Shelton, Conn.   Distribution of Radical Literature.

FACTS DEVELOPED:

At Shelton, Conn.

Reference is made to letter from Chief of Bureau, dated August 12, 1921, initialed TFB-AS. relative to the distribution of the Communist leaflet "The Tulsa Massacre", in the Town of Shelton, Conn. Under instruction of Acting Agent in Charge EDWARD J. HICKEY, Agent called on the informant in this matter, L. deK. HUBBARD, Operating Vice-President of the Sidney Blumenthal Company, Shelton, Conn., on the above date. He stated that the leaflets were distributed on the principal streets of Shelton during the night of the 6th. or the early morning of the 7th. of August, 1921. He thas no information relative to the persons or organizations responsible for the distribution. As far as he knows there is no local organization of the Communist Party in the Town of Shelton.

Agent then called on Chief DONOVAN, of the Shelton Police Department. He stated to Agent that he had been unable to get any trace of the persons responsible for the distribution of the leaflet. He is of the opinion that there is no local organization of the Communist Party in his town.

Both of the above mentioned persons stated that they would communicate further with this Office in case they obtained any additional information.

This investigation is closed.

REFERENCE: Copies to this Report forwarded to
2-Washington, 1-Hartford.

ORIGINAL.

WJF-jpm

July 13, 1921.

Honorable Frank R. Brandegee,
United States Senate,
Washington, D.C.

My dear Senator:

Referring to your recent letter which had as an enclosure a dodger circular titled "THE TULSA MASSACRE" copies of which were being distributed in sections of the State of Connecticut. I am sure you will be interested in knowing that the parties responsible have been detected and apprehended.

For your information I enclose a copy of letter from our Agent in Charge at Hartford which goes more fully into detail.

Respectfully,

Encl.

Director.

BS 202600 - 2253 - R